THE WINNING WAY

THE
WINNING WAY

Antony Ball
Stephen Asbury

Jonathan Ball Publishers

Johannesburg

© Stephen Asbury
  Antony Ball

First published in 1989 by
Jonathan Ball Publishers
PO Box 2105
Parklands
2121 Johannesburg
(011) 880-3116/7

ISBN 0 947464 09 3

Designed and typeset by Book Productions, Pretoria
Printed and bound by National Book Printers, Goodwood, Cape

To Colette and Sarah for their love, support and understanding through this frenetically busy period.

To Anne for her counsel and her contribution.

CONTENTS

AUTHORS' NOTE

This book has been over a year in the making — a very busy year in which we have also been expanding our own unit of Deloitte Haskins & Sells consulting practice. The project as a whole — the research and particularly the writing — took a great deal more work than we originally anticipated. But while it has been far more demanding than we expected, it has also been far more rewarding. We have wandered a fascinating trail through the boardrooms and across the shop floors of some of South Africa's very best companies, talking along the way to super-performers across a broad spectrum. In the process we have learnt a very great deal about business — especially business in South Africa. For all of this we are profoundly grateful to all those people in the Winning Companies who gave so freely of their time and who were, almost without exception, willing to part with sensitive information that was not for publication. This book is fittingly a celebration of their success. We are grateful also for our firm's enthusiastic support, without which the project would have been simply impossible. We thank our colleagues too: Craig O'Flaherty, Gavin Fraser, Paul Aucamp, Claudia Koch, Michael Rossiter, Anthony Hewat, Di Soutter, Duncan Campbell and Desiree Rosenfield; their contribution to the content has been enormous, their forbearance of our frequent absences longsuffering, and their noisy encouragement continuous. What more could we have asked for?

We thank also our long-suffering secretaries: Fiona Flockhart and Evelyn Miles. They transformed the script from untidy handwriting to an impeccably typed document and kept us focused on the important task of managing our own business with constant nudging and frequent reminders.

We stand now on the threshold of a decade that will be as daunting and as exciting as any in our country's history — perhaps even more so. In that context, each one of the full range of scenarios for South African business in the 1990s offers challenge above all else. We look forward through this publication and in our work to helping South African companies master those challenges.

Antony Ball
Stephen Asbury

Johannesburg
July 1989

CHAPTER ONE

INTRODUCTION
THE NEW BASICS

SUCCESS

It's a perennial discussion. In boardrooms and shebeens, at golf clubs and dinner tables the talk will turn to success — business success and how to achieve it. Our fascination with success is endless, our curiosity insatiable. Views will diverge and opinions will be strong. But conclusions will generally be few.

What drives corporate success? Why do some companies consistently outperform their competitors? Does corporate success necessarily follow from outperforming the competition? There are, of course, a thousand answers — depending upon whom you listen to, or what you read. As business consultants, we set out to find the excalibur of success, and particularly business success in the South African context. We began by revisiting the obvious sources:

The Academics

Academics play a vital role in the creation of corporate wealth. We are both products of business schools and keep up to date with business literature. We know the territory. However, for the purposes of our enquiry, we believe the academics to be two levels removed from corporate success. Firstly, they are generally more concerned with management technology, i.e. techniques for managing, than they are with corporate wealth creation. The application of this technology may bring success (and we will show dozens of examples where it does), but the link is not sufficiently direct or integrative to pull together all the factors driving corporate wealth. Secondly, academic enquiry is often not well rooted in the rich earth of the real world.

1

The Financial Analysts

We spoke to a number of analysts: people trained to seek out shares in companies which are likely to move — upward! In summary, they tell us, it is all about industry exposure and about management. The recipe, therefore, is to choose a good road and make sure you have a good driver. True, but we needed to know more.

The "Excellence" Industry

Peters and Waterman's book *In Search of Excellence* has spurred the "excellence" industry. Most businessmen — worldwide — are by now familiar with this book and the eight important lessons learned from its study of America's best: bias toward action; close to customers; autonomy and entrepreneurship; productivity through people; hands-on, value driven; stick to the knitting; simple form, lean staff; simultaneous loose-tight properties.

Fashionable criticism of this fine work usually focuses on the poor record of many of America's best, following publication of the book. Michelle Claymen's research published in the *Financial Analysts' Journal*, May-June 1987, shows that out of a portfolio of 29 of the 36 publicly traded shares in these companies, 18 underperformed the S&P 500 index. The inference one is tempted to draw is that the findings aren't valid. We don't support this, for the following reasons :

- The research focused on lessons to be learned and therefore, by definition, focused on positive factors, i.e. "what to do's" rather than "what not to do's". Many of the companies in their sample must surely have been doing a few things wrong.
- The eight lessons were not common to *all* companies, i.e. some companies were not applying certain factors.
- Markets have shifted in rapidly changing environments. Some excellent companies needed time to adapt. Their poor performance was therefore a temporary aberration (remember the research focused on the long-term). Some of the under-performers (such as IBM) have already bounced back.
- Some of the excellent companies may have become complacent and forgotten their lines — ceasing to apply themselves to some of the things they were doing well.

The issue that we take with the research is a contextual one — that is, the American economy, societal values, scale of business undertaking, regulatory framework, levels of management sophistication and other factors are all very different to ours. Our advice to South Africans would therefore be to apply these lessons, but apply them with caution.

We tried them all: the academics, the analysts, and the authors. We had gleaned some pointers, but the answers were incomplete. There was nothing for it but to undertake in-depth research of our own.

THE WINNING COMPANIES

If we were to find the real answers we would have to go and do a bit of "horseback" research — what one of our interviewees called "get-off-your-arse-and-have-a-look" research. We decided to get out there and talk to South Africa's success models. We selected a group of top-performing companies and drew some invaluable lessons from them and the people that ran them.

In selecting these companies, we gave serious thought to what we wanted to learn. So we applied the following criteria in selecting the companies:

- We were out to learn something from companies that had passed the acid test of commercial success, by making piles of money for their shareholders.
- If the lessons were to be valid, the companies must have shown that they could do this on a sustainable basis.
- For the purposes of this book, we were interested in those things done by companies at operating level to build competitive advantage in their marketplaces. Consequently, holding companies were excluded from our sample. Our thinking was that managers at holding company level need to manage their businesses by a different set of rules. Nevertheless, we resolved to interview some of South Africa's leading holding-company executives anyway to hear their views of the key factors for competitive success. One of those executives, it turned out, was Warren Clewlow of Barlow Rand, who confirmed our view of holding company management as a huge corporate chess game. Anton Rupert, Warren Clewlow, Derek Keys and

Gavin Relly, the late Dr Fred du Plessis and Jan van der Horst are the corporate grandmasters. They engineer the real synergies so vital to the success of conglomerates. They install management expertise and discipline in their subsidiary companies, thereby offering their shareholders a degree of certainty in their returns — returns therefore that will however often be lower by virtue of that lower risk profile. South Africa's master holding companies like Barlow Rand, Anglo American, Rembrandt, Sanlam and Malbak have unquestionably made an enormous contribution to the success of a corporate South Africa. A study of holding company success, fascinating as it would be, is another exercise altogether and does not form part of this book at all.

- If the lessons were to be translatable, then there would be little point in selecting companies where the success factors were very specific to their own business context. We believed mining and exploration companies to fall into this category.

We therefore used as a basis David Carte's 1987 *Business Times* Top Companies Survey. He calculates the all-in-return to shareholders for all JSE listed companies as follows: The share price of each company as at 31 August 1987 was taken and compared to the share price of that company five years earlier. (Due allowance was made for capital issues and share splits.) This figure measured the capital gain over the five-year period. All dividends paid during this period were added to the capital gain. Finally, a 12 per cent interest factor (reinvestment of dividends) per annum was added. This gave the total all-in-return over the five-year period. David excluded cash shells and "thin trading" companies from his analysis.

We then discussed this list with financial analysts and commentators with the objective of:

- Adding top-performing unlisted companies and top companies which had been listed for less than five years. (A measure of subjectivity seemed unavoidable here.)
- Eliminating companies that had been included due to their start from an exceptionally low base.

4

- Making a final selection of about 30, which would include companies from all significant sectors. (Certain sectors had obviously performed better than others; we didn't want to find ourselves researching eight retailers and no transporters — we wanted a spread.)

The list we finally settled on is as follows:

Retail and Wholesale	• Pick 'n Pay • Edgars Stores • Cashbuild • Foschini • Ellerine
Motor	• Toyota South Africa • Volkswagen of South Africa
Insurance	• Liberty Life
Engineering	• Edward L Bateman • Stocks & Stocks • Cape Gate Fence and Wire Works
Beverage	• The Beer Division of The South African Breweries • Suncrush
Food	• Irvin & Johnson • Langeberg Co-op • Cadbury-Schweppes (South Africa)
Transportation	• Tollgate
Chemicals and Oil	• Trek
Banks and Financial Services	• Sage
Clothing, Footwear and Textiles	• Seardel Investments Corporation • SA Bias Binding Manufacturers (SA Bias)

Tobacco and Match	• United Tobacco Company
Electronics, Electrical and Battery	• Altech • Plessey SA
Office Supplies	• Mathieson & Ashley • Waltons Stationery
Hotels	• Sun International
Cement	• Pretoria Portland Cement
Packaging	• Sun Packaging

We then hounded the Chief Executives of these companies and were able to elicit the participation of all but:

- Irvin & Johnson, Langeberg, and Cape Gate — all of whom preferred to avoid the publicity that the research would necessarily bring.
- Edward L Bateman, who were too busy to see us.
- Sun Packaging, whose senior executives were not in the country for long enough to be pinned down.

In the course of writing this book the 1988 *Business Times* Top Companies were announced. When National Bolts came out top, we resolved to add them to the list as a last minute inclusion. Regrettably they too were too busy to see us.

We therefore ended up with 24 companies, which we believe have a lot to teach us. We would be the first to admit that our basis is not rigorously scientific — perhaps these 24 companies are not the Top 24, but 24 out of the Top 50, or Top 100. But so what? We were out to learn lessons, not to prove a scientific theory.

Mindful of the difficulties we had had when we started our quest, we were determined that the research should be each of the following:

- **Practical** — the lessons should be translatable into action.
- **Focused on corporate success** — once translated into action the link between that action and corporate wealth creation should be direct.
- **Integrative** — taken together, the lessons should pull together all the relevant management disciplines.

- **South African** — the lessons should be drawn from South African sources.
- **Positive** — the lessons should be in the nature of "what to do" rather than "what not to do".

We began by gathering and reviewing all publicly available information on each company. This provided us with the basic understanding and research agenda for each company. Our next step was to interview the Chief Executive. Based on the outcome of this interview, we would set up further interviews with executives, managers and others further down the line. We then spent a good deal of time think-tanking the strengths of each of these companies. In distilling the success factors, we tapped into the combined brainpower of our colleagues.

THE WINNING WAY: THE NEW BASICS

What did we find? Did a pattern emerge from the wealth of data we collected? What *do* South Africa's winning companies do so well?

We were delighted — and reassured — to discover that the Winning Way is no hidden path revealed only to the chosen few. We learned that the Winning Way is the fundamental way, the *management* way. There is no secret to it; the Winning Way is via the basics. South Africa's best companies have made it to the top by applying themselves to nine basic factors:

Turning strategy into action. The super-performers — each in their own way — have powerfully effective processes for setting strategy, and powerfully effective processes for implementing it.

Giving customers what they need. Customers are the source of almost everything the winning companies do. Extraordinary efforts are made to understand the customer — and to deliver what the customer needs.

Liberating human potential. Our top companies have learnt that success follows from setting people free to perform in the workplace.

Welcoming change and encouraging innovation. Change does not upset the super-performers. They welcome it. They foster innovation, new organisational forms and processes as well as new products and services.

Managing the fundamentals. South Africa's winning companies have learnt to identify the few key activities that set them apart from their competition. They enhance their skills in those areas, and measure their results simply but accurately.

Doing things properly. Professionalism and thoroughness are the hallmarks of the super-performers. In ways that their customers value, these companies simply do things properly.

Managing stakeholder relationships. The top companies understand the importance of maintaining strong relationships with their stakeholders — suppliers, employees, unions, bankers and others, as well as customers and shareholders.

The right kind of leadership. The leaders of our winning companies know that the South African context demands leadership skills that are very different from British, European or American models.

Building strong corporate cultures. South Africa's super-performing companies are turning on the power of corporate culture. These organisations have strong and consistent shared beliefs about their businesses.

There is no doubt about it — these are the basics. But they are not the old basics applied in the same old ways. You will see, as we did, that our winning companies are applying the basics in uniquely South African ways — ways that are right for our unique environment. In the super-performing companies, the old basics have been reshaped and redefined — they have become the New Basics for South African business.

We hope that you will find the discovery of the New Basics *in action* in South Africa's winning companies as exciting as we have.

CHAPTER TWO

MASTER YOUR DESTINY

"War is a simple art; its essence lies in its accomplishment."
Napoleon Bonaparte

STRATEGY DELIVERS

Twenty years ago United Tobacco Company (Utico) enjoyed some 65 per cent of the lucrative South African cigarette market. With brands like Commando, West 85, Gold Flake, State Express and Gold Dollar, Utico had grown from humble beginnings in Johannesburg in 1905 to a large, organised and highly profitable manufacturing machine. And prospects looked rosy; the white market continued to grow, and the slumbering giant — the black market — was astir. Utico was a comfortable, clubby sort of place to work — a gentleman's company.

A decade later Utico was in deep trouble. Anton Rupert of Rembrandt, their aggressive competitor of the past 10 years, had capitalised on their complacency, overtaking them with professional marketing and superior product quality. By competing on all fronts Rembrandt had left Utico with only 20 per cent market share. Utico's new management, led by Bruce Edmunds, assisted by [parent] BAT took a hard look at the company's strategic direction. The result was radical. Called "The Drive Policy", the strategy demanded concentrating all their resources on just four brands selected on the basis of their viable brand positioning and their upward sales trends in emerging market segments. Support was to be withdrawn from all 11 remaining brands that didn't match these criteria. Even big sellers like Gold Dollar were to be left to die.

Out were to go their economists, planners, researchers and other corporate staffers that a niche player cannot justify. Led by Benson and Hedges Special Mild, the four Drive Brands have since wrought a remarkable turnaround for Utico. Over the five years to 1987 the company provided shareholders with an outstanding average return of 45,7 per cent per annum.

Strategy has delivered the goods for Utico. And in different ways it has delivered the goods for all of our top-performing companies. Each of these top companies has developed powerfully effective strategies that have played a major role in creating wealth for shareholders. Some of our top-performing chief executive officers claim not to worry too much about strategy. Others swear by the formal strategic process they employ. **Whether formal or informal, the fact of the matter is that strategy is alive and kicking in South Africa's best companies.**

Perhaps, at the outset, we should dwell briefly on the meaning of this much used — and often misused — word *strategy*. The word has military origins of course, but in the business context strategic issues and plans are those that have a direct bearing on the future performance of the company as a whole. Initiatives that move whole companies (like whole armies) are, by definition, *strategic* initiatives. In business terms too, strategy has different meanings at different levels; *business unit* or *competitive strategy* is concerned with the performance of operating units and takes its cues from the cut-and-thrust of competitive activity in one or more related product/market areas; while *corporate strategy* operates at a higher level, at say holding company head-office, where the imperative is to arrange the interrelationships between business units so that each may derive maximal competitive advantage in its own operating arena. Business unit strategy is about outperforming the competition. Corporate strategy is about engineering real synergies, about realising unrealised value amongst a group of business units.

But isn't strategic planning out of date? Don't people do other things now? What about strategic management and scenario planning? By reference to the top companies we will see that strategic planning isn't out of date, but that it is only a part of strategy, and that, to be effective, strategy must be much more

10

than strategic planning. We will see that strategy must be led by a powerful vision of what you want your organisation to be, that strategic thinking isn't only a talent bestowed upon the fortunate few — that it can and should be a deliberate exercise that is best done by people undistracted by the din of operations. While we will describe some of the very formal strategic processes in operation in some of the top performers, we will see that the "informal" approach offers a very real alternative, and we will attempt to understand which process is best for which business. We will talk about gathering the information that must form the basis for strategic decision making, and we will show how the top performers have used that information to define their core strategy and their desired competitive advantage.

Above all, towards the close of this chapter, we will see that strategy is nothing without implementation. Our super-performers will show that there is much that can be done to improve the chances of successful implementation: focusing on a few important things, ensuring that the structure and systems in place favour realisation of the strategy, communicating the planned changes to employees and supporting them through those changes. But let us begin at the beginning — with Vision.

The Big V

Most of us have heard the story about Sol Kerzner scouring Bophuthatswana in a helicopter until he found the site for Sun City. It actually happened.

> *In the latter part of 1977 Sol had been researching the prospects in Bophuthatswana. A number of potential sites had been mooted but Sol was not completely satisfied with any of them. Early in 1978 Sol and his childhood friend the late Baba Selsick, then an architect with the firm SKM, boarded a four-seater helicopter and made for the Pilanesberg. When they finally spotted the valley where Sun City stands today Sol was unequivocal : "This is it," he said. "No question about it." They touched down precisely where the foyer of the hotel is today.*

Everyone said Kerzner was crazy. But Sol had a clear and visionary picture of what he wanted to create, and, as it turns out, the cash that has flowed from Sun City has funded the birth of an international hotel and leisure empire.

There is a similar vision story in each of our super-performing companies. Winky Ringo is taking Mathieson & Ashley (manufacturers of Dashing, Offex and Anglo Dutch office furniture) into the electronic office — the office of the future. Chris Seabrooke had a clear view of a restructured garment accessories industry —restructured on SA Bias's terms. Frankie Robarts had a vision of Waltons being bigger than DRG. Vic Hammond now carries the flame lit by Adrian Bellamy in the early eighties — to turn Edgars into a decentralised, market-focused retail powerhouse. Peter Searle has brought to Volkswagen the vision of a high-quality, market-oriented future. Bruce Edmunds had a clear picture of United Tobacco Company fighting back Rembrandt's onslaught. Gerald Haumant at Cashbuild, Robin Hamilton at Suncrush, Bill Venter at Altech, Albert Wessels at Toyota, Raymond Ackerman at Pick 'n Pay — each of these men possesses a powerful vision of his organisation. Vision focuses attention on what the organisation wants to be and do. And the vision should look as far into the future as possible. It should take the long view. As Aaron Searll of Seardel says, "What's 30 years in the life of a business?"

Of course it's not enough just to have vision. We've all met the dreamers who will set the world on fire — one day. You have to communicate that vision so that the whole company, and especially your top team, has a clear picture of the organisation that you are all trying to build. Express the vision in value-laden language and talk about it often. Translate your vision into a set of hard objectives. And then act on the vision — achieve those objectives through strategy.

Strategy Needs Top Level Commitment

We get a little worried when we hear that a client or prospective client has a Strategic Planning Department, or that there is a staff person designated Strategic Planning Manager. Those kinds of structures give the impression that strategy — "strategic planning" — might have been delegated to a convenient place away from the Chief Executive's office or hijacked by the planning department. Strange as that may sound, it's a surprisingly prevalent arrangement. And there is a role for the strategic planning manager — a process intensive role. But don't charge him with strategy itself. Strategy must start at the top, with the Chief Executive. And it must be driven from the top. Piet Beyers, MD of flagship subsidiary of Cadbury-Schweppes, Cadbury's (Pty) Ltd, talks about top management commitment:

> *"A lot of the things that one talks about can slide without you really noticing it — unless the Chief Executive keeps on focusing on them, keeping them to the fore, creating structures to keep focusing on them."*

In our client organisations, and in the super-performers, we have seen the power that top management commitment can bring to the strategic process. While we know that implementation of strategy is a complex task that needs the co-operation of many people, we know too that implementation will not succeed without the Chief Executive's committed leadership.

And conversely we have seen good strategic thinking wasted, superb opportunities squandered, solely and directly as the result of an individual's lack of commitment. **Strategy is the job of the Chief Executive. He must initiate it, lead it and drive it.** One of the key components of Volkswagen South Africa's amazingly successful strategy for the latter half of the eighties and early nineties has been a programme to change the culture of the organisation. Peter Searle, VW's Managing Director, played a major role in formulating that strategy — and a major role in driving it home. Literally for years now Searle has phoned the person responsible for the change programme, Leon de Klerk, at least once a week to find out how the process is progressing.

Meyer Kahn of SAB says it all in his own inimitable style:

> *"Shit rolls downhill. You start here and it impregnates the whole organisation."*

Mental Space

What conditions favour strategic thinking? Where and how do

our top-performing chief executive officers formulate these winning strategies?

Visit Aaron Searll at Seardel's corporate head office. He and his corporate team of four executives, their secretaries, "three gardeners and two kitchen ladies" operate from a magnificent estate high above Constantia on the slopes of Table Mountain. Built by an American millionaire in the 1930s and called after Monterey, California, the baronial mansion is set in huge, forested grounds. There are fountains and trim, terraced lawns. Inside, behind leaded light windows and dressed sandstone archways, a minstrel gallery looks down from under a hammer-beam roof into the Great Hall — "perfect for our group cocktail parties". The boardroom table fits elegantly into the old library. There is oak panelling everywhere. Searll's office is upstairs, in what was formerly one of the bedrooms. It's a large room. The big wooden desk and table at its right are piled with files. This is a place where work gets done. But it's furnished very personally. Searll's flying licence hangs in pride of place. There are family photographs alongside the current business texts on the bookshelves, an exquisite Lalique figurine on the mantlepiece. Aaron is very modest about it all. "Just look at this," he says, "It's unbelievable. We're very lucky." Well, to misquote our own great Gary Player, fortune favours the prepared mind, and a working environment like Monterey must surely favour that mental preparation. Searll has distanced himself from the hum of operations, and has given himself space to think.

Visit Guy Luyt in Pretoria Portland Cement's elegant modern offices in Parktown. From floor to high ceiling, the windows give out onto lovely gardens. Luyt's office is quiet: mental space. Visit Vic Hammond at Edgardale. It's one of three enclosed offices in a building that accommodates 1 300 people. Hammond's carpets are deep pile, the light is soft, almost low. Garment industry journals and fashion magazines cover a reading shelf against one wall. The office is quiet: mental space. Harry Oppenheimer's office is on the first floor of Anglo American's 44 Main Street headquarters. As one would expect, it is elegantly furnished in the best of taste. A collection of silverware fills a glass case to one side. There are paintings and *objets d'art*. The office is quiet,

14

insulated from the city traffic below: mental space. Dr John Temple's office at Plessey has magnificent views of the mountains above Kirstenbosch Gardens. It too is hushed: mental space.

Not all our top-performing Chief Executives work in such tranquil surroundings. The open windows of Raymond Ackerman's wonderfully memento- and award-cluttered office admit the noise of Main Road, Claremont. The door is closed as we talk, but from time to time people wander in in very informal style. The door of Hugh Mathew's office at Foschini is open to a typing pool.

At Cashbuild, Gerald Haumant's tiny office is positively busy. The door is open. People put their heads in and have short conversations, confirm times for meetings. The phone rings frequently. Gerald answers it himself — no-one screens his calls. No mental space here. We know that Haumant is a thinker, but where does he do his thinking? We guess he thinks in the car, for he travels between his office and Cashbuild's rather distant branches several times a week. Cashbuild executives spend time at Mabula Game Lodge several times a year. There's plenty of mental space available there. We don't know where Hugh Mathew does his thinking, but we guess that Raymond Ackerman thinks on planes — he's been to the United States 72 times.

There's another aspect to mental space too. A number of studies have shown that decisions made under high levels of stress will tend to be of lower quality, and that risk aversion in decision making tends to rise with rising stress levels. In other words you are less likely to make good, balanced decisions when you are under stress. So de-stress. Delegate more, do less yourself, give yourself more time. Try to make your office environment less hurried, more relaxed. As we travelled from winner to winner in our research we were impressed with the relaxed feel of many top Chief Executives' offices. They almost all had more time available for us than we had asked for, or had scheduled.

Chief Executive officers do it in different ways and with different styles. But the message is, if you want to think strategically and make quality decisions, give yourself the mental space to do so, either by insulating your everyday working environment

from the daily pressures of operations, by physically getting away from it all, or by simply doing less — whatever works best for *you*.

When we think of mental space we think of the Chief Executive of one of our client organisations. During the 18 months that we have been working with them the combined effects of greater decentralisation, greater delegation, and his greater confidence in a more developed management team have allowed him to create for himself significant mental space. He spends more quiet time in his office on his own. His desk is clearer. He is visibly more content and more relaxed. And above all, he is now thinking strategically about his business.

Strategic Head, Operational Legs

Our research into the super-performers showed a clear pattern. All of these companies separate strategic thinking from operational action. **At whatever level strategy is being drafted — and that could be at corporate, business unit or functional level — the people responsible for the strategic concepts are not the people who will have to implement the detailed strategies that flow from the strategic concept.** There's an important rider here though. While strategic initiatives don't originate at operating level, operating management is nevertheless very involved in fleshing strategy out and in planning implementation. More of this later.

This distinction between thinking and doing seems to be particularly important in South Africa where, by virtue of the shortage of management and perhaps because of a rather macho approach to shouldering workload, line managers tend to be very busy people.

At group level in Cadbury-Schweppes, Chief Executive Peter Bester sees himself as the architect of strategy — more of a thinker than a doer — but his experience at Cadbury-Schweppes, and previously, is that he works best when he has a strong operations man close by. SA Bias's Chris Seabrooke talks about this too. He believes that every business should have, at the top, two clear-thinking people, one hands-off and one hands-on. Chris designates himself Executive Chairman. His hands-on man is Philip Coutts-Trotter, the Managing Director. The closeness of this relationship is the basis for turning strategy into action at SA

Bias. It is a relationship that works despite evident potential for conflict — both men have big egos — for it is a relationship that is founded on trust: trust that Chris will not interfere in operations and trust that Philip will always look after the interests of shareholders. After all, Philip is himself a substantial shareholder in SA Bias Binding Manufacturers Limited. There surely can be no better way to ensure that an employee looks after the interests of shareholders than to make him one. (This is discussed in Chapter 4.) Naturally they spend a great deal of time together, but the role distinction suits the respective talents of the two individuals. Seabrooke brings his cool and impressive intellect to bear on the broad strategic issues; Coutts-Trotter checks, translates and marshalls resources with keen, practical intelligence. Dwight Eisenhower used to say, with considerable self deprecation, that "any damn fool can be a strategist, but it takes someone who knows armies to get the food, the ammunition and the fuel there on time so the attack goes through." We don't buy Eisenhower's proposition on strategists, but we're with him on the rest.

Classical Strategy — the Formal Way

"Strategy is an absolutely central part of the Plessey ethos," says John Temple, Managing Director of Plessey's South African operation. "It really is a big thing in our lives and it's one of those things that have come to us from Plessey, England. In January 1986, when Sir John Clark (of Plessey Plc) rejected GEC's 1985 take-over bid, one of the cornerstones of his counter-argument was that Plessey's strategic management process was vastly superior to the GEC system, and that was the main reason why Plessey's results and ratios were vastly better than GEC's and that if they were taken over by GEC the company would go down. He regarded the strategic planning processes as the key to all that."

In certain parts of the Plessey business worldwide that strategic planning process looks far into the future. Where there are particularly long lead times 10 and even 15-year scenario planning is formally tackled, especially with what are called the enabling technologies, which need a great deal of research and development before they find production-line application. Gallium arsenide and diamond integrated circuitry, for example, are already under development, but are only expected to yield commercial returns in the next century. In South Africa, Plessey's development programme does not need to look as far ahead as that, but a comprehensive five-year plan is drawn up every year. "And it's not long-term planning," says Temple. "We do proper strategic planning." By that he means that Plessey's strategies for the next five years are formulated top down, by assessing the prospects for each of the firm's products and in each of the firm's markets in the light of the firm's current and future operating environments. The process begins in May every year with a detailed and wide-ranging environmental scan. Key issues facing each division are teased out and summarised. The top management team — comprising about 10 people — usually get away from the office for a few days at the critical point of the environmental review. "We develop environmental guidelines. The divisions then go off with their own management and think through the strategic issues of product and market and then the resources needed to service those products and markets."

Temple's boss comes out from England to review those findings — division by division — so providing a critical link into the group's experience and activities worldwide. "Then from May through to September the solutions, the strategies, the preferred strategies, the analysis of options, and so on, goes on," says Temple.

Strategies are tested using a sophisticated computer model (originally built by Temple himself) to ensure that the selected strategies will yield the best possible results in the years to come. In October the Plan is presented to Plessey UK. There is much review and debate. "It's not done in the form of an inquisition. It's done in the form of 'You know that's jolly interesting. Have you thought of this? Can't you add that?' There's tremendous backing and support for it."

The result is the POST Plan — the Plessey Operational Strategic and Tactical Plan. It becomes the Bible for the year ahead. Directly from it flow certain Action Plans. All other Action Plans follow from the budget. Ah, the budget. We've often heard it said that there must be clear separation between a firm's strategic planning and budgeting processes. **While we agree that the strategic plan must be much more than a set of financial projections, we believe that the budgeting exercise must follow directly from the strategic plan.** Plessey certainly do it this way, as do Cadbury-Schweppes and Foschini. The first of the five years covered by Plessey's strategic plan is called the Budget Objective year, and it forms the basis for a top-down approach to the detailed Budget. The Budget itself is calculated on a bottom-up basis and is tested for reasonableness against the Budget Objective, line by line. After all, as Temple says,

> *"How do you know you've arrived when you didn't know where you were going? Bear in mind the Budget Objective was done on a theoretical top-down modelling basis. You've got your concept of a perfect company, now you've got to check that you can actually have that. Gaps between the Budget and the Budget Objective are simply eliminated by re-doing the Budget until it is in line with the Budget Objective. It works like a dream. It is a key factor for our success."*

Alternative Strategy — the Informal Route

Our discussion with Robin Hamilton, Executive Chairman and controlling shareholder of soft-drink bottler Suncrush Ltd, opened with an interesting preamble on the disappearance of his competition (Pepsi-Cola), the importance of distribution, and the limited usefulness of current cost accounting. We asked Hamilton whether he would like to work through our agenda, which had been faxed to Durban a couple of days in advance. He agreed. The first item was on strategy: *The overall strategy which Suncrush employs to address its markets and the strategic management processes by which the strategy is implemented.*

There was a long pause. He looked across the table from under bushy eyebrows, "I ran into a bit of a brick wall on Item 1. I mean, it's not my kind of language really and when I read that it isn't very clear to me." One of us mumbled something apologetic about the jargon, but knowing that Suncrush has been a darling of the financial press for years and has performed exceptionally well over a sustained period, we persisted, saying that there must be *some* kind of system that Suncrush has for deciding what to do.

"In terms of marketing," said Hamilton and referred us to Andrew Beggs, Suncrush's Marketing Director, who would be interviewed later in the day. Not wanting to let it go, we referred to the interesting ways that other top performers turned strategic thinking into action. Hamilton sidestepped again, by talking about their current strategic thrust into the black market. Our meeting with Beggs confirmed that Suncrush indeed has a clear and farsighted approach to marketing strategy, but Suncrush does not have a process for setting and executing business strategy. They have thought about it but they remain unconvinced. They just don't think they need it.

Our experience with Aaron Searll of Seardel was disturbingly similar. Although he referred to their published Mission Statement as a very clear and important communication of the group's strategy, he explained that there is no formal strategic management process at Seardel, and no annual weekend "in the green".

> "I think you evolve strategy, just through experience, and also reading and learning what others are doing."
>
> "There is no annual weekend 'in the green'?"
>
> "No, because tomorrow something else is happening and I've seen so much time wasted in these four-day seminars. I don't know what those guys achieve quite honestly — I really don't know — other than making them tired and confused. I really don't believe in it, rightly or wrongly. I think that sort of thing may apply at government level or where you are dealing in a highly capital intensive industry, say mining, where you have to take long decisions which have four or five years' worth of implications, but we don't have that kind of thing."

The management theorist might be tempted to dismiss Searll's and Hamilton's approaches to strategy as naive, even dangerous. But these men have built businesses that have consistently outperformed almost all others, certainly all others in their respective industries. And they ain't idiots either; Hamilton has a degree in Maths and Physics; Searll is currently completing a part-time Doctorate in Business Administration at a Swiss business school. It's not that they don't know about strategic planning, they just don't think they need it. "What for?" they ask, and in doing so they help us to an important (and for us rather surprising) conclusion: if you're a Suncrush or a Seardel you can get to strategy without going via strategic planning. The evidence is right there, in their results. But Plessey couldn't do without strategic planning, nor could SAB, or Altech. How do we decide who can and can't do without strategic planning?

Suncrush and Seardel operate in very different businesses but share a number of common characteristics. Both companies experience highly cyclical demand for their products. The seasonality in the soft drink business is overwhelming: consumption graphs show two peaks, a massive one over the Christmas holidays and a smaller one over Easter. Seardel's major activity is garment manufacture — also heavily seasonal, and with a fashion component as well. In these businesses cyclical change is the order of the day. They have got used to it; they have learned to accommodate it. A second common characteristic is that both companies are run by their effective owners. Thirdly, both Suncrush and Seardel have flat, decentralised management structures. And fourthly, and perhaps most importantly, both companies have, over long periods of time, developed strong, internally consistent organisational cultures.

Familiarity with cyclical change, owner managed, flat decentralised structure and strong culture — what does this all add up to? We'll talk much more about culture later in the book, but essentially a strong organisational culture can in many ways substitute for formal co-ordination and control systems in an organisation and in any case should underpin and energise them. Combine informality with decentralisation, fast communication and rapid decision making and you have an organisation that can cope with rapid and frequent change — a flexible organisation. Flexible organisations, like Seardel and Suncrush, don't need strategic planning. That's not to say they don't need strategy — Hamilton and Searll are both great thinkers, both know what they need to be doing — but they don't need formal systems for developing and implementing that strategy.

The Right Route to Strategy

We've seen that on the one hand Plessey and Cadbury-Schweppes use the classical strategic planning model as a formal basis for their process of strategic management. We've seen too that Seardel and Suncrush at the other extreme are breathtakingly informal in their approach. What do the other top-performing companies do, and how do you decide what is best for your own organisation?

Twice a year Cashbuild's executives and senior management — about 20 people in all — disappear for a few days to Mabula, a game reserve in the northern Transvaal. An invited lecturer will speak on a predetermined topic, whereafter the team "think-tanks" around the topic to isolate the five most important issues that flow from it. Each individual is given a project that deals with some aspect of one of these key issues, and has to report back to the group at the next meeting in six months' time. The topic may be on any aspect of the business, from people, through marketing to "ranging" — the selection of stock ranges. At a recent conference, discussion centred on raising the barriers on entry into the industry. The process is loosely structured and fairly informal.

The Altron group also has an almost paperless strategic process. Strategic information and strategic initiative flows up and down the group structure through a hierarchy of strategy team meetings, of which the topmost comprises Bill Venter and his executive deputy chairmen, Neill Davies, Richard Savage and Don Snedden. Only action-point minutes are kept. Teams meet regularly and team members are expected to act promptly and report back. Communication of strategy is by representation of individuals at meetings of teams lower in the hierarchy — a hierarchy that reaches right down into the operating companies, where Technology Development Task Teams are working on new product projects.

SAB's strategic planning process is as sophisticated as you will find anywhere. But Meyer Kahn maintains that "it should be turned on and off depending on requirements." The plan form-alises a lot of informal thinking, but planning isn't done just once a year. "It's absolute lunacy to do it that way," says Kahn, who believes that planning can become a "terrible chore" down the line unless you introduce an element of interest. Consequently

SAB varies the process from year to year to keep it fresh, to inject a measure of excitement. Kahn holds that strategic planning is a line management function; SAB doesn't have a strategic planning department.

Foschini have had a fairly formal system of monthly management and strategy meetings since 1982. In the latter weeks of 1988 they began developing Mission Statements for group companies as a move towards greater formality of the strategic process. Strategy is highly decentralised in Pick 'n Pay. Regional managers set their own strategy within guidelines provided by Head Office. And at Head Office the top management team discusses strategy on a regular but informal basis.

Clearly, although every organisation needs strategy, different kinds of organisations need different strategic planning processes at different stages in their organisational life-cycles. What pointers can we find from the super-performers? To take up Aaron Searll's points, planning is more important for companies that have slow feedback from their strategic decisions and that feel the effect of a strategic move long after the decision is taken. Pretoria Portland Cement, for example, must decide to invest in a new cement factory 10 to 15 years before they think they will need the additional capacity. They must plan that capacity expansion pretty carefully.

To a lesser degree the same applies to Plessey, and to Cadbury-Schweppes, where the lead time on installing new manufacturing technology tends to be long. For these companies strategic planning is appropriately a big, formal exercise that occurs annually. Pick 'n Pay, Suncrush, Seardel and Cashbuild, however, have much quicker strategic feedback. They look at strategy more frequently and less formally.

Moreover, the emphasis of the strategic management process is going to be different for different degrees of both centralisation and formalisation. Small owner-managed firms are generally highly centralised in terms of decision making, and fairly informal — there are relatively few policies and systems.

These firms don't really need strategic planning, but as they begin to grow they will feel the need to decentralise. And, initially at any rate, decentralisation typically demands increased formalisation. In our experience organisations in this phase usually need consolidation planning, a largely internal exercise that tends to focus on organisational weaknesses and system building. When the internal problems are in hand, the organisation's strategic process can shift to being more strategic in the true sense. The focus of strategy should move outside the organisation, to the changes that are occurring in the company's markets and environment. Good old-fashioned strategic planning is probably appropriate here. Most medium and large South African companies are in this phase; they are only partially decentralised, and they have become fairly formal in their processes and systems. They tend to be fairly rigid, responding rather slowly and deliberately to new threats and opportunities. They are likely to change only reluctantly.

Most organisations will, we believe, benefit from increasing decentralisation. But increasing decentralisation calls for increasing co-ordination and control. How can you effectively improve co-ordination and control without putting in more and more systems that will eventually turn your business into a bureaucracy? The answer is by building a strong organisational culture. As we said earlier, a strong culture will provide you with the informal control and co-ordination: to further decentralise and "informalise" or "de-bureaucratise" your company is to make it more flexible. As you do that your strategic management process is likely to focus on strengthening your corporate culture and managing organisational and individual values.

The message that we get from listening to the super-performers, and comparing them to other companies that we have worked with is pretty clear: **unless your organisation is truly flexible — which few are — you will benefit from a fairly formal strategic management process. The cornerstone of that process will be some variant of classical strategic planning.**

Process and Product Benefits

Of course the most tangible outputs from a well-conducted strategy exercise are the strategy itself and the programme for its execution. These are the *content* benefits. But time and time again, with clients and with the super-performers, we have seen the benefits that flow from the strategic management *process* itself. **Whatever its intensity or level of formality, at whatever levels in the organisation, whenever strategic planning involves members of planning teams, in meetings or workshop sessions there is an almost immediate improvement in team spirit and communication.**

At Edgars, where strategic planning takes place informally throughout the year, the figures are regarded as unimportant. The exercise is more directive than definitive. Strategic planning there is the responsibility of the Group General Manager: Corporate Services, Fred Haupt, who explains that "planning is about allocating resources and people are your most important resource". Haupt firmly believes that the planning *process* is in fact more important than the product that results from it.

Building a Knowledge Base

The super-performers base their strategic decisions on information; information about their environments, their markets, their customers and their competitors, and themselves. When SA Bias planned their moves on the garment accessory industry they took real time and effort to understand the industry, the market and the competitors. They learned about technology and product development. They paid particular attention to industry structure, looking carefully at buyer-supplier relationships and at the ways value was added to products as they flowed through to the end user.

The clear picture they developed led them to a strategy truly elegant in its simplicity; to cut the wholesalers out and to integrate back from trading to manufacture through acquisitions. Their knowledge of the players in the industry allowed them to identify the operations they wanted to buy. The original hit-list contained the names of no less than 35 companies. They have subsequently acquired about 17.

When Peter Bester took over as group Chief Executive of Cadbury-Schweppes Ltd in late 1984, he and his top team began a complete strategic re-evaluation. Bester's business background is enviably diverse: starting out as a chemist, he moved through to production at TW Beckett, spent time as Marketing Director of

Royal-Beechnut and moved to Zimbabwe where he ran the Meikles group — one of that country's largest conglomerates with businesses in hotels, tea, textiles, engineering, supermarkets, department stores and building supply. He has come to the conclusion, though, that there is no formula for success in business: "You've got to look at each situation as a unique business proposition. I came into Cadbury-Schweppes without any preconceived ideas of what had to be done. We actually started out with a very systematic analysis from which we drew certain conclusions about how the business had to be changed. It really was looking at the business in relation to its environment. On the environmental side we saw clearly the South African economy heading for major trouble.

"The rand was just in the process of its initial massive slide. One could see the signs of interest rates rising, and so on. The internal analysis showed that the Cadbury-Schweppes business as a whole was dominated by its confectionery business, which in turn was dominated by its chocolate business, which was highly import-dependent. It was oriented entirely towards the upper-income white female consumer. It's a very capital intensive business. It had been suffering the disadvantage of under-investment for some years."

A further problem was the rather comfortable non-competitive management style that the group had developed over the years. In retrospect the way forward for Cadbury-Schweppes seems obvious — as it always does when the strategically important information is systematically laid out. The confectionery subsidiary, Cadbury's (Pty) Ltd, would lead the growth of the group. But Cadbury's needed to shift its emphasis towards confectionery's growth markets — young consumers and black consumers. That would take time. And in the meantime the group was poorly balanced to provide good returns. Acquisitions were required, including companies that were in fast-moving consumer goods, were oriented towards confectionery or drinks, were not import-dependent and had low capital intensity. Several prospects were identified, one of which was Bromor Foods, manufacturers of Brookes Oros and Moir's Jellies. The final imperative was to shift the group towards a market-oriented, performance-based culture that encouraged innovation. Three years on, those information-based strategies have been substantially achieved; the confectionery company has refocused its marketing; Bromor has been successfully acquired and integrated. The culture change is well under way.

We talked earlier about the informal alternative to classical strategy. We saw that very flexible organisations — like Suncrush and Seardel — that are highly decentralised, have strong cultures and operate in industries with fast feedback on strategic decisions, may not need formal strategic planning. But here we raise a critical caveat. **While we say that you may not need formal strategic planning, we don't believe you can do without a system to collect and analyse strategically important information about your markets, your customers and your competitors. Whether your strategic process is formal or informal you cannot make good strategic decisions without good strategic information.**

Core Strategy — the Strategic Concept

Raymond Ackerman's Damascan experience was at the hand of Bernardo Trujilio of National Cash, Dayton, Ohio — the supremo of supermarketing in the United States of the fifties and sixties. Ackerman added what he heard about supermarketing at one of Trujilio's famous seminars to what he had learnt about marketing from Professor Hutt at the University of Cape Town. It all dovetailed perfectly with the ethics of customer care and courtesy drummed in to him in his early days in the Ackerman's stores: "Put the customer as Queen. To support her make a table with four strong legs: administration, merchandising, sales promotion/social responsibility, and people." As Ackerman says, "The philosophy of the table is really what's built Pick 'n Pay. The table is like a technique to achieve the strategy. The strategy isn't to make as much money as possible, or to be the best or the biggest, the strategy is consumer sovereignty." Pick 'n Pay's core strategy couldn't be clearer or simpler.

Suncrush, too, have a clear and simple philosophy: to put Coke within arm's reach of the consumer's desire. The product must be available, acceptable and affordable. From this, all else follows. Passenger transporter Tollgate espouses a classic low cost core

27

strategy: to give the customer what he wants (punctuality, speedy delivery, frequent departures, cleanliness and comfort) at the lowest possible price. Waltons' strategy has been even simpler: to take over loss-making stationers and turn them around. Utico to focus all their resources on only four block-busting cigarette brands. SA Bias: to cut out wholesalers and integrate backwards with acquisitions. Cashbuild: to dominate the cash-and-carry wholesale building materials market. SAB: to offer the consumer a choice of consistently high-quality beer brands.

Each of the super-performers has a clear and simple concept of its strategy. Each Chief Executive can express what he is trying to do in two or three sentences. A short, simple statement is powerful because it can be communicated. Every Pick 'n Pay employee knows about making the customer Queen and the four legs of the table. They all know about it because it is easy to visualise and understand. They all know about it because they are told about it again and again. It has become part of life at Pick 'n Pay.

Competitive Advantage — the Lynch-Pin of Strategy

It's one thing to define your core strategy. It's another to flesh it out to a useful level of detail, to set out all the detailed strategies, business by business, or function by function, that must be pursued to give force to the core strategy. Competitive advantage is the bridging concept. It is the starting point for the translation of strategy into action because it defines the basis upon which you will compete. It defines the ways in which you are going to outperform the competition. It helps you understand the things you must excel at, the core skills you must develop to win. We think of competitive advantage as the fulcrum, the lynch-pin of strategy. **All that precedes competitive advantage in the strategic process is deductive — distilling ideas from a mass of information. All that follows it is inductive — turning those key ideas into the many, many actions that will realise success. We believe that it is as important to be clear on competitive advantage as it is on strategy. If you don't know how you are going to outperform the competition then you probably won't.**

As we examine the ways in which the super-performers strive to outperform their competition, you will notice that most of their definitions of competitive advantage are concerned with providing value to the customer. They are essentially marketing thrusts. We believe that to be entirely appropriate. It follows naturally from the question of what *value* is to the customer, a question that your earlier information gathering will have carefully addressed. Since detailed strategy flows mainly from desired competitive advantage, we see that the marketing function will be the vanguard of strategy in almost all companies. We will take a closer look at how the super-performers handle marketing in Chapter 3.

Willards' competitive advantage centres on product and marketing innovation. Take the successes of Crinkle-Cut and Flanagan's, for example, which were both locally developed and which each created an entirely new brand category. Pick 'n Pay's competitive advantage has customer care as its foundation. They aim to look after the shopper — both in and out of the store — better than OK Bazaars or Checkers do. Pick 'n Pay's niche marketing approach and decentralised decision making flow directly from their commitment to customer care; that way the company can better tailor each of its many offerings to the needs of particular groups of customers. Seardel's Searll also talks decentralisation, but believes in market domination, aiming to dominate the product areas in which he competes so that he can play the game pretty much by his own rules.

In most of the country there is no direct competition for Coca-Cola. Nevertheless Coke-bottler Suncrush is up against dozens of other products in their fight for "share of throat". As their strategy says, they aim to make their product accessible and available to the consumer, so they must have faster, deeper and cheaper distribution systems than the opposition. Their product has to be colder too. As Suncrush's Marketing Director Andrew Beggs says, "There's nothing more unrefreshing than a warm Coke." They also aim to make their product affordable, so they work long and hard at improving efficiencies at their plants. Despite not being the largest soft-drink bottler in the country (SAB subsidiary Amalgamated Beverage Industries is bigger), Executive Chairman Robin Hamilton reckons Suncrush is the most cost-effective.

Waltons is now the largest stationery business in South Africa. The only way they believe that they can compete with focused niche players is by offering a superior service and a complete range of products. They aim to offer the best service in the stationery industry, where service is measured in terms of range and availability of stock, speed of delivery, quality and efficiency of administration and timely advice to customers of impending price increases. As for product range, Mark Davis, Waltons' Financial Director, explains that even if their pen is more expensive than the niche player's, the customer will probably take it as part of a larger order. "What we want to do," he says, "is make it much easier and more pleasant to buy from Waltons than from anyone else."

Cadbury's celebrated 50 years of manufacturing in South Africa in July 1988. In their glossy anniversary brochure, Managing Director Piet Beyers wrote "Quality and innovation have always been the cornerstones of our success. Our glass-and-a-half logo endorsing our product quality is no idle boast and the popularity of our new brands has proved the value of innovation." Cadbury's competitive advantage is based on quality and innovation. From these simple ideals flows the company's detailed strategy.

The super-performers teach us that you have to define the basis of your competitive advantage — and then you have to work at it. Carol Scott and Maureen Jackson built Imperial Car Hire on the basis of service. They resolved to offer better service than their competitors, and they worked, day and night with fanatical zeal, to achieve that aim. At the other end of the passenger transport business, bus operator Tollgate does all in its power to keep the cost of its operation low. Yes, it must give its passengers what they want — frequency, punctuality, comfort, etc, but at the end of the day it competes with SABTA taxis on price.

Volkswagen has made quality its consuming passion. Utico fights Rembrandt with strong brands. Edgars drives its competitive advantage on better merchandising and better service. "Give the lady what she wants," says Chief Executive Vic Hammond. As the industry leader, SA Bias's position in garment accessories is similar to Waltons' in stationery. They want to "make it so darn easy to buy from SA Bias", so they offer a range of products that is beyond the resources of any of their competitors and they offer service that no competitor can match — deliveries are guaranteed within 10 days of order and are often made within five. Willards regard product and marketing innovation as the key to their success. SAB's Beer Division concentrates on quality. Pick 'n Pay compete by offering superior customer care. Mathieson & Ashley's office furniture operation aims for superior quality and timely delivery. Each of these companies has defined just how they plan to beat the competition. In a broad sense they are *positioning* their companies in the context of their industries.

MAKING IT HAPPEN

Strategy first became fashionable in the 1960s. In those early days Igor Ansoff, Bruce Henderson, Peter Drucker and their co-pioneers strove to draw conceptual frameworks for analysing corporate performance and defining strategic options. The emphasis was on strategy formulation; the conceptual framework and analytical techniques focused on *what* the corporation should be doing. Strategic planning became an accepted necessity. Management began to get that warm feeling that comes from knowing that things are under control, that the future will be as it should. In the seventies, however, strategy started to lose some of its lustre. The fact of the matter was that not all the well-laid plans were working properly. Things *weren't* happening as they should have been. The understanding began to dawn that careful and deliberate implementation of a strategy is as important as, or perhaps even more important than, strategy formulation. The emphasis was shifting towards the *how*. Now, as we go into the 1990s the balance has tipped even further; while there is still dazzling work being done on strategy formulation (particularly by the field's undisputed guru, Michael E Porter of the Harvard Business School), more and more attention is being given to implementation. As SAB Beer Division's Graham Mackay says:

> *"If it were fairly simple to write down a success formula and also very simple to implement it — and that's more to the point — then everyone would do it. Well obviously it isn't. It's by no means simple to decide what to do, and it's even less simple to implement what you decide to do."*

Good strategy will deliver, but only if it is well implemented. The road from strategy to success is often long and hard. In the remainder of this chapter we'll see how the super-performers travel that long, hard road.

People Implement Strategy — Involve Them

People implement strategy — people at all levels in the company. But they can't contribute if they don't know what is required. Yes, it certainly helps to tell people what the company plans to do, what the strategic initiatives are, but the most powerful technique for building people's commitment to a plan is to involve them in the planning.

At Altron strategy team meetings go right down into the middle management levels of the operating companies. People at every management level are involved in making the decisions that they will have to implement. Involvement is an important feature of Edgars' strategic process — probably the most important feature. Recall Fred Haupt saying that the process of strategy is more important than the product. That's because the process gets people involved, and involved people are committed people. As Peter Searle says of Volkswagen's quality initiative, "Everyone needs to appreciate that it's their responsibility." Talk to your stakeholders too about your strategy. Clearly there will be confidential information that no outsider should have access to, but your customers, your suppliers, your shareholders, your union, and even — perhaps especially — your bank manager will be much more "on board" if they know in which direction you are headed. Cashbuild's entire start-up strategy hinged upon the backing of their key suppliers — or Royal Suppliers as Cashbuild called them. Cadbury's involved the union in their programme to improve workers' understanding of the concept of profit.

Show and Tell — the Big V Again!

There's another powerful way of communicating your strategy to those around you: demonstration. Demonstrate by your own behaviour as a manager the things that need doing. Do them yourself. Ask people about the issues that are important to the strategy. Emphasise in your behaviour, in your conversations, in

32

the agendas for meetings, that there are a few important things that everyone should have foremost in their minds.

Peter Searle talked about Volkswagen's efforts in building the commitment and co-operation of their dealers: "Bringing people on board requires that they see a behaviour change on your part. One seeing is worth a thousand hearings." VW brought the dealers into the factory to show them the changes. Searle was actively involved in dealer tour guiding duties. Be sure, though, that your behaviour is consistent. If you are trying to improve customer orientation in your organisation, make sure you are the most customer-oriented person around — all the time! One small slip will be seized upon by the cynics and used to undermine the credibility of your programme.

Focus — and Courage

The super-performers focus their attention and their resources on what needs to be done. Unrelenting and undistracted follow-through is the order of the day.

As Cashbuild's Gerald Haumant says, it's a question of discipline:

> *"Nobody's got our strong discipline and that's also one of our key factors for success. We stuck to our knitting, like they say in* In Search of Excellence. *We really stuck all along to what we knew best, which was the cash and carry business. We've never deviated from it, we've never bought a truck; credit is about one half per cent of our turnover. All those temptations were great. We rather grew at a slower pace, limited our growth, but didn't deviate from our mission, which was to saturate the cash and carry market."*

Recall Utico's Drive Strategy; to focus their attention and *all* their resources on their four best brands. In fast-moving consumer goods a brand dies if it isn't supported. They withdrew *all* support from their other 11 brands. It was risky. What if the trends they were following (like the "move to mildness") didn't materialise? What if they had misread the positioning of the favoured four? It took discipline and it took courage, especially, says MD Bruce Edmunds, because many saw it as folly: "I can recall some blokes who came to see me asking me if we were trying to commit suicide."

The Short Agenda — Less is More

Time and time again, when talking about implementation, our super-performers come up with a critical message: **Don't try to do too much.** When Vic Hammond took over from Adrian Bellamy at Edgars, he resolved to concentrate on only two things: merchandising and decentralisation. Chris Seabrooke says that the short agenda has been one of five factors that have helped SA Bias achieve its goals. Seabrooke's agenda listed only four activities: to change the industry structure through acquisitions; to shift SA Bias's focus from trading to manufacturing; to build a very wide range of products; and to offer the best service in the industry. The latter two items flowed directly from SA Bias's desired competitive advantage, the former two from a close understanding of the industry economics. Waltons' core strategy was to take over loss-making stationers and turn them around. Implementation of that strategy has been facilitated by strict adherence to a fairly simple formula that is easy to understand and easy to replicate. When we asked Peter Searle about implementing Volkswagen's major strategic reorientation, he explained the need to provide a sequence to it "because you can't do it all at once". Cashbuild keep it simple too. From all of the issues thrown up at their biannual strategy indaba they pick out the five most important. Projects are then defined to address only these five issues.

And of course, the agendas of all these super-performers are concerned with action — getting things done. As Waltons' Frankie Robarts says: "We take far more action than investigation." **Short, focused, action-oriented agendas turn strategy into action.**

Take Time to Plan and Time to Do

Gerald Haumant of Cashbuild estimates that the practice of strategy takes 5 to 10 per cent of all his time. Furthermore he expects each of his senior executives to spend about 10 per cent of their time on self-development — which includes leading the special projects identified as part of their strategy process. Our formal strategic managers like Plessey and Cadbury's, invest a very great deal of time in formulating strategy and planning implementation. They can't afford not to. Our informal strategists don't deliberately plan strategy sessions but, over the course of the year, they probably devote an equivalent amount of time to strategic thinking and informal discussion. And be they of the formal or the informal camp, our super-performers are at the business of strategy throughout the year. **Developing strategy and turning it into action is a continuous pursuit. It's not once-off strategic planning that they do, it's ongoing strategic management.**

An action plan must obviously have a programme. That means activities must be programmed for completion by dates that are as tightly defined as possible. Cadbury-Schweppes' 1987/88 strategic plan contained the following activities for the introduction of new moulded (slab chocolate) products, each with a specified deadline:

- To launch at least one new variant every year for the next four years
- To launch bite-size CDM (Cadbury's Dairy Milk) in 1988 period 7.

Senior Volkswagen executives have programmed visits to dealers. When they arrive on the forecourt they ask passing customers two questions: "How is your car?" and "How is your service?" It's a programmed activity in their strategic shift to customer orientation.

But we shouldn't plan to deal with our agenda too quickly. A number of the top performers spoke about this. As Chris Seabrooke of SA Bias says, "The reason the switch of the business to manufacturing moved quite well was because we didn't rush it. We expanded each area pretty slowly, not trying to do it all in one year." One of the special strategy projects defined by Cashbuild executives two or three years ago was systematically to raise the barriers to entry into their industry, the idea being to make the job of a prospective new participant in wholesale cash-and-carry building materials more difficult. They identified a number of entry barriers that might be erected, but in line with their short-agenda policy chose only five, of which the two most important were tying up exclusively with the major suppliers and bagging the best store locations. And instead of trying to work on all five at once they ranked them in priority and have only been working on one per year. Their strategy to raise the barriers to entry to their industry will have taken at least five years to bring fully on line.

The strategies of many of our super-performers include planned changes in their corporate cultures. In Chapter 10 we'll be talking much more about culture, which we regard as the single most important factor for business success in the 1990s. The point here though is that changing a corporate culture takes a long time. Cashbuild have been at it for six years. Cadbury's and Plessey have both been on culture change programmes for about three years — and have by their own admission both got a way to go yet. When it comes to culture change though, Volkswagen sets the standard. Peter Searle attributes the vastly improved performance of his company to the cultural shifts they have achieved towards quality and customer orientation. He expected it would take time. Volkswagen's culture change programme has a 10-year time scale — mid-eighties to mid-nineties.

Aaron Searll provides a nice coda for this section on time:

> *"There's a philosophy I learnt from the Japanese: business is a long, long term exercise. The Japanese talk in terms of 30-year, 40-year cycles. It's a long-term thing. The Americans think in terms of every quarter, therefore they make the most atrocious mistakes. They've got to report quarterly growth. I mean, how can you do that? You end up doing all sorts of things — making silly decisions. So we take our time. Do it properly and take your time."*

Structure Enables Strategy

To take up the issue of decentralisation again, Edgars Chief Executive Vic Hammond's strategic agenda listed only two items: merchandising and decentralisation. Clearly, merchandising is fundamental to retailing — but why decentralisation? Decentralisation was one of the key thrusts set in motion by Hammond's predecessor, Adrian Bellamy. Bellamy and his team (which included Hammond, who was Managing Director of Edgars Stores Retail Trading at the time) had decided to reorganise the group into three separate chains, Edgars, Sales House and Jet, so that each could focus on a distinct segment of the retail clothing market. In order that each chain should develop a separate image and culture that suited its target market, Bellamy began the process of decentralising everything, including the support services. It was, for South Africa, radical stuff in its day; each chain was to have its own procurement, store operations, human resources finance and marketing functions. After Bellamy left in 1983 to run a worldwide chain of airport duty-free shops, Hammond took decentralisation to its logical conclusion. Edgars, Sales House and Jet now even have separate boards of directors. For Hammond, decentralisation has been a key factor in the implementation of Edgars' strategy.

Of course when people talk about decentralisation they are not simply talking about location, they are talking about decentralised responsibility and authority — decentralised decision making. Seardel has a small corporate head office; Aaron Searll doesn't hold much with centralisation:

> *"My belief is in a decentralised business. We have 25 companies, we have 25 Managing Directors. Each one runs his own business and we must get out of the way. This builds an entrepreneurial spirit, which in turn builds a lot of talent. Rewards are paid on performance and on results and we get out of the way!"*

Pick 'n Pay, too, is highly decentralised, to allow the group to focus on its market niches, and the needs of the customers in those niches, in a concentrated way. Operational General Managers (those responsible for hypermarkets and supermarket regions) have almost complete autonomy in the running of their businesses. Decision-making will in future be pushed even lower down in the organisation, so that each individual supermarket manager can decide how best to serve the customers in his own catchment area. Already though, the general managers operate very independently — as evidenced by the number reporting to Managing Director Hugh Herman. He has 23 operating general managers and 11 corporate general managers reporting to him, a load that can be bearable only by virtue of Herman's limited involvement in daily operational matters.

SA Bias operates on a decentralised structure too. But a key element of their strategy is to offer a broad range of products, a one-stop service to garment manufacturers. Therefore they need a co-ordinating group marketing function. In general, when these group functions provide services that are the primary elements of strategy there may be justification for a centralised or partially centralised operating structure. Of our super-performers, only Tollgate has an explicitly centralised structure. Their passenger transport operations are divisionalised regionally into the western Cape and the eastern Cape, and then tightly centralised. Tollgate's structure has been designed to enable its low cost strategy. Centralisation offers Tollgate a number of cost advantages; bulk procurement (especially of fuel) carries discounts; a large-scale centralised operation can afford a very sophisticated routing system, allowing for optimal utilisation of vehicles and manpower, centralised maintenance is more controllable and more efficient (maintenance costs run at about 10 per cent of total costs) and helps optimise the lifespan of vehicles.

Our most immediate example of the power of decentralisation comes from our own firm — the consulting practice of Deloitte Haskins & Sells. Initially our assignments were resourced from a pool of professionals who shared qualifications and experience in accounting, finance, information systems and general management. Between 1984 and 1986 that pool grew relatively slowly from six to about 12 people. In the latter part of 1986 the firm was reorganised into four focused business units: financial management, management information, decision systems and strategic management. The now decentralised structure has stimulated and accommodated explosive growth — the 30 months subsequent to the reorganisation saw the professional complement rise to around 60, with a concomitant improvement in profitability.

Measure What You Want to Happen

So you've set your short, focused agenda. You've structured your organisation to support your strategic thrusts. You are on your way down the yellow brick road towards your preferred future. How will you know whether you are on the way to where you want to be? Volkswagen's Peter Searle is very clear on this:

> *"If something is important, set a goal with your people and agree on how you're going to measure it. And apply those measurements. Even with motivation of people you've got to decide what's important and find a way to measure it."*

Quality is VW's priority. "How do you measure quality?" we asked. Quality was one of the easier ones, said Searle. They measured defects per car, customer warranty statistics, customer survey statistics — an enormous number of quality measurements. Today there are many measurements of customer satisfaction. Even employee morale can be gauged by tracking absenteeism, staff turnover, requests for training, participation in quality circles, participation in cost-saving programmes, the number of suggestions coming from employees. "These," says Searle, "are all measures of how motivated people are." Searle's arch-competitor, Brand Pretorius of Toyota, goes even further:

> *"If you can't measure it, you can't manage it."*

The lesson is that even the soft factors like motivation and customer satisfaction can be measured. It's not easy, but if something is important, the trouble you take to measure it will be richly repaid.

Reward What You Want to Happen

Measurement and reward go together in a powerfully motivating two-punch combination. The clear message from our super-performers is: Measure what you want to happen and reward people when it does.

Chapter 4 deals with motivation and reward in more detail, but we mention them here as key elements in the implementation of strategy. We have seen that several top companies have very effective ways of translating broad corporate objectives, strategies and action plans into measurable performance objectives for individuals. Philip Coutts-Trotter, Managing Director of SA Bias, regards this tailoring of personal goals to corporate objectives as being critical to the successful implementation of their strategy. Seabrooke, Executive Chairman, maintains that Coutts-Trotter is "one of the best-paid executives in South Africa". Setting personal objectives sounds unrealistic in textbooks; classic cascading from corporate level down through business units, into divisions, right down to departments and sub-units, to product groups and production areas. Liken it to that huge pyramid of champagne glasses (the flat ones, not the real ones) that is inevitably built in a shopping centre somewhere in South Africa every year. And it's not easy, but it can be done. Cadbury-Schweppes, for instance, do it very effectively indeed. The formal systems are of necessity quite complex if they are to be effective, and are easier to design for managers than for workers, although companies like Cashbuild have developed effective systems at the lowest levels too.

Recognition as Reward

The alternative to these formal performance measurement and reward systems is, of course, the informal way. **Whether they have formal performance measurement systems that are linked into the strategic process or not, the super-performers all use the informal reward systems. "Strategic behaviour" is rewarded with awards, citations, certificates and plaudits. And informal doesn't mean *ad hoc*; these programmes are carefully thought out so that the right behaviour is publicly recognised and encouraged.**

Pick 'n Pay, for instance, have a "PIP award" that encourages employees to take Pride In Performance. In 1987 Wellington Hlengwa, who works in the Shelley Beach store, found a diamond worth R1 500 on the floor of the supermarket. He handed it to his manager who returned it to a very grateful customer. Wellington received a PIP Award — no money, just recognition, and his story told in glowing terms in the company's in-house media. All of Wellington's 22 000 colleagues got the message that honesty is valued at Pick 'n Pay.

Culture Power and Leadership

Our exposure to the top performers has convinced us that **a strong corporate culture is fundamental to winning business performance, particularly in South Africa as we go into the 1990s.**

40

Chapter 10 is devoted to corporate culture, but we make the point here that successful implementation of strategy becomes more feasible if the right culture is built around that strategy, to support it and enhance it. We will see in Chapter 10 that companies like Pick 'n Pay, Suncrush, Cadbury-Schweppes and Volkswagen have done just that with telling effect. We will see there that **culture building starts at the top of the organisation — with the Chief Executive. He has to know what kind of culture he wants, and he must steer the management of culture. And so it is with strategy and its implementation. With foresight, energy and sensitivity the Chief Executive must turn strategy into action. He must make it happen.**

---

19 Steps Towards Mastering Your Destiny

1. Develop a clear vision of what you want your organisation to be and do. Communicate that vision to those around you.
2. Translate the vision into hard objectives.
3. Commit yourself to the process of strategy.
4. Give yourself the mental space that real strategic thinking needs. De-stress. Do less.
5. Shield strategic thinking from the din of daily operations, but involve operating management in the strategic process.
6. Choose a strategic process that suits your company and your industry.
7. Tap in to the *process* benefits.
8. Don't rush it. Take time to plan and time to do.
9. Build a knowledge-base about your markets, your customers and your competitors — and about your own company.
10. Articulate a clear and simple concept of your strategy, of what you are trying to do.
11. Define your competitive advantage — the competitive basis on which you will deliver value to the customer — and position yourself in your industry accordingly.
12. Draft a short, action-oriented, time- and responsibility-specific agenda.
13. Put in the right operating structure. Decentralise wherever you can.
14. Measure what you want to happen — and reward people when it does.

15. Involve people in implementation.
16. Talk to your stakeholders about your strategy.
17. Constantly emphasise the important strategic thrusts.
18. Support your strategy with a strong culture.
19. Keep the focus. Have courage.

CHAPTER THREE

GIVE THE LADY WHAT SHE WANTS

"Give the lady what she wants."
                    Vic Hammond, Chief Executive, Edgars

Lois Wagner is a Brand Manager for Cadbury's. Ask her about Tempo and her face lights up with excitement:

"The night of the launch in Jo'burg we sold every single box of stock we had — to the guys there at the launch. That night Peter van der Lith, our key accounts man, could have walked out of there with orders for 20, 30, 40 thousand outers. It was just unbelievable."

Tempo, of course, is a chocolate bar. The launch that Lois talks about was its launch to the trade — buyers of the major wholesalers and retail chains. The "outer" is the trade package. It contains 50 bars. So at the Johannesburg launch alone, Peter van der Lith could have taken orders for a cool one to two million chocolate bars. The trade took them and the consumer bought them — fiercely, almost passionately. During its peak period Tempo was selling one million bars per week, a figure limited only by a shortage of stock. The bar had been received with an almost fanatic enthusiasm. When stocks ran out irate store keepers and traders threatened never to buy again if they weren't supplied with Tempo immediately.

A rumour began circulating that Cadbury's had adopted a new marketing strategy: create a huge demand and then withdraw the product. Consumers wrote, phoned and even telegrammed the company to demand satisfaction for their Tempo cravings. Sharon Cohen wrote from Craighall Park: "This is a desperate plea from a desperate woman in desperate need. I have become addicted to a very rare, very precious commodity, something that cannot be bought at any price, something so precious it cannot even be stolen!! WHERE HAVE YOU HIDDEN ALL THE TEMPO BARS?? You addict an entire population, then once we are enslaved, you torment us by playing hard to get!!"

In April 1988, a year after Tempo's debut, Cadbury's launched another new chocolate bar, called Cabrio. Although a companion-product to Tempo — both are made by a production technique called "sheeting" — Cabrio has a different mix of ingredients, and is subtly but carefully pitched at a different market segment. It outsold Tempo by 59 per cent in the first two-month post-launch period. Sensation outstripped sensation.

How does Cadbury's do it? What has made Tempo and Cabrio such phenomenal successes? Is it fluke, or fortune? Good luck or great intuition? We believe that it is none of these. The successes of Cabrio and Tempo — and a host of other Cadbury's products over the years — are the results of a top-class marketing effort, an effort, though, that is no more than the artful and deliberate application of marketing fundamentals.

Marketing has no secret spells. Cadbury's competitors know about marketing too. Willards Foods, South African Breweries and Foschini are all magic marketers in their fields. Even passenger-transporter Tollgate and cement manufacturer Pretoria Portland Cement regard marketing as the key to their success. Marketing techniques are available to all. But, as with any tool, the techniques themselves are of little value; it's only their skilful application that creates value.

The rest of this chapter is devoted to looking at those techniques, and how the top performers apply them in their businesses. We will see how they approach the definition and segmentation of their markets, how they go about building up an intimate understanding of their chosen segments, and of the forces that shape and drive demand in those segments. We will see how they will go to almost any lengths to learn about their customers, and their customers' customers. We will examine the strategies that they have adopted to attack their chosen markets, and we will see how each tries to dominate its market segment by closing out the competition. We'll see too that success is not enough for the top performers. They strive for consistency. They are constantly tracking the trends to avoid being caught unawares by a shift — sudden or gradual — that changes the rules in their particular ballgame. We will see too how these top companies have developed the "soft skills" that critically underpin any marketing enterprise; a genuine customer orientation, a desire to be physically close to the customer, and a deeply founded attitude of service and post-purchase follow-through. While we will be drawing on the experience of many of the super-performers, we will closely examine the way things happen at Cadbury's, long renowned for its marketing expertise.

The Star of the Show

There's no doubt about it. **South Africa's top-performing companies regard marketing as their central pursuit.** These organisations are led by what the market wants. Phrases like "We are market driven", "Marketing is the key component of our strategy" and "We're a marketing company" are catch-phrases with all the super-performers. And it's not just lip-service. As the examples in this chapter will show, whether they are in fast-moving consumer goods or industrial commodities, these companies give marketing top billing.

Segment Your Market — Find a Niche

Cashbuild, the cash-and-carry building material wholesaler, and its former Managing Director, Albert Koopman, are now famous for the company's trailblazing and courageous move to participative management. But current Managing Director (and Koopman's right-hand man from the start), Gerald Haumant, attributes the company's success not to their people policy but to their marketing approach. In the late seventies Metro, anticipating a slowing in the growth of their cash-and-carry food wholesaling business, resolved to apply their merchant skills to new product areas. We don't know whether they formally segmented any of the industries or markets they looked at, but they undoubtedly identified a promising niche for cash-and-carry wholesale in the building material business. Koopman, already with Metro, was assigned to the project. He brought in Haumant, who had several years' experience in the building material trade. They started on a small scale, test marketing a limited range of building products in existing Metro stores. It took time, but having analysed the consumer needs and demographics and the economies of the building material industry, they were convinced that they had identified an open niche.

"Traditionally, this industry was one that required credit and delivery," says Haumant, "so we took the counter step. We had a conviction." Their conviction has been admirably vindicated. From the small test start in Metro Stores, Cashbuild today has over 50 outlets all over Southern Africa.

Pick 'n Pay also have a very clear understanding of their industry and the way that it is segmenting. This should come as no surprise: Raymond Ackerman introduced supermarketing to South Africa in the mid-sixties, and has almost single-handedly transformed it from a tiny niche of retailing to a R10 billion industry of its own. And as the shape and size of the industry have changed Pick 'n Pay have introduced new chains, new store formats and new shopping concepts to attack a wider range of segments: Price Club is a cash-and-carry wholesaler; Pick 'n Pay Hypermarkets carry a wider range of goods than the traditional supermarkets, a range that includes building materials, auto spares, and which at one time even extended to discount petrol; Pick 'n Pay Pantries are new, full-range food stores, much smaller than traditional supermarkets and located as convenience outlets.

Edgars, too, has segmented the family clothing market and has separate chains to cater for each broad segment — Sales House, Jet, and Edgars itself. Likewise, Foschini, which apart from the high fashion chain of that name, also has Pages, Markhams and jewellers American Swiss. These are all big-segment examples of entire chains of stores addressing large and fairly self-evident market segments. But the process of segmentation and niching goes much further — right down to the level of the individual consumer.

Infinitesimal Segmentation — Get Your Slice

Segment your segments. Find niches within niches. The process

can be an infinitesimal one, progressively cutting the cucumber into ever thinner slices until you find the piece of the market to which you can most effectively apply your skills and resources, which you can turn into an almost personalised opportunity.

Think about the market for chocolate bars, or "countlines" as they are called in the industry. It's part of the confectionery market, which is part of the "impulse" part of the food market, which is part . . . see what we mean? Segments within segments, slices of slices. And we can go much further down than the segment called "countlines". Let's see how Cadbury's did just that, and in doing so laid the foundations for winning marketing strategies for Tempo and Cabrio.

Segmentation, at whatever level of detail, can only be done on the basis of information. Segmentation is, after all, no more than the identification of sub-groups through recognition of their mutual differences, differences that can only be detected with information. So you have to know a *lot* about the market or sub-group that you wish to segment. And Cadbury's knows a *lot* about the chocolate bar market.

Know Your Customer. Find Out What She Wants

Lois Wagner, Tempo Brand Manager, has been in the business for years. To complement her own experience and the generally available trade information, such as the IBIS (Nielsen) figures, she routinely commissions her own market research. Lois's knowledge of chocolate bars, and the people that buy them, is unbelievably detailed.

Where did Lois start the process that would lead to a strategy for her new countline? She pulls out the Tempo file. Her first document was called "An insight into the countline consumer". It is dated 26 July 1985. It summarises Cadbury's knowledge of the chocolate bar market as a whole. But even in summary, the information is rivetingly specific. We pick out a few phrases from the section headed "The Market":

- Psychographically they (the consumers) are more likely to be status-conscious persons, who use certain brands to project a desired self image to others in order to gain approval for who and what they are.

- There is a strong degree of brand loyalty as consumers know what they like and what they want. They have distinct preferences but they do enjoy a variety of brands and have a repertoire of firm favourites. One or more of these favourites is purchased on an average two to three times a week.
- Consumers tend to eat the bar on their own, most often as a mid-afternoon snack in order to satisfy their hunger, or for eating while watching television.

Pretty penetrating stuff! The document goes on to discuss the differences between countline brands as perceived by the consumer. Factors such as ingredients, taste, texture, effect (filling/ no filling), size, shape and wrapper design have emerged as being those which influence hungry mid-afternoon munchers in their choice between a Bar One, a Lunch Bar or a Campus Crunch. Lois climbs right inside these choice factors. She and her team have built an expert knowledge of the range of ingredients that go into chocolate bars worldwide. They know which combinations of ingredients have been used in obscure British and American products. They understand the dimensions of "taste", as it applies to chocolate bars. They know the countless textural variations between "soft and creamy" and "crisp and crunchy". But they go much further than that. They climb right into the customer's head.

To these physical choice factors they add some of the emotional factors that motivate the consumer's brand choice. These ever-pragmatic Cadbury's people start to get a little esoteric here, for they begin to talk of things like guilt ("the effect the brand has on figure and skin, breaking the social rules") and rebellion ("against socio-norms and amongst younger females against the traditional female stereotype"). Lest you suspect that this is no more than mere conjecture, may we assure you that Cadbury's don't guess if they can help it. Lois Wagner tells of a fascinating piece of research they conducted a while ago:

> *"We did a whole lot of usage and attitudinal research to try to find out what motivates consumers to purchase chocolates, the psychoanalytic reasons as to why people actually purchase chocolates. We used a psychologist who did very in-depth one-on-one interviews that lasted about two hours each."*

From that research the marketing team developed a model of the "rational/irrational" psychological process that a consumer goes through in making his or her decision to purchase.

What Lois is telling us is that **you can only give the customer what she wants if you've taken the trouble to find out what she wants. Our other top-performing marketeers also go to almost absurd lengths to establish what particular bundle of rational and emotional benefits is demanded in each of the niches they serve.** Utico sells its cigarettes almost entirely on lifestyle-based extrinsics. SAB's beer is marketed on lifestyle, each brand offering a different image to reinforce its target consumer's self perception. Volkswagen and Toyota, too, surround their products with extrinsics. Sun International are explicit: "We sell adrenalin and excitement. We'll take you on the roller coaster."

Nichemanship — Define Your Offering

There are many, many examples of successful South African nichemen. We recently had difficulty making last minute car hire reservations for a spontaneous peak-season visit to Cape Town. A car was finally located at Bright's Car Hire, a 70-year-old family business, according to the Bright's man who brought the car out to the airport. A 70-year-old car-hire business in Cape Town? Well Bright's started as South Africa's first taxi operation, running Model T Fords. From there they extended their service over the years to car hire, and further into a unique little market niche — the collecting, transporting and assisting of the scores of foreign seamen and fishermen who visit Cape Town when their ships call at the port. Bright's will arrange collection from the ship (by helicopter if necessary), shepherd the visitors to immigration, assist them in finding medical attention, take them to airports, and so on. The Bright's people that were encountered were quite remarkably friendly and helpful. Perhaps that explains why they remain unchallenged as the leading provider of transport and assistance to Cape Town's visiting seamen.

Bright's have defined their niche, and they serve it well. Nichemanship starts at the point in the process where you begin to define your product or service offering — that bundle of benefits that is going to satisfy your target customer. You've collected and analysed a mass of information about your customer, about his motivations and needs. Your task now is to see which of your competitors is offering what to whom, so that you can identify a unique position for your product — a position from which you are offering something that is different from all the competitive products. **Defining your product offering and positioning it relative to the competition, and in the mind of the consumer, are the final steps in the nicheman's approach to winning marketing strategy.** It's the point too when science becomes art — after all, the mass of information that you have gathered about your chosen market segment is available to any competitor that chooses to collect it. As Piet Beyers, Managing Director of Cadbury's, says:

> *"The key is, what do you do with that information? How do you think? How do you convert it into competitive advantage?"*

Beyers goes on to review where they were, in information terms, before they developed the positioning for Tempo and Cabrio:

> *"Of course we had the demographics showing where the bulk of the people are going to be. And by the way — and it's a big by the way — they're going to be black. But almost more important than the numbers is what kind of people they are going to be, what their lifestyles are going to be, what an ordinary day is for them, whether the target consumer is white or black, urban or rural. How are they going to spend the day? What are their needs going to be during the day? What's going to excite them? What's the interaction with their friends going to be like?"*

So a picture of the target consumer begins to emerge — her lifestyle, her needs, her aspirations. Beyers goes on: "Given that, we must determine what is available to the consumer from our range of products and from the competitors' products. That's obviously a very easy exercise."

He says it's easy, and it is — if you choose the right dimensions along which to compare the products that are on offer in the marketplace. It *is* easy when products are compared in terms of

50

the key factors that the consumer uses when making her choice of brand. *These* are the relevant drivers of demand. *These* are the grid lines you must use when drawing the map of your marketing territory. And don't assume that these fundamental factors are cast in concrete for ever and a day. They will be gradually changing all the time, shifting in importance relative to each other, disappearing altogether, appearing out of nowhere. **Never stop finding out about the customer. If you think you know all about her today, remember that she will be different tomorrow. Avoid surprises. Track the trends.**

Cadbury's had picked up the trends. In 1986 the countline business was increasing in importance relative to the other two components of the chocolate market as a whole — moulded slabs and assortments. And Cadbury's traditional strength was in moulded slabs, where it had over 50 per cent of the market. Cadbury's was strong in a shrinking market segment. And in addition there were three fundamental shifts occurring within the countline segment itself: a shift to younger consumers, a shift to black consumers, and a shift towards the "big eat" product — the one that fills the tummy.

Beyers draws the map of the countline territory. He locates Cadbury's, Wilson-Rowntree and Beacon chocolate bars, each by brand name, on the axis between "big eat" and "indulgent". Lunch Bar and Bar One are at the big-eat end of the scale; Flake and Aero are indulgent. He points to the "big-eat" end of the scale: "So we said, if we want to be a player in this business, this is where we've got to focus our new product development, cause that's where the growth is. All the lifestyle pointers in terms of the biggest section of the population are there — all the nice concepts like eat on the run, street food, that kind of thing. It's the lifestyle of the mobile, individualistic teenagers and 20-year-olds. That's where the future is."

So they looked at the technology. What was technically possible in manufacturing terms? They began the process of specifying both the intrinsic and extrinsic qualities of the product. The intrinsics would determine what the bar would be made of and what it would taste like. The extrinsics would give the cues to the image and personality of the brand, and to how it would be marketed. The gaps on Piet's map of countline country indicated that two new countlines should be developed, for launching three to six months apart and positioned directly against competitors' leading brands. The respective products were codenamed "Helix" and "Barry". (Lois Wagner explains that "Barry" is derived from the name of the engineer responsible for putting in the new sheet-process manufacturing equipment. With a blush, she declines to explain where the name Helix comes from.) On 20 May 1986 Lois produced a document entitled "Countlines — New Product Opportunities". It specified in detail the formulations of each product and the benefits, both intrinsic and extrinsic, that each would deliver. It set out a target date for the launch, and detailed interim dates for finalisation of pack design, wrapper photography, etc. It set out a preliminary brief for the advertising agency which talked about how the brand personalities would be created, and what the communications strategy and launch programme must do. It presented the preliminary creative strategies for both products — strategies that summarised the target markets and the consumer needs that the products would respectively satisfy. It talked about the choice of the names, and the designs of the wrappers. It's the kind of document that competitors would kill for.

Piet and Lois and the rest of the Cadbury's team had taken the purchase dimensions that their research had identified and overlain them onto the mass of information they had collected on their market segment. They had sliced through the information along those lines and had examined the cross cuts for gaps left by the competition. They had defined two new products to be positioned in those gaps. From here on there would be a thousand decisions, a thousand tiny steps along dozens of different paths — all converging on launch day.

Tracking the Trends in Fashion Retailing

Let's turn our attention to the fashion business. Does Seardel do market research? Aaron Searll again: "I'm not interested that Mrs Cohen from Sea Point is going to buy a size 30 blue whatever it is, or the lady from Soweto — what her preferences are. It's not material."

Searll doesn't trouble himself with demographics or psycho-analysis. Nor does his regular customer Hugh Mathew, Deputy Chairman of Foschini. They don't need to. They have all the market research information they need right inside their own businesses. They support the fine art of fashion buying with the pure science of actual sales figures, figures that they assiduously collect in the normal course of their daily operations. They learn from their mistakes, season to season to season. They base their decisions on established facts. Hugh Mathew explains the concept rather well:

"We haven't set out to identify people demographically. In the end people will show their preference through their selection. There you sit with a blue suit and a red tie. I've got a greenish suit. There's a preference. Now it could be that you also have a suit like this and I also have a suit like that, which means that if we were the only criteria, both are very acceptable. But there may be another person with a cream suit, and you and I don't have a cream suit. So straight away cream is not in the same degree of acceptance as our two suits. Now he might have bought his in Johannesburg and we bought ours in Cape Town. So Johannesburg sold a cream suit — we don't know to whom, but we know it sold a cream suit. And if it sells another and another and another, you'd better put cream suits into Johannesburg. So by following the absolute measurement of the elements of the merchandise performance to sales we believe we identify the demography of our outlets in terms which enable us to build up a merchandise plan for each outlet.

So we don't have to know that there are more coloured people in Cape Town than there are in Bloemfontein. What we do know is that the size performance in Cape Town is very different from Bloemfontein. We don't have to know that there are more blacks that buy from Markhams in Carletonville (would you believe, in spite of its having gone CP) than there are buying from Markhams in Cape Town. But we do know that the colour preferences and the sizings and the price ranges in Carletonville Markhams are very different from the same measurements in for example, Wynberg, Cape.

So all we have to do is to know that Wynberg, Cape performs along those criteria (colour, size, price, etc.) in one kind of way, and Carletonville performs in another kind of way, for us to be able to plan how we will construct the merchandise requirement for those shops, and then to buy the merchandise and distribute it accordingly. And then we're working on facts. Now the trick comes when there's a change in fashion. You're wearing a striped shirt, I'm wearing a plain shirt.

But what the buyer's got to be able to do is to determine from his observations that the garment which sold well last spring, isn't going to be the identical garment this spring because of the change in fashion. But the person who bought that garment last spring is going to buy this garment this spring. So all the statistical information that I have on that garment — which is fact — I'm going to transfer onto this garment.

And if I find, for example, that I had planned to clear 80 per cent of my stock last spring and I cleared 90 per cent, then I obviously underbought. I misjudged the quality of the appeal. So I must take that into account when I plan this garment. And of course there's the risk — because I could be wrong. That's the whole trick. So I do that bravely because I know enough about this garment and I know enough about my country, and I go overseas and I look at the fairs and I look at the fashion magazines and I actually look in the shops and I come to the conclusion that whoever bought that garment is going to buy this one. Now all I do is I forget about that garment — and I transfer the facts and plan this garment. The truth of the thing is the merchandise you sell."

Foschini invests real effort and expense in collecting and sorting volumes of sales data. There are, after all, over 600 stores in the four chains that the group operates. Some R20 million is spent on data processing every year. (Remember, though, that Foschini is also in the banking business. It has a debtors book of around R200 million, which absorbs a fair proportion of its computing capability.) It has come a long way since the days when it had 140 punch clerks capturing merchandise information. Today there is on-line point of sale invoicing which debits the customer and updates inventory instantaneously. As for the future, consultants from the United States are helping plan a huge customer database that will provide even more sales information and afford the opportunity to market to certain classes of customers much more directly.

Foschini have a few important pointers for us here. Firstly, they are clearly "horizontal marketers". Horizontal marketers don't worry much about arbitrary racial, social or cultural distinctions between customers. They group their customers on the commonalities of those customers' needs. Seardel, Edgars, Pick 'n Pay, SAB, Cadbury's, Willards, Utico, Volkswagen, Toyota, Cashbuild and many others do the same. The distinction between black and white customers is not particularly useful to them. They believe that there is no justification, business or otherwise, for any marketing approach other than a horizontal one. Secondly, they track the trends from the information that is already available in the business — hard sales information that is readily available. They do internal market research to improve the quality of their marketing decisions.

Dominate Your Niches

The super-performers believe that niche dominance must be the fundamental objective of any niche marketer. For dominance brings independence. The dominant player is much more able to impose his own rules upon the game.

Most of our top performers would agree, including Aaron Searll of Seardel.

> *"Growth? The strategy there was to be in products where we could have a dominant share of the market. We set out to have a major share of each product group we're involved in, and we've certainly achieved it in clothing, toys and consumer electronics."*

Meyer Kahn and Graham Mackay of South African Breweries, Terry Rolfe and Jeff Liebesman of Natbolt/FSI, Sol Kerzner of Sun International, Frankie Robarts of Waltons, Chris Seabrooke of SA Bias — all would go along with Searll on this. These companies all have massively dominant positions in their chosen markets. SAB controls very nearly 100 per cent of the clear beer business. Natbolt is about the only industrial fastener manufacturer of any size left in the country. Waltons has made office stationery its own. Sol Kerzner — one way or another — has sewn up the hugely lucrative casino business in this part of the world. By a variety of means they have all effectively and systematically closed out their competition. South African Breweries is famous for its aggressive response to new competitors — all were either acquired or forced to retire. Natbolt, too, systematically bought up its competitors during the depressed years between 1982 and 1985. Sun International has joint ownership and operation treaties with the Bophuthatswana government which exclude other casino operators. These great companies have staked out their territories and made them their own.

You might argue that these heavy-calibre examples are a little academic and have no real relevance for you. You can't buy out your competition or make treaties with governments. How can you possibly "stake out your territory and make it your own"? Don't despair! There is a way. In fact there are many ways, including those big-gun methods cited earlier. The super-performers suggest three ways here that are available to any size of operation and that would be classified under marketing.

Firstly, and this goes back to an earlier section of this chapter, **define your niche so that you can dominate it, even if you are not a large player in the context of your industry as a whole.** It's that concept of segmenting and resegmenting the segments until you've defined a niche to which you can bring a unique and superior set of capabilities. Build your own ballpark, even if it is small, and play the game there according to your own rules. Secondly, **whether you are in consumer or industrial goods, you must build your brands. You must firmly establish the name and personality of your product or service in the mind of the target consumer.** Your communication strategy must wrap your bundle of benefits in the strong identity of your product or company name and image. Aaron Searll knows about brand building:

56

"We have a brand called Speedo in our apparel section which is an international brand. When children go to buy a racing costume they ask for a Speedo. It's become a generic."

Even accountants know about brands. UK accounting standards allow companies to value brands. Hanson Trust Plc, the huge British-based corporate raider that commands respect on both sides of the Atlantic, increased its borrowing capacity by billions by valuing the brands of its subsidiaries.

Seardel have built dominance in the competition swimwear niche by building a very strong brand. Any prospective new player in that market has to overcome an enormous obstacle in the minds of his target customers. The brand is so strong in fact that the barriers to entry are probably insurmountable. Searll has made competition swimwear his own.

Brand building takes time. It requires a long-term view of the product and its place in your business. In consumer products it is done with "direct marketing spend" — the advertising budget. Cadbury's are committed to increasing their brand-building efforts. "Direct marketing spend will always grow. We will spend brand-building money as planned, irrespective of short term profit needs," says Beyers.

Thirdly, **you must out-offer your competition. You must simply provide a more attractive bundle of benefits.** That's not as trivial as it sounds. If you've done your homework like the people at Cadbury's did for Tempo and Cabrio, you will know what benefits your customer is looking for from the product or service that you provide. Then you must *deliver* those benefits. Delivering those benefits must be the consuming preoccupation of your organisation. If your customer wants quality, *deliver* quality — make your organisation fanatical about quality. If your customer wants service, *deliver* service.

Carol Scott took Imperial Car Hire from nowhere to a major-league South African operation. Her secret? Better service than the competition. Imperial was on call while the competition slept — literally:

"If anyone wanted a car at midnight, we delivered it. If they wanted a chauffeur, we supplied one. We bent over backwards

for our clients, and gained the reputation of being the company with the best service. All our saleswomen carried pagers so they could deliver at any time, anywhere."[1]

Charmfit, one of the Seardel subsidiaries, manufactures Triumph bras and girdles. Triumph is the biggest selling bra in the country. Searll believes that its success is built upon the strength of brand in terms of design and quality, and on customer service. "Customer service?" says Searll, "Critical, absolutely critical." Charmfit have service teams that call on Triumph stockists to check inventory for them and call for replenishment stocks immediately. They want their stockists to be sure that the Triumph shopper will always find her size in any style. That service, Searll says, builds enormous confidence, goodwill and trust between his organisation and its customers.

What is owning a car all about? Owning a car is about *reliability*. When you climb into your car in the morning you don't want to be asking yourself "Will it work?" You want to be sure that it will work. You want reliability, and reliability means product quality. Product quality then is a key strategic deliverable. It is central to competitive advantage in the motor industry. As we will see in Chapter 10, there is probably no company amongst our top performers that has dedicated more time and energy to improving the quality of its product than Volkswagen.

But how do you improve quality and service? How do you outperform the competition in these areas? Yes, you can put in sophisticated quality assurance systems, complex service procedures, but will these do the trick? How can you get a handle on such soft concepts?

Working on the hard systems and skills will help. Volkswagen ensure that their welders are trained to a high level of proficiency. Imperial girls carried pagers. **But the real way to deal with soft concepts is to develop soft skills and soft systems like customer courtesy, customer closeness and customer care.**

Courtesy, Closeness and Care

Our super-performers are big on the soft marketing concepts.

---

1 *The Executive.* December 1988/January 1989.

They take them very seriously. It's a cliché, but for them the customer *is* always right. Pick 'n Pay are famous for their slogan "The customer is Queen". As he talks to us, Raymond Ackerman leans forward and looks us earnestly in the eye:

"Another thing that is wrong with me, which is either a fault or a good thing, is courtesy.

When I got out of university I had a blue suit and a white collar. And my father said to me 'The first job you do for six bloody months — you think you're a clever boy coming out of university, none of us retailers went to university — you're going to greet customers for six bloody months in our Corner House store.'

And my job was to say 'Good morning, madam.' And if she was pregnant I had to give her a chair, and I had to show them where the departments were. And for six months with a B.Com that's all I did. And he said 'I'm not moving you out of there until I feel it's so steeped in you that you'll say good morning to every member of staff and know their problems, and they'll know you care. And every customer will know that someone is greeting them. This philosophy has really helped build our company. It's become part of my being."

Note how Ackerman has difficulty distinguishing between courtesy for customers and courtesy for staff. He's really talking about courtesy to everyone. Inconsistency would mean insincerity.

At electronic manufacturer Plessey, customer relationships are a key component of selling strategies. John Temple likes to meet and entertain customers. He estimates that he has entertained 500 to 1 000 customers in the three years since taking over as Managing Director. His customer entertainment is programmed ahead on a routine basis.

"Major effort is made here in Cape Town. We like to bring people to our factory. We like to show them around the factory, give them lunch, talk to them, show them the company. But because we can't bring everyone from the Transvaal we do it in the Transvaal on a regular basis as well — once a month. We have public relations lunches. And we do it in all the main centres as well from time to time — Port

Elizabeth, Durban and so on. And generally speaking I go round and host those myself, but if I can't get to all of them, particularly in the outlying areas, then one of our directors will go."

Temple sees this face-to-face contact with the customer as being far more cost effective for his business than "background advertising", which he regards as being hopelessly unfocused and so a total waste of time and money. He told us of a recent visitor to the factory who was "not particularly pro-Plessey, being under the spell of one of our major competitors". The visitor was welcomed at the gate with a prepared VIP name tag, with his name on it, met at reception by his host for the day and taken to Temple's office to review the printed programme for the day's activities. There he was presented with a professionally produced and bound document that contained all of the technical material that the visitor might take away with him. The visitor admitted to being "bowled over" by the professional and personal attention he had received. We understand that the reaction is not unusual from Plessey's visitors.

The way Plessey cares for its customers is very different from the way that Pick 'n Pay does. That difference makes perfectly good sense — Plessey is an industrial marketer, Pick 'n Pay is in fast-moving consumer goods. Aside from the obvious differences in the products they sell, the two companies offer very different bundles of benefits. Their market environments are quite different too — John Temple's visitors wouldn't include many pregnant women. On top of all of that their styles are different. Ackerman is probably more naturally outgoing than Temple. Nevertheless, each in the ways that are appropriate to their particular businesses, both companies take great care with their customers.

Getting close — physically close — to the customer is important for most of our top performers. And if their customer is on-selling, the top performers like to get close to their customers' customers. Cadbury's doesn't sell chocolate to consumers, it sells it to wholesalers and traders. But it likes to get close to the consumers themselves, and it recognises that as being an ongoing process. Says Managing Director Beyers:

60

"Closeness to the customer is a journey — not a destination reached. You can easily fall into the trap of talking face to face with the trade but relying on numbers and secondary information when it comes to the consumer. We're trying to break that by saying we need to get our management to talk directly to the consumer."

All the marketing people, up to the highest level, go out into the shopping centres on a regular basis to talk directly to the consumer.

Other super-performers do just the same. Willards MD Mike Benn spends at least one day a week pounding pavements visiting outlets. Frankie Robarts often spends Saturday morning serving customers in one of Waltons' retail outlets. You've heard about MBWA — management by wandering around — well this is MRBWA — market research by wandering around!

Another technique that Cadbury's management use to stay close to the customer is the procedure that has recently been instituted to handle consumer complaints. Customer complaints are very important. Studies done in the United States and elsewhere show that customers tell twice as many people about bad experiences as good ones, so you'd better look after that unhappy customer; she could badly damage your image. In the past, Cadbury's complaining customers have been sent a personalised letter and a complimentary parcel. But Cadbury's knew that all its competitors did just the same. So as part of its continuing endeavour to outperform its competition, the chocolate-manufacturer is going a step further, and a big step at that. It still sends the parcel and the letter, but in addition, about four weeks later, a member of senior management telephones the consumer. Each senior executive is routinely allocated several people to telephone, so the consumer might hear from the Financial Director, or the Production Director, or the Managing Director. Beyers says that it's amazing how consumers react.

"We convert what was a slightly negative feel, following the purchase of a defective product, turning it around 100 per cent to a very, very positive effect. At the same time the process gets the whole senior management talking to the consumer on a

regular basis. It helps to entrench a caring-for-customers attitude."

Customer courtesy, care and closeness are really all to do with attitude. In a recent Plessey staff newsletter, under the headline "Let's give customers the big 'C' touch", John Temple wrote:

"Never let any telephone near you ring more than three times. Answer it. If it is a Customer or anyone from outside, do all that you can to help the caller. Get the correct person to ring them back if you cannot help them yourself. Check up afterwards that they were fully helped.

Never write the word Customer anywhere without a capital 'C'.

Look out for people who do something special for a Customer. Tell your director about him or her.

We will be making awards to people who 'go the extra mile for a Customer'. Please join me in Caring for our Customers."

John Temple's article is part of a much larger exercise. Temple is deliberately trying to build a customer-oriented culture at Plessey, for he knows it is culture that shapes the behaviour of individuals within organisations. Chapter 10 will show that if you want a market-oriented, customer-caring organisation, you'd better build a strong culture that supports those values.

---

10 Steps to Winning Marketing Strategy

1. Know your customer.
2. Segment your market according to the customer's perception of value.
3. Segment the segments until you have defined a niche you can make your own.
4. Define the bundle of benefits — intrinsic and extrinsic, rational and emotional — that you are offering your customer.
5. Position your offering so that it is unique in the customer's eyes.
6. Dominate each of your niches. Build your brands. Out-offer the competition.
7. Avoid surprises. Track the trends. Use the information you've already got.

8. Get close to the customer — and stay close.
9. Develop soft skills in courtesy and care for customers.
10. Build a strong customer-oriented culture.

CHAPTER FOUR

LIBERATE YOUR HUMAN POTENTIAL

"If you put a gorilla in a cage, it's hardly likely to get in on the act, okay?"

Meyer Kahn, Managing Director, SA Breweries

Wherever we went, we found an enormous focus on liberating the human potential that existed within the super-performers. Incidents like the one related by Dennis Smit, Divisional General Manager of Suncrush, abound:

"Last year I think I undercatered for distribution at the Rustenburg plant. In fact what happened was that near Christmas we had an incredible peak in Rustenburg, and I had drivers coming back — I know this sounds like bad management, but we were in trouble, we'd had a fantastic sales month. On Christmas Eve, the last driver was in at 1.00 am on Christmas Day. And on New Year's Eve, the same driver was in at 1.00 am. Okay, that's bad management but we were in trouble. We had planned for growth, but nothing like the success that hit us there. And that's the sort of commitment you get — I'm talking about black guys here. A lot of the company's success has come from guys who are prepared to bust their backs."

Philip Coutts-Trotter, Managing Director of SA Bias recounts the observation made of his company by a firm of management consultants.

"The amazing thing about your company is that you have a whole lot of mediocre stars ... they don't appear to be

super-intelligent or massively intellectual, yet they are performing like 'mega-stars'."

The same might have been said of many of our super-performers. **Surely this must be a company's most powerful source of competitive advantage? That is, getting the people in the organisation (and remember, an organisation is nothing more than a collection of people) to move from a level of working merely to live — to pay the monthly bills — to a position where work takes on a whole meaning of its own. Where people will bust a gut and outperform even their own expectations.** Our super-performing companies have demonstrated to us in a very practical way the fine art of liberating human potential.

We would like to distinguish this from motivation, a subject that has been much written about. The word "motivate" suggests a push. **The super-performers have shown us that uncaging the gorilla is about unshackling and liberating latent potential within all organisational members. It is also about empowerment: going to extraordinary lengths to ensure that the individual is given the best chance of succeeding.**

In this chapter we will show some of the things done by super-performing companies to liberate their human potential. We will show that individual dignity and respect are treated as a religion; that individual needs are catered for; that people are vested with autonomy and freedom; that red tape is anathema; that people need work to match the size of their spirits; that people need to have demands placed on them; that the pride of winning is chest-busting stuff; that what constitutes a "fair deal" is rather generous; that communication is likened to the conductor that carries the electricity through these high performance systems; that, yes, South Africans love hoopla; that culture management is the order of the day in top companies.

The overriding theme that we hope will come through is that even in South Africa, rational man is dead. In fact, he never really existed. The people who keep organisations going demand a special sort of attention, which appeals to needs for dignity, respect and individualism. In appealing to these needs, super-performing companies have shown us that this appeal is made at least as much to the heart as to the brain.

A point before we begin, is that there will be no liberation without leadership. Unless organisational members find in their leadership an example that they can hold onto and which captures their imagination, there will be no release of energy. The example must be powerful, exciting and consistent. The concept of inspired leadership is so fundamental to the principle of liberating human potential that we develop it in Chapter 9.

DIGNITY AND RESPECT

Immediate physiological needs such as eating and drinking aside, a human being's most basic needs relate to dignity and respect, to feeling good about himself and what he does in life. How easily we forget this in South Africa. Just think of the tea lady who lives in a rented tin shack in the nearby township. She comes to work in smart Sandown offices and serves tea in bone china teacups with silver teaspoons to frantically busy executives in Gucci shoes. Extend this to the worker on the floor. How is he supposed to identify with the concept of product quality when there's no quality in his own life? And extend this further. The same person might be expected to treat customers with dignity and respect. Logic tells us that this just doesn't add.

And this explains why some of our companies go to extraordinary lengths to improve the quality of their employees' lives, both in and out of the workplace. As Peter Searle put it when talking about liberating the human potential of Volkswagen:

> ".. it meant that we had to start addressing a lot of community problems, because they were really impacting on us. It was out of a recognition of a worker's basic needs that we got into things like housing and education ... seeing that employees were getting good wages and not living in shanties."

It explains why most of the super-performers not only have housing schemes for their workers, but push their local authorities into housing programmes, into electrification and water reticulation programmes. South African managers like to think they are macho. It also explains why real men who run companies like Pick 'n Pay, Cadbury-Schweppes, Mathieson & Ashley and Volkswagen will proudly claim to pay their workers a higher than average industry wage. Why they support the "living wage" campaign. And it's not about social responsibility. It's about basic economic common sense.

RECOGNISING THE NEEDS OF THE INDIVIDUAL

The rise of the Me Generation has been a fact of life in most western countries. Individuals demand to be treated as such, to have their rights as individuals and to have their individual needs met in the numerous social systems in which they operate. This extends naturally to the workplace.

In the super-performing companies there is an enormous respect for the individual needs of employees. The leaders of super-performing companies have discerned the spillover of this trend into South African society. They see it as natural to meet the need in their people for dignity and respect.

Winky Ringo, Executive Chairman of Mathieson & Ashley, developed the concept of "the make me feel good goodies bag". He explains it as follows:

> "For years I fought vigorously the demand for, say, a Mercedes-Benz. How stupid I was to fight it. It's plus minus R20 000 over five years for a guy that is going to produce millions for shareholders. How important it is to his family, friends and customers. Management must recognise the need for this 'make me feel good goodies bag' ... People are the same as you and me. What I want, they want. And within the parameters of profitability, we will help give these goodies ... I love giving goodies."

Robin Hamilton, Executive Chairman of Suncrush, thinks of meeting the needs of the individual from the point of view of "selling jobs to people" constantly. He reckons that if you think of it from that point of view, you get around to thinking what he really wants. He explains:

> "If you're trying to sell a job to a guy — you've got to think 'What does he really want?' Let's look at the motor car. The average guy would like to do some very strange things, and own strange motor cars. And I sat here one day and thought 'Why don't I devise a system that takes care of that want and

also takes care of the company's needs?' It's actually developed into a fairly complex thing. And over the years the guys have been able to indulge in their particular fantasies, as far as motor cars are concerned, at no great extra cost. You'd be amazed at what people do — I mean accountants get through eight cars in three years!"

Super-performers also recognise the need to extend this understanding of individual needs right down to the lowest paid worker. Cadbury's is a good example. Ever tried to get from North End to Kwazakele in the middle of the night? Cadbury's management arrange SABTA transport for night-shift workers.

EMPOWERMENT THROUGH AUTONOMY AND FREEDOM

In Chapter 5 we'll tell you more about Suncrush and its capacity for shrugging off failure. One of its senior executives, Dennis Smit, spent some time managing Suncrush's operation in Rustenburg. He told us the story of how he and a colleague decided to improve distribution logistics by designing a new trailer system. They spent about R100 000 on the system, only to find that the damn thing didn't work. Not only did he live to tell the tale, but he actually advanced considerably within Suncrush. The point here is that the concept of freedom has real meaning for him. He is not the sort given to lyrical prose, but had this to say:

"The freedom — I don't think it exists elsewhere. I've not seen it. The freedom to go bootlegging, to make a real mess of something — to me that is valuable, that's golden, that's a thing to cherish."

In the super-performing companies we found people down the line empowered to use their own initiative to get things done and try things out. Vic Hammond, Chief Executive of Edgars, has an interesting view of power within the organisation. He maintains that the higher you go, the less power you have. How so?

Adrian Bellamy, formerly Chief Executive of Edgars and arguably one of South Africa's foremost professional managers, began the decentralisation process at Edgars. The group had grown in spectacular fashion under the entrepreneurial direction

68

of Sydney Press. Control from the centre became cumbersome and Bellamy started pushing responsibility down the line. The process was vigorously supported by a professional bureaucracy — financial and planning systems, management by objectives, etc. Hammond has taken the process to its logical conclusion. Each of the retail chains — Edgars, Jet and Sales House — now has its own board of directors. Within the parameters of a negotiated budget and strategic plan, these boards are autonomous. And within each of these companies responsibility has been pushed right down to the lowest level of decision making. We saw this in action: a 25-year-old buyer approving a multi-million rand buying order.

This sort of stuff scares the hell out of many managers. **The truth of the matter is, however, that the sort of control exercised by people like Vic Hammond is more potent than any other form. It is not an abdication of control, but rather a way of releasing the combined energy of an organisation in a directed way. If one looks closely at companies that have successfully managed a decentralised decision-making structure, a number of supportive processes are evident. These processes achieve the advantages of centralisation-control, co-ordination and integration — whilst making provision for the advantages of empowerment through autonomy and freedom.**

Training, Training and More Training

There is little need to fear that the subordinate assuming responsibility will screw-up if he is properly trained for the job. The super-performers show this to be such a substantial point that we develop it more fully in Chapter 6.

Dennis Smit, of Suncrush, explains what we mean:

> *"The general manager and his factory management team decided that we needed to try and push decision making down to the lower levels in the factory management structure, and in so doing give greater responsibility and authority to what we call line managers — in fact the first level of managing in the factory. We went through massive training programmes to develop these line managers to take on these additional responsibilities. We've spent a lot of time and effort conduct-*

ing assessment centres, trying to establish what the real training needs are, and we used some top professionals to help us to run what we called coaching skills programmes — firstly to help the managers to develop, and secondly, to help them develop their subordinates in turn."

What he told us here was that not only is training critically important, but managers develop people. The responsibility for training and development cannot be totally abdicated to a training department. Managers themselves must climb in and get involved.

Supportive Control Systems

We found that our decentralised super-performers supported autonomy and freedom with rock-hard control systems, from strategic planning through to budgeting, timeous financial reporting and human resource management systems. This firmly supports the contention that autonomy and freedom are not dewy-eyed concepts — they do not presume a *laissez-faire* management philosophy. They demand the discipline and rigour of control systems.

Budgeting is a religion in most of the super-performers. An enormous amount of time goes into budget preparation. The process here is critical — the people in whom the autonomy and freedom have been vested need to take ownership of the figures. And they need to know that variances will be thrown out and dealt with timeously.

We also found in place human resources management systems. Whilst these vary considerably in their degree of sophistication, the decentralised company recognises how important it is that all their people know what is expected of them — certainly in terms of performance — and that at the end of the year they will be measured against these expectations. Simple? Yes, but too often we see that either these systems are absent or they become bogged down to the extent that the tail starts wagging the dog. It becomes a bureaucracy that develops an exasperating momentum of its own.

Yet we are frequently reminded that performance is based not only on ability, but on attitude. We found a number of further supportive processes to deal with this.

Focusing the Mind: Directed Incentive

We pick up on the concept of directed incentive below. Here we merely point out that **incentives, both financial and non-financial, are seen by the super-performers as a control tool. But they need to be directed at desired behaviour.** Mathieson & Ashley, Waltons Stationery, SA Bias and a host of other companies which genuinely push authority down the line, reward salesmen on margin, not sales; senior management on longer-term, rather than shorter-term measures; and lower level managers on specific non-quantifiables rather than financial results.

In Chapter 10 we'll talk more about developing a performance-based culture. That is, a culture that stresses performance at every level in the organisation. We'll show there that a performance-based culture begins with directed incentive.

Control, Co-ordination and Integration Through the Glue Called Culture

Time and time again control through culture was shown to be the most complex, yet most potent form of organisational control.

It works a bit like this: a person can be trusted to perform because the culture and values of the company provide the pathway to making the right decision. And the culture is so strong, that it becomes the predominant force guiding behaviour. Each time he behaves in accordance with these values, he has an instantaneous sense of satisfaction. It's as if the pathway were vividly clear and each step down this pathway brings an enormous sense of satisfaction — like one step closer to the honey-pot.

This form of control is about more than behaviour. It's about attitude and frame of mind. This makes it all the more powerful. More on this in Chapter 10.

The lesson here is clear. Empower your people at the lowest level — and unite them with this glue called culture.

It came as no surprise to us to find the most illuminating example of people empowerment at Volkswagen. In discussions with workers, top management got a real sense of the frustration workers feel when things go wrong on the production line — as they inevitably do — and the line moves on. At the end of one of the lines they installed a big board with lights. If a worker experiences difficulty, he pushes a button. The lights flash and the line stops. A team moves in immediately to sort out the problem. Quality problems are resolved at source. We asked Peter Searle how long it took for the button to be pushed after it was installed. It was five minutes. When asked what the problem was, the worker grinned and said, "I just wanted to see that it works!"

Keeping Out the Red Tape

SA Bias makes more than R10 million in attributable earnings. It employs more than 1 500 people in more than 20 companies in eight different locations. Given all of this, we found the lack of red tape remarkable. So do the employees, and they love it. Two of the senior executives explain:

> *"An individual in this organisation has a lot of flexibility to make things happen very quickly. One is not tied up with the normal bureaucracy that one can get in larger companies."*
> John Dew, General Manager, SA Bias, Cape

> *".. from a senior person's point of view, it [the success] is the lack of red tape and the ability to move forward and take risks, obviously within reason, and try to achieve something through their own efforts."*
> Nigel Martindale, Group Management Information
> Systems Manager, SA Bias

John Dew tells the story of the practical application of this principle. He explains how SA Bias had always been fairly strong in woven labels. They detected a swing in the market from printed to woven labels and were able to swiftly purchase the most advanced electronic equipment. By the time the competitors had made their purchasing decision, key customers had already been tied up.

Bureaucracy has become a value-laden word. If one traces the history of the concept, it can be seen that it was an initial response to organisational complexity. It was a method of creating order and efficiency in big organisations. And it was based on a turn-of-the-century understanding of man — man as an all-rational being. It soon became associated with the battery of systems, procedures and red tape that inevitably surround a system that aims to order organisational activity around the rational model of man.

The technology of organisational theory has thankfully undergone a series of changes. As we stated earlier, organisational theorists of today clearly understand that man is not rational. He is driven more by the heart than the brain. And most people — particularly the high-performance species (which most Chief Executives like to keep in stock) — are intensely demotivated by red tape. Why?

What happens is that bureaucracy develops a persona and momentum of its own. It unwittingly, but rigidly, regulates the conduct of work in an organisation. Your competitor buys a new machine which reduces the cost of production of the widget by 20 percent. You need to get one fast. But first of all, you've got to complete the capex proposal pack. You don't know how to do their favourite IRR calculation, so you ask for help from your favourite accountant. He's too busy, so you give it a bash yourself. Then you get to the section that asks you to quantify the benefits. A bit damn difficult. You have to wait for the next board meeting, only to get it chucked back at you because there are errors of both logic and arithmetic in the proposal. So you resubmit. And by the time you've bought the machine, it's simply too late — you've lost a whole lot of important things called customers. And money. You are so demotivated at this point that you start cursing the company. Unfortunately it doesn't end there. Talking your company down is analogous to talking yourself down. Any psychologist will tell you that there are few things more damaging to an individual's self-esteem than down-talk. The mind, which as we know is an incredibly powerful thing, starts telling you that your life-work is for the benefit of a bum organisation. All this will help get your motivation well below zero.

Another important implication of too much red tape, particularly as it relates to human resource systems, is that it factors out the inherent competitive nature of man. Referring to formal processes, Meyer Kahn explains:

"What you do is you inhibit the business. I can't believe that when you put people in blocks, specific blocks, with specific responsibilities, and very detailed and specific job specs, that they in fact grow in that. I'm a firm believer that one must be flexible enough. If you put a gorilla in a cage, it is hardly going to get in on the act, okay? They must be allowed to stray and assume responsibility and create conflict, because part of the conflict I have always considered to be healthy . . . I'm not arguing against organograms and job specs — don't misunderstand me. I'm saying that if they are too specific then you handcuff people. Certainly as far as the people that I manage are concerned, I try and make it as loose as possible. If there is a loose ball, I am interested to see who is going to pick it up. That has to tell me something. And inevitably among my senior management if there is a loose ball, you can hear the crashing of heads, because everybody rushes around. It doesn't matter who the ball belongs to."

While this macho competitiveness might not suit all organisations, the message is clear: **bureaucracy stifles, so don't define people's jobs so precisely that you factor out the freedom to engage the brain or the inherent competitiveness of man.**

The sad truth is that red tape is probably an inevitable consequence of success. It has become almost a cliché that the early success of an organisation derives from the drive and energy of the entrepreneur. He and bureaucracy do not co-exist comfortably. One of the reasons why he got going on his own probably related quite closely to his chaffing at the bit of less rigid organisational controls. This highly centralised, yet informally run organisation becomes a bit uncoordinated when it reaches a significant size. The entrepreneur starts getting advice — from the financial press, his auditors, his accounting department and the management consultants he probably hired — that he must start formalising, and quickly. The professional managers take over and in marches the bureaucracy and starts ordering the way work is conducted in the organisation.

The response of our super-performers to this phenomenon presents us with three interesting lessons.

74

Suncrush is one of the few organisations we know that has crashed through the growth barrier without wheeling in the bureaucracy. We asked all sorts of questions about the formalised processes we would have expected in an outstandingly successful organisation of its size. To our surprise we found that this superbly strategically positioned organisation did not have a documented strategic plan. Whilst managing its people so well, it was thin on human resource management systems. Its cost structure is bang on target, yet its cost control systems are loose. We were aghast.

Digging a little deeper, we found ourselves coming back to the whole question of value management. As we showed in Chapter 2, **all successful companies need a strategy, but not necessarily a strategic plan — no matter how big you are — if the strategy has been so well communicated through discussion and through the behaviour and attitude of the senior people that everyone knows where the company is going. You don't need complicated human resource systems if people are empowered yet controlled by values. And you don't need restrictive cost control systems if cost consciousness is something of a religion in the organisation.** We follow up on this in Chapter 10.

SA Bias is another good example. It has clearer strategy than we have seen in most organisations, but no formally documented strategic plan. But all the people we spoke to there know it almost by rote. Since Philip Coutts-Trotter climbed into the saddle in 1981, it has acquired something like 17 companies — mostly small operators in a fast-moving environment with virtually no formalisation at all. Part of its success with these acquisitions (and it has been an extremely successful acquiror, unlike most South African companies) derives from the deliberately slow pace at which it has nurtured them into its more sophisticated style of operating.

The second powerful lesson we learn from the super-performers is that if you must have bureaucracy, give it a pretty face and make it user-friendly. Edgars is a good example, as pointed out earlier. Adrian Bellamy introduced a professional bureaucracy, but got computers to deal with the administrative burden associated with it. He also realised that the creative folk wouldn't sit very comfortably with this bureaucracy, so he ensured that these people were supported by people who could relate to it. For example, in Edgars you will find buyers and merchandisers sitting next to each other, right brain and left brain respectively. The merchandiser wades through the budgeting and costings whilst the buyer gets high on fashion. "In fact," says Fred Haupt, Group General Manager: Corporate Services, "I sometimes think we give these creative people too much of an easy ride through the admin."

The third successful response to the red tape virus is to administer a potent antibiotic. That is, engage in a drastic response by excising the headless beast from the system. This response requires courage and a steady hand. A timid approach will merely tamper with the symptoms.

John Temple, Managing Director of Plessey South Africa, presented us with an interesting example of this approach. As we will relate more fully in Chapter 7, he found everyone pushing memos around the place to justify their actions. A copy of every memo, he instructed, was to be sent to him. Quite quickly, the river of memos dried up to a trickle.

Heads Down, Busy, With Loads of Meaningful Work

In most advanced western countries, middle management have been labelled "the endangered species". Advances in information technology, methods of business organisation and the enormous cost pressures associated with global competition have resulted in a closing of the gap between strategy and operations. Middle management have been squeezed out.

South Africa hasn't followed suit. The vast educational gap between those involved in strategy and operations, our isolation from the global game and our uncompetitive economy may be reasons for this. We often refer to South Africa's middle managers as "the neglected species"; they play a role of critical importance in South Africa.

Firstly, they represent that critical interface between strategy and operations. This means that they regulate the pace at which an organisation can get things done and change direction. It also means that they set the pace and influence the drive of people at the front line and on the factory floor.

The second important role of middle management is to filter information both up and down. Senior people generally hear little more than information provided by middle managers. And the front-line and factory floor generally hear little more than what they are told by middle management.

The South African middle manager is stereotypically someone with a matric, and probably also a post-matric qualification. He's anything from 30 to 50 and earns between R40 000 and R50 000 per annum. He drives a mid-range company car. Taking everything into account, he probably costs the employer between R60 000 and R100 000 per annum.

It's these people that are in the office at 08h30 and on the starting blocks again at 16h15, with lots of talk in between, but not too much to do. Attitude surveys show time and time again, that what these people want most is to have their heads down, to be busy, and to have loads of meaningful work. It does wonders for their sense of self worth, self respect and self esteem. It also stops all the down-talk, which is an unfortunate by-product of middle management boredom.

Most South African companies are not getting their pound of flesh, because they haven't thought critically about this large piece of overhead. Not so with some of the larger super-performers, such as Edgars, Liberty Life, Toyota, Beer Division, Plessey, Pick 'n Pay and Foschini. These companies have structured themselves appropriately at the middle management level and can say quite confidently that their middle management have their heads down, and are busy with loads of meaningful work.

Their middle managements, the regulators of pace, information and motivation, are charged up, motivated and willing to face inevitable changes. This is a rich source of competitive advantage.

PLAYING ABOVE YOURSELF

At the most basic level, we know that people will not consistently perform above what is expected of them. This is not being cynical about the nature of man, but rather being practical — performing consistently beyond expectations probably means that one is not being rewarded for it, or that someone higher up finds it all a little threatening. So in the super-performing companies, managers develop a good understanding of what people down the line are capable of. This involves understanding the person and the content of their work. This is why people like Vic Hammond go to extraordinary lengths to understand computer technology, and Bruce Edmunds, Managing Director of Utico (an accountant by training) to understand marketing (he is a voracious reader of marketing books): so that they can understand what people in these functions are capable of.

Those who have played competitive sport will understand clearly the exhilaration of "playing above yourself". The same applies in the work place and our super-performing companies know all about this, about getting the team to play consistently above itself. **Playing above yourself is about expectations — the expectations that the organisation has of its people and the expectations that those people have of their own abilities. Managers of super-performing companies constantly manage these expectations by setting them high. In meeting these expectations, people start playing above themselves and feel part of a winning team.**

TAKING PRIDE IN BEING PART OF A WINNING TEAM

The people at Plessey explicitly think of themselves as a winning team. John Temple, the Managing Director, puts it like this:

> *"We're not a country club. We're more like a rugby team playing a hard game. And winning is important — we want to win every lineout, we want to win every scrum. We want to score all the tries. And we want to talk about the great game we played."*

Frankie Robarts, Managing Director of Waltons, resented being interviewed. He let us know that ever since Waltons had become successful, everyone wanted to pick their brains. We weren't allowed to use a tape-recorder, but we were able to jot down the few things he told us.

Much of Waltons' success derives from its formidable record in buying poorly performing companies and rapidly turning them around, usually with the same people. We pressed him on this. His response was as follows:

"Yes, we've bought some crap companies and managed to turn them around with the same people. They (the same people) stay and pull together because what they see is something being done properly and in an exciting way. We're a winning team — that's why all you parasites want to pick our brains — and there's nothing quite like being part of a winning team."

We've all experienced the feeling of pride in being part of a winning team. The exhilaration is like a form of warm adrenalin. And it feeds on itself, because the more you think you're a winner, the more likely you are to be one.

And people in super-performing organisations jealously protect this pride. Meyer Kahn describes this graphically:

"You become so damn proud, that it simply burns a hole in your arse when some other oke [competitor] gets ahead of you in anything."

REDEFINING THE COMMITMENT/REWARD EQUATION

Philip Coutts-Trotter, Managing Director of SA Bias, sees the commitment/reward equation in terms of perceptions of what constitutes a "fair deal".

"You can't drive people unless you reward them. Money is not the key. The key is making people feel they are getting a fair deal. A chap is instantly demotivated if he feels he's getting a shit deal."

The world over, managers have come to realise the power of directed incentive. That is, providing financial incentive to perform in accordance with organisational objectives. Super-performing companies, like SA Bias, have taken note of some critical trends and events which have caused employees to redefine their understanding and expectation of what constitutes a "fair deal". Some of these are:

Changes in Societal Values

How times have changed. Some 30 years ago, it would have been unheard of for a mere employee to explicitly state his expectations regarding his deal. Since then there has been a consistent challenging of authority and status quo (in society generally, and spilling over into organisational life).

South Africa has not been entirely sheltered from this trend. It currently manifests itself in a prevalent attitude which is far more sympathetic towards the demands of the individual in the organisation and rewards him for value created for shareholders. It's an attitude that now understands and accepts what was previously unstated by the employee, that is, "If you want all my talent and energy, I want my chop." This prevalent attitude provides fertile ground for redefining expectations as to what constitutes a fair deal. Fred Haupt, Group General Manager: Corporate Services of Edgars, expresses it like this:

> *"We are well on the way to implementing a philosophy of fairness. That is, if you create wealth, we'll give you some of it."*

The Exodus of Skills

Need we be reminded of this tragic phenomenon. Sydney, Perth, London, New York and San Francisco gain all the time at South Africa's expense, as so many of our managers trade wealth, security, friends and family for political security.

Simply stated, the rate at which a developing country develops is so critically dependent on having the sort of people who make things happen. Those that stay behind are in a position to expect (and demand) so much more. And this is what is happening. The people that bring in the goodies carry a price tag. This is being bidded up exponentially. And this trend will continue.

The same applies to technical skills, be they accounting, information systems or operations. These people are starting to specify their price tags and the organisation that wants the best of these professional skills is having to pay more and more for them.

Entrepreneurial Revival

We firmly believe that South Africa is experiencing an entrepreneurial revival. We perceive a general spirit of young smarts, who are prepared to run the risk of going it alone. They are leaving the big corporations in droves.

Why is this? We believe the listing boom and foreign disinvestment played an important role. For so long this country was locked into a psyche of believing that only the big could make money. Then all of a sudden company after company came to the JSE boards, spitting out hundreds, if not thousands, of paper millionaires in the process. When we think back to the heady days of 1987, we think also of all those clients of ours that set their sights on getting there too. It certainly focused the mind.

Foreign disinvestment came at much the same time. From the point of view of rekindling the entrepreneurial flame, the timing was propitious. It added fuel to a process that was up and running.

What we've witnessed in our super-performers is not only an understanding of the unstoppable force of the entrepreneurial revival, but a willingness to run with it and lead it. They understand that if they want entrepreneurs in their organisations, they are going to have to reward them accordingly.

Meyer Kahn believes there are three things needed to liberate the potential of senior managers: creating an environment in which they can prosper; providing them with enough security to allow them to take risk; and affording them the opportunity of becoming rich. On the latter, he had this to say:

> ". . . I mean, the guys are entitled to be rich if they succeed. I'm a firm believer that a professional manager has as much right to accumulate wealth as an entrepreneur, because that is what he is. Now that is relative, and I suppose if you take into account the pension fund, plus the security of tenure, the power that goes with being a professional manager and the tom that our guys have made and hopefully will continue to make, that is rich by professional standards. It doesn't compare with the American syndrome, but compared to the standards of South Africa, I think that our guys are the richest in the country. And I really believe that. I wish they were 10 times richer, so that I would be 10 times richer. Rich is good."

As far as senior managers are concerned, at least 12 of the super-performers believe their senior people to be the top-earning executives in the country. They can't all be right! But it is interesting that they claim this. And that they quite genuinely wish they were earning more. This is a major change! Whereas 10 years ago, we are quite sure the view would have been to pay as little as you could get away with, it is now to pay as much as you can get away with!

DIRECTED INCENTIVE

Our top companies have in place reward systems which include directed incentives, based on a careful assessment of the commitment/reward equation. Piet Beyers, Managing Director of Cadbury's, explained lucidly the power of the directed incentives.

"The situation with bonuses is that whereas we have no guarantee, we [senior managers] have the potential of earning 40 per cent of our annual salary. Now that's very generous — and also not very generous because you have to work damn hard to get there (laughs). . . . I've certainly seen with a lot of individuals a very targeted focus on the targets. They say 'What are we going to do? These are the numbers. How are we going to drive to get those numbers?' Because it can mean 40 per cent of his yearly salary. That's real money."

Affording Top Management the Opportunity of Becoming Rich

It's close to universal amongst the super-performers that they afford their top management the opportunity of becoming rich. The top people are generally the people vested with the greatest freedom to make the bottom line happen, and nothing quite focuses their minds more than having a financial interest in that bottom line.

We are so convinced of the power of this sort of incentive that we specifically consider it when conducting a competitor analysis. In understanding what drives that competitor, at the top of our list will be this: "Are the top people getting a chop, and if so, what do they have to do to get it?" That helps enormously in understanding what to expect from them in the market place.

Meyer Kahn, once again in his inimitable style, puts it like this:

"I firmly believe that a professional manager is entitled to f . . . you money. In fact, a top executive that does not have f . . . you money is not a top executive."

Pushing Opportunity Down the Line

Most of the directed incentive schemes are targeted at the top echelon of management. However, companies like Edgars, Mathieson & Ashley, Waltons, Liberty Life, Kersaf, SAB's Beer Division, Suncrush, Pick 'n Pay, Cashbuild, Edward L Bateman, Foschini and Seardel will tell you that this is only the start in the implementation of a principle. We will see these companies pushing the principle deep down into the organisation.

Edgars currently have 140 people participating in their scheme. It works a bit like this: Managers negotiate financial targets with senior management. Once they hit 30 per cent over target they automatically clock into the scheme. The amount earned in year 1 is split into three: In Year 1, he gets the first third. If he meets the target in Year 2, he gets the second third. If he's around in Year 3, he gets his final third. So if he's performed really superbly, in Year 3 he will get his third share for Year 1, a third share for his Year 2 performance and a third share for Year 3. Each of these will differ in size and they can amount to 70 per cent of his salary. Their objective is to have a scheme like this operating throughout the group within six to 10 years.

Waltons got special JSE approval to issue up to 10 per cent of their shares to employees. These shares are issued according to a set of loose criteria, but essentially to reward outstanding performers for long service and loyalty. This applies to everyone — including the tea-lady. Mark Davis, the Financial Director, tells the story of R3 000 worth of shares issued to a secretary. At last count these shares were worth R80 000.

Raymond Ackerman explained that Pick 'n Pay's whole policy of consumerism could never have worked without employees at all levels being correctly motivated. He focused on the importance of this one:

"One of the major aspects which I feel has built the morale of our company has been our share policy. From the time we started, and subsequently as we have grown, we have issued shares to hundreds of our staff at all levels and this has really created a climate of belonging. I am a great believer in paying not only the correct salaries, but also giving people a share of the profit and most importantly, a share of the business. As a

matter of interest, we started our share scheme before we went public in 1968, shortly after we started, so as a private company, shares were given to certain executives and those shares have grown enormously, as can be appreciated. We have been public since 1968 and our share price has grown very strongly. Many of my colleagues are very strong shareholders in the company and this obviously increases their motivation and attention to the interests of the company."

It is well recognised that Liberty Life has most of the best life people in South Africa, and possibly in the world. Another feature of their senior management is that many of them are young, and certainly most are far from retirement. Dorian Wharton-Hood explained the problem:

". . . If you have a chap of 45 who is a general manager, it is very difficult to have a really top class man under him, because he's going to have 15 to 20 years to go before that chap retires, unless he can see a possibility of moving sideways."

They have started a programme of moving people sideways. However, he believes that the share incentive scheme has gone a long way towards keeping some of their younger people. He explains:

". . . the share option scheme goes quite deep — that's very important, so they are involved and they do have a piece of the action. In fact, the one scheme goes right down to the bottom of the organisation."

Cashbuild have a bonus system that extends from the Managing Director to casuals. It's complicated as hell, but they've taken the time and effort to make sure that everyone understands it. They also have a wealth creation scheme, which measures how much wealth was created in the business and then allocates a portion of this to employees. Employees then vote on how they want to spend it. This year they are looking at allocating it to a company housing scheme. They understand that the principle of participation *at all levels* is difficult to operationalise, but it doesn't mean

84

that there isn't a way of doing it. As they say, where there's a will there's a way.

COMMUNICATION, COMMUNICATION AND MORE COMMUNICATION

In Chapter 7 we will show how super-performers manage their communication processes. In this chapter, we will deal with the importance of communication and the role it plays in liberating human potential.

The concept of communication in the organisation first appeared in the business literature in the 1960s. The human resource school were heavily influenced by the thinking of psychologists, who have conclusive evidence that any social system degenerates without the free flow of information between elements of that system.

Not surprisingly, we found communication to be something of a religion in our super-performing companies. These organisations are alive with communication — upward, downward and lateral — alive with workshops, company newsletters, meetings, memoranda, phone calls, plane trips and plain old hanna-hanna. It struck us that this seemed to be the conductor that carries the electricity around these high performance systems. We were told time and time again that without communication, there is no co-ordination, no trust, no ventilation and no understanding.

Co-ordination

The dislocation between critical business functions is so prevalent as to be clichéd. The bean-counters don't understand that it costs money to make money, the marketing folk want to sell the product at all costs, the operations people don't understand that they are producing for customers. The strategists, dear God, don't understand what happens on the ground.

When a company launches a new product, it's pretty inevitable that the launch will be all the more successful if marketing, sales, production and finance have been able to provide inputs in some kind of group forum. This is so because time and time again studies in group dynamics prove that the power of the group is a multiple of the power of the individual. The problem is that groups tend to be cumbersome and fraught with hidden agendas. No matter how much you communicate, they will remain cumbersome — although there will be some improvement over time. But through communication, the hidden agendas are dealt with; they become explicit, and are explicitly resolved.

Not surprisingly, we found in our super-performing companies a lot of plain and simple communication — the most powerful weapon to deal with dislocation. Toyota is an excellent example. Here we were surprised to see the extent of differentiation between marketing and manufacturing. The marketing company is headed by Brand Pretorius in Johannesburg, and the manufacturing company by Ralph Broadley in Durban. Both report to Managing Director Bert Wessels, who then reports to Dr Albert Wessels, his father. This provides a medium of co-ordination. But all agree that communication here is the key. And not only the formal kind either — the daily informal flow of words delivered by telephone, in person and by letter. In this way they have their cake and eat it. Manufacturing and marketing, which require inherent differences in management processes and cultures, can go their own way, yet always pull in the same direction.

Participation

We draw the distinction here between the concepts of autonomy and freedom and participation. Autonomy and freedom are about pushing decision-making down the line. Participation is about getting people to make a contribution in a decision-making process. The two don't always go hand-in-hand — many companies which allow autonomy are not participative, in which event the company develops all sorts of power-plays and fiefdoms. **Participation is about getting people to play a meaningful role in decision-making, with the objective of eliciting their energy and support for implementing that decision.**

Our super-performing companies are full of participative processes. This is essentially a strategy to action concept. The relevant point of this juncture is that without communication, there can be no participation. The amount of time that participation requires in the form of workshops and meetings, meetings and more meetings often puts companies off the process, or causes them to take short cuts. Short cutting the communication process can cause the whole exercise to backfire.

One of the enriching aspects of our consulting work in recent years has been in getting participative processes going deeper down in organisations which have large black staff complements. In discussion groups we have found blacks to open up, communicate and relish the opportunity of contributing to decisions which affect their working lives. These discussions seem to take forever as the people get involved in the minutae of the decisions. But the result! The energy released by this participation is astounding. This has frequently caused us to question our western business ethic of short, clipped sentences, one-line instructions and one-minute managerism. People down the line need loads of communication time if participation is to mean anything. Certainly our study of Cashbuild reinforced this. The amount of time spent in communication in CARE groups, venturecoms, meetings, meetings and more meetings is an absolute prerequisite for effective participative processes.

The importance of putting in communication processes when embarking on a participative management approach is critically important for another reason. Peter Searle, Managing Director of Volkswagen, portrayed this graphically:

> *"What happens, of course, when you start supporting a participative process, is that an enormous amount starts bubbling to the surface and you lift the lid, and of course all sorts of goggas start jumping out."*

Gorbachev would undoubtedly agree.

Part of the solution, of course, lies in communication, communication and more communication. Open, honest, sincere communication. And Peter Searle is adamant that you can't abdicate this entirely to the union — you need to communicate directly to the worker.

Trust

Trust, unfortunately, does not come out of thin air. Trust between people takes time (in years) and multiple and repeated episodes of communication. It is only in this way that people come to understand each other, their values, the boundaries of their responsibilities, their competencies, their weaknesses and their points of reliability.

Ventilation

Employees' grievances, however unreasonable they may seem, are legitimate from their point of view. Management has the option of either putting a lid on them and letting them ferment and decay the soul of the organisation, or creating the right fora to flush out these grievances and address them head-on. Companies such as Mathieson & Ashley, Toyota, Volkswagen and Suncrush realise this and build it into their culture. Nine times out of ten, they will tell you that these grievances are resolved amicably. People actually like kissing and making up. Such is the power of communication.

In taking over Anglo Dutch, Winky Ringo, Executive Chairman of Mathiesen & Ashley, faced the usual dilemma: how much to tell his people about the proceedings. This, together with the usual tension surrounding mergers and take-overs, caused a lot of the Mathieson & Ashley people to tense up. Alan Zimbler, a Non-Executive Director, told us how Ringo went around the country pacifying the troops:

> "... Winky would come along and we'd have an open forum with Winky there. They could say whatever they wanted. They could say 'Winky, you're a f...ing bastard.' And some of them did just that. His tolerance of that sort of thing is wonderful. He could listen to it and talk about it. He would allow them to ventilate."

Mike Benn, Managing Director of Willards, reckons that a fair amount of conflict is inevitable and, if handled properly by communicating, can be healthy. Talking about cross-functional meetings, he explains:

> "You tend to have a fair amount of conflict, and conflict is healthy, provided it is handled properly. It brings to the fore the problems of the company — the frustrations — and releases them. At meetings I've managed there has been conflict. And we talk through those conflicts. The result is that

at every meeting I've managed there has been a happy group of people knowing that the problems are behind them."

Understanding

We referred earlier to the diversity of the people of South Africa — in culture, race, tribe, upbringing, educational standards, political perspectives and a whole lot more. The racial diversity is further compounded by the rigid segregation of people from birth. English and Afrikaner have precious little understanding of each other's perspectives, not to mention black and white. People rely on stereotypes and make little effort to understand one another.

Yet in any large industrial organisation in South Africa there are people with differences in values and philosophies that take on cataclysmic proportions. For example, AWB and ANC supporters working cheek by jowl! Ouch! And literally cheek by jowl because it's often the worker who identifies with the ANC and his first line supervisor who supports the AWB. Quite clearly the task of bridging the gap is enormous. But it begins with communication. By getting people to talk to each other. It sounds a bit lofty, but we've seen it work. We had the opportunity of listening to Tlhopheho Modise, a PG Bison executive, who makes it his job to talk to conservative folk about a black man's perspective. He tells the story of his efforts at such a gathering in Piet Retief, and how the men he spoke to really listened. Many of them internalised what was said. It changed their lives to such an extent that their wives asked Tlhopheho to come and talk to them. Their husbands had left them behind and they wanted to catch up.

Volkswagen addressed the gulf in understanding early on. They run a programme of Interaction Groups to reduce tensions between foremen and workers. Foremen are formally trained in intergroup dynamics. They are then put into groups of 10 workers and encouraged to talk about non-work related topics, usually over lunch hour. Participation is entirely voluntary, and anyone can pull out of a group at any time. To their surprise, they've found a lot of common ground. For example, most people find themselves in dual income families — child care is a problem and they swop experiences. In the Eastern Cape, fishing is big. Fishermen love telling stories. Most people also enjoy a punt at the races. So they swop information on horses and form.

What our super-performing companies realise is that the opportunities for communication and interaction outside the workplace are scarce. Without communication and interaction there is little hope of breaking down the stereotypes. Organisations wanting harmonious relationships in the workplace simply have to create the opportunities.

The gulf in understanding between management and worker of the purpose and functioning of a commercial undertaking is enormous. If workers live off union rhetoric, they are likely to believe that management pockets the money. Many of the super-performers make a point of providing them with a model of the organisation as it exists in a market economy through one of the many programmes available. It's not saying that the workers have to accept that viewpoint, but presenting the way management understands it. At worst, it's a starting point.

ANOINTING THE HEROES

When we started our research, we were quite adamant that all the hoopla spoken about in *In Search of Excellence* wouldn't work here. We couldn't have been more wrong and must ascribe this to our inherited English reserve. The fact of the matter is that the super-performers are full of hoopla and celebrations. **The objective, of course, is to anoint the heroes; for the company to put an employee on the pedestal and say "We want to tell you that we think you're a bloody hero." It's a hearty pat on the back, which the chap is awarded in the public forum — in front of his mates and it spills over into his community. Wherever we saw this in action, we were in awe of its power. It *really* does work.**

Volkswagen have started a process of "citing" people for great deeds. One way of citing people is to award them a "Custom Builder" badge. Clive Warrilow, Marketing Director, tells the story of an award being made to the Humansdorp dealership,

90

Dirk Ellis Motors,[1] in recognition of their customer service achievements. The dealer made sure everyone was there, including Toutjie, the cleaner, who was lent a suit for the occasion. The dealer made sure Toutjie stood on a pedestal upfront to get the award, which included a badge, a cup and some money. But most important, the honour of being told they were the best in front of a hundred or so people. Said Warrilow:

"You know, it's quite an unnerving experience. It can make a grown man cry."

We could recount a hundred similar stories from super-performing companies. What we learn from these is that it's not the monetary value attached to the award that's important. What is important is the public recognition that it is made in the person's own environment, amongst his mates, that it is for some significant achievement and that he has some memento to remind him and his mates of this fine achievement. People love it!

CULTURE MANAGEMENT

Philip Coutts-Trotter, Managing Director of SA Bias, expressed this lucidly:

"I aim at decisions that are going to bring together the objectives, ambitions and dreams of the people of SA Bias together with those of the shareholders. I place equal stress in my book on the attainment of personal goals for the people as achievement of shareholder goals."

Alan Zimbler, Non-Executive Director of Mathieson & Ashley, refers to people's attitudes and beliefs as the "bottom part of the iceberg". We think this is an appropriate analogy. The top part is the hard data — age, sex, qualifications, work experience, etc. It doesn't tell you an awful lot about the person.

What we found in many of our super-performing companies was

---

1 Dirk Ellis Motors is a story in itself. The people there embraced the core concept of customer service early on and have turned themselves into one of VW's best dealers. The size of the dealership has expanded rapidly over the last few years — Humansdorp is not a big place, but the size of the operation would seem more appropriate to Johannesburg.

an extraordinary effort to understand people's attitudes and beliefs and then to build a robust value system (culture) around these and the dictates of the marketplace. It's a slog of a process, yet those that have successfully gone this route swear by it.

We pick up on this concept later as it pulls together many of the concepts discussed in the book.

PUTTING THE PIECES TOGETHER HOLISTICALLY

One of our colleagues met a chap who was doing some interesting organisational development work at SAB's Beer Division. Organisational development, the burgeoning new technology of getting change processes going in organisations, has been of particular interest to us in recent months. He had an impressive career in this technology, including more than a decade of working with some world masters in North America. We invited him to come and talk to us about some of his ideas. It was at a time when we were having real difficulty conceptualising some of the findings of our research. He spoke to us about his thesis, and everything just seemed to fall into place.[2]

The thesis developed from asking the question "Why is it that organisations seem to be unmanageable today when we know more than ever about the art and science of management?" Our difficulty in conceptualising the research stemmed from the multitude and varied array of techniques and tools used by the super-performers. So many differences, yet they are all liberating their human potential. Why is this?

The answer to the question is that organisations have developed sophisticated tools, but have not been able to put the pieces together holistically. This is exactly what we found the super-performers were doing. They were putting together the pieces of puzzles in a holistic way. They understand their organisations clearly and know exactly what is required in the various places. Volkswagen has only recently been able to introduce workers to 6M training. Had they tried earlier, resentment would have been created. The climate wasn't right. They also understand the need

---

2 We subsequently convinced him to join our team. He has changed the way we approach our work, by factoring into all our work the people development implications of strategic change. The effect has been powerful.

to get the basic industrial relations processes in place before embarking on their culture management programme. One of the reasons for Liberty Life's success has been its "tough" climate. Times have changed, and they are now trying to make people more caring. Would they have got to where they are if they had done this 10 years ago? Probably not.

The lesson is that the organisation is like a lump of jelly. You touch it in one place and the lump wobbles. This is exactly what the tools and techniques of organisation development do to your organisation. We have found that the super-performing organisations are able to apply the *right* tools and techniques at the *right* time.

---

12 Steps to Liberating Your Human Potential

1. Rational man is dead. People respond to appeals to the heart at least as much as appeals to the brain.
2. We need to move away from words like "motivating" and "stimulating", which suggest a push. Instead we must talk about liberating, uncaging, unshackling and releasing. It requires a leap in thinking, but then it delivers a leap in performance.
3. The need for dignity and respect is paramount and, in South Africa, not always easy to meet. Most white managers have got used to painful affronts to this need at a societal level and develop blind spots at the organisational level.
4. Empowerment of people requires pushing decision making down the line. There is no reason not to do this — there are powerful ways of keeping "control" whilst doing this.
5. Keep out the red tape. It corrupts the soul of the organisation, renders it inflexible and keeps it firmly on its heels.
6. Keep people busy — particularly your middle managers. If they are demotivated, your whole organisation will follow suit. Nothing demotivates them more than plain old boredom.
7. Get a Winning Team concept going. People love being part of a Winning Team, and it's only a Winning Team that can play above itself.
8. Redefine the commitment/reward equation. The marketplace, in the form of people's perceptions of the equation, has changed radically over the past few years.

9. Communication is the key to co-ordination, participation, mutual trust and ventilation. It takes time, it can be tedious and it can be tricky. But you've got to have it.
10. Anoint your heroes. Public recognition is inexpensive to the organisation, but rich to the individual. They love it.
11. Develop a culture that builds on the attitudes and beliefs of your employee body and meets the dictates of the marketplace. It is the most elusive, yet most powerful form of organisational control.
12. For any organisation at any time, there will be the right set of tools and techniques for liberating human potential. Find them and apply them.

UNLOCK THE GATE, EMPOWER YOUR PEOPLE AND YOU WILL HAVE ENGAGED YOUR MOST POWERFUL SOURCE OF COMPETITIVE ADVANTAGE

CHAPTER FIVE

RING IN THE NEW

It looked as though 1985 was ending on a downbeat for Willards Foods — the food division of Utico Limited. Not only were they struggling to source sufficient high grade potatoes, but arch-rival Simba, already ahead with bigger and more established buying capability, had snapped up market share with its new product, O'Grady's. Within six months of launch, O'Grady's had taken 20 per cent of the R200 million[1] a year chip market. Willards MD, Mike Benn, had his back to the wall. In an attempt to snatch some breathing space, Benn called in Alan Bunton of Grey Phillips Bunton Mundel and Blake, then undisputedly the front-runners of South African advertising. Grey Phillips' brief was simply to produce the most exciting chip concept for the hungry youth market. Bunton delivered and Greedy Boys hit the racks in supermarkets and cafés with enough crunch to keep the Simba Lion at bay — for a while at least.

Looking for a new product to take on O'Grady's, Benn and his Utico Managing Director, Bruce Edmunds, headed for the USA. What they discovered there were kettle-fried chips, sliced thin and slow fried the old fashioned way in huge vats of oil. On returning home they found that the kettles at around R250 000 each would be far too expensive to import. So they gave the original turn-of-the-century drawings of the kettles that they had found in the United States to a local Pretoria precision engineering shop and got them to knock together the equipment for R25 000 each.

At the same time they went back to Alan Bunton at Grey Phillips and asked him for a concept for the new product. This

---

1 *The Executive*, December 1988/January 1989.

time the idea had to have legs; a fast-burn starburst like Greedy Boys was a fad — it wouldn't hold lasting market share. The day before Christmas 1985, Bunton came up with Flanagan's. The product was launched with an initial marketing budget of R40 000 — a paltry sum in the world of fast-moving consumer goods. Small beginnings, but only 18 months later Willards had eight kettles working flat out. The marketing budget had grown to R1 million per year. The big-bag plain-salted old-fashioned kettle-fried chip was the new market leader. Willards couldn't meet demand even without introducing new flavours. At the 1988 Paris Food Product exhibition, Flanagan's won a Golden Oscar against products from 15 other western countries. Golden Oscars recognise outstandingly innovative and commercially successful products in seven categories, as rated by the retail trade. Flanagan's was voted the best South African product across all seven categories; and the world's third best grocery product in its class.

Willards and Simba have been trading blows in snackfoods for years. It has been toe-to-toe stuff and the bout is far from over, but at this stage the heavier and more experienced champion is slowly losing ground to the faster and hungrier challenger. Simba's share is slipping. Willards attributes its success in the snack foods market to more aggressive marketing and sharper, more frequent and more successful product innovation, for, aside from Flanagan's, Willards had dealt punishing blows with Crinkle Cut, Ghost Pops and others. For Willards, innovation is a key strategy.

Innovation isn't just about new products, though. Innovation is really about change. And the ability to change is now a critical attribute in the South African business context. It is essential to survival in these ever more turbulent times. In everything a company does, in every facet of its business, in its products and in its processes, it will have to innovate. Even successful companies — especially successful companies — will need to innovate. Remember the adage "Success breeds failure"? To fail to change is to remain static and to be left behind.

This chapter on innovation will look at how Willards and other top-performing South African companies go about new product and new process innovation. We will see that innovation is much more than bright-idea, blue-sky inventiveness, that it can and should be a deliberate process that takes its cues from information: information about the marketplace, the customer and the competition, information about the broader environment and information about the organisation itself. We'll see how top companies try very hard to avoid reinventing the wheel, but that when they do transpose ideas or products from one situation to another they adapt them carefully to the new specifics. We will see that although the super-performers regard mainstream innovation as a deliberate and rational pursuit, they also let intuition have its say. We will examine how the best companies create conditions that foster an innovative spirit within their organisations by structuring for innovation; by tolerating failure; by putting people under pressure to take short cuts; by disturbing the routine and breaking the rules. We will learn that innovation can not only be encouraged but also managed — very effectively.

Above all, hopefully, we'll come to understand that innovation must be rewarded — and rewarded in the right way, and that if these things are put in place carefully so they support and reinforce each other, the organisation can create a climate of innovation so consistent and so strong that innovation — the right innovation, the innovation that the organisation wants and needs — just begins to happen.

Look for Clues. Take Your Cues

We talk a lot about information in this book. In Chapters 2 and 3 on strategy and marketing we saw how important good information is to making good strategic and marketing decisions.

Good information improves all decisions — including decisions on what and how to innovate. Fortunately these innovation decisions don't each need a completely new set of data. It may be necessary to rearrange the information somewhat from case to case, but once you have in place a way of collecting salient facts about your own company, your customers, your marketplace and your competitors and about your wider operating environment, you will be well placed to spot the clues to what and how you should innovate. The trick of course is to recognise the clues when you see them, and to know how to respond to them; to turn clues into cues.

Think about Volkswagen's Citi Golf. In introducing the "Jumbo" Golf and the new Jetta, Volkswagen was consciously moving upmarket in terms of size and price. They knew they were vacating a very interesting segment at the bottom of the market. So they gave some thought to how they could keep the old Golf alive and cracked the concept of the Citi Golf. Peter Searle:

> *"The styling design was done by a mixture of three groups; people in the advertising agency had some good ideas, our own styling people and some of our marketing people here. It was a hotch-potch. Between the three we tortured out this red, yellow and blue concept. And of course the story has even surpassed our dreams."*

A clear understanding of the structure of their market, and of the needs and aspirations of the consumer in each market segment led logically (via some inspired new livery and advertising) to the zappy red, yellow and blue runabouts so favoured by working girls and boys throughout the land. It's classic lifecycle extension stuff; Citi Golf production has now risen from 25 cars a day to 80, and may soon be increased to 120 a day. Not bad for a product that is technically 15 years old.

Our super-performers provide many examples of new product innovations and innovative approaches to problems that spark from knowledge of their markets and environments. We read earlier of Cashbuild's start-up strategy in cash-and-carry building materials, of Cadbury's deliberate and careful development of two brand-new chocolate bars, Tempo and Cabrio. Suncrush, one of the most innovative of our super-performers, has developed a highly innovative approach to distributing soft drinks through the thousands of tiny spaza (backyard) shops in black townships.

The fashion-conscious reader will recall that tartan was in vogue for the winter of 1988. Top performer SA Bias was the only apparel accessory manufacturer able to produce tartan ribbon. Why? Because SA Bias had anticipated the swing to tartan in time to install the necessary machinery. They had the flexibility. This focus on the changing needs of their *end-user* market has stood SA Bias in good stead. A good few years ago they foresaw the trend towards clothing labels being used as a design feature.

Once again they installed the right equipment in good time, so that today most of the labels you see sewn snugly onto the back pockets of jeans have come out of one of SA Bias's factories.

Electronics manufacturer Plessey has just developed a new machine that is a direct response to trends in the broader environment. Called the "Votemaster", this little table-top console is billed as "The computerised solution to weighted voting in Regional Services Councils and other similar bodies". It is swipe-card activated and designed to register, calculate and display the outcome of a weighted-vote poll. Plessey's Market Development Director, Willy Gibbens, explains that in the course of their regular wide-ranging assessment of the South African scene they had realised that Regional Services Councils were on the way.

They targeted a level of business for the RSCs without knowing what they might sell to them, and proceeded to develop relationships with and an understanding of the RSCs. A couple of days after visiting the factory, an RSC member called back to enquire about a voting system. He outlined what the system would need to do and asked Gibbens whether it could be done electronically. Willy laughs, "As a marketing guy I said 'Yes, of course it can.' How it was going to be done I didn't know. A mock-up with lights and dummy keys was ready for presentation to the customer five days later."

Edgars provides an example of innovation that was stimulated by looking not only outward at customers and competitors, but also inwards at the organisation itself: Edgars, like Foschini, sells a large proportion of its turnover on credit. Remember the jingle "Lots of super fashions, lots of time to pay"? It works very well, but it means that Edgars has lots of time to finance a huge debtors' book. Edgars currently has 1,7 million account holders, and a debtors' book worth R200 million. At an averaged cost of borrowing, that book cost them about R30 million in 1988. Quite an interest bill! The issue had been debated many times over the years, but the company had consistently resisted the temptation to charge interest on credit purchases. They know their market, they know their customer and they know what "value" is to their customer. So they know that their customer will not be happy to see an interest charge on his or her account. How could they raise just a little more money from each of their account holders? Vic Hammond, Edgars' Chief Executive, told us how they came up with the Edgars Club concept. Each and every account holder would automatically become a member at a monthly fee of R2,00. The regular club magazine would feature interesting and colourful articles. The magazine would carry advertising that would at least cover its costs.

Hammond estimates that the Club concept will bring in R18 million in 1989. That goes a long way towards covering the interest bill.

Shifting Demographics

Most of the new ideas we looked at in our previous section — Citi Golf, tartan ribbon, cash-and-carry wholesale building materials, and so on — came from looking for clues in industry and market structures. What about some other sources? Well, South African demographic changes are as fast and profound as any anywhere. Rapid urbanisation and shifting income patterns are challenging almost every South African enterprise. In response, Suncrush, for example, is going the informal route with its spaza shop distribution system. SAB is already selling 50 per cent of its production through shebeens.

Changes in Perception

Think about changes in perceptions of cigarette smoking. In the good old carefree days before health became an issue for smokers, cigarette marketing focused on *lifestyle* — the image of the brand and the aura around it. Men's men smoked Paul Revere; thinking adventurers, Camel; jet-setters, Peter Stuyvesant. But now health awareness has added another dimension to cigarett marketing. Sure, the cowhands still ride the canyons of Arizona, our khaki-clad hero still flogs his faithful Land-Rover through tropical rainforests, beautiful people still week-end hysterically in Acapulco, but there is also a growing set of new archetypes — a plethora of new, lighter, healthier brands. Utico responded early to these changing perceptions; Benson & Hedges Special Mild was launched in 1978. The brand's superb positioning, consistent message and creative sport sponsorship have fuelled soaring sales figures — growth has been at 15 to 16 per cent per year. Benson and Hedges Special Mild is regarded in South Africa as the definitive mild cigarette.

Incongruities

Explore the incongruity, says management guru Peter Drucker,[2] between reality as it actually is and reality as it is assumed to be. Robin Hamilton, Executive Chairman of Suncrush, does this all the time. "You've got to test the assumptions," he says. When his team were exploring ways to reduce their distribution costs, they went right back to the beginning. They examined the long-used procedure of having the delivery truck follow the same outlet sequence as a sales representative in a car. Hamilton:

> "Our first big breakthrough was our understanding that the route taken by the man who pre-sells, who is in a car — I mean it sounds absurd to find this out after so many years — is convenient for him, but it's not necessarily the route the truck should take, because the truck is a different thing, it's much bigger."

When they started measuring respective distances travelled by the pre-seller's cars and by the delivery trucks, they found some crazy anomalies. Between a set of particular outlets in Rustenburg for instance, the pre-seller drove his car 300 metres down the street. But the truck physically couldn't go that way; it had to travel 5,5 kilometres to get to the same outlets! Reality was not as it ought to have been. Divisional General Manager, Dennis Smit, who previously managed the Rustenburg operation, recalls how they then re-planned their delivery procedure:

> "We said 'You've got to look at your bombers — the fighters can get anywhere.' We saved kilometres. In Rustenburg, it used to be 380 km for our trucks to service the town. We got it down to about 100 km."

When you consider that the Rustenburg route is driven twice a

---

2 Peter Drucker, *Innovation and Entrepreneurship*, London, Heinemann, 1985.

week by large and very expensive trucks and that it is only one of many routes that service 15 000 Suncrush customers around the country, you can begin to appreciate the kind of cost savings that resulted from simply testing the assumptions.

Process Need and Organisational Innovation

When Peter Drucker talks about innovation from process need, he explains that it "does not start out with an event in the internal or external environment. It starts out with a job to be done. It is task-focused rather than situation-focused." He goes on to give a number of examples of technological innovations that have improved the way that people or companies do things. Our super-performers do provide examples of this kind of innovation. Edgars, for instance, has developed outstanding direct-marketing capability in response to the need — or opportunity — to make use of its huge database of existing account holders. However, we would like to use Drucker's heading to draw your attention to a class of non-technical innovation that we believe is critically important in South Africa — and will become more so in the years ahead. We are talking about *organisational* innovation.

In 1982 Cashbuild, then five years old, had grown from three stores to 12. Pre-tax profits had leapt to around R700 000, up from R140 000 the previous year, and R40 000 the year before. Albert Koopman's three-cornered philosophy of value, innovation and commitment was clearly bearing fruit. The economy, and the building industry with it, was booming. Forecasts predicted 1983 to be another record year, and as it progressed the company expanded its operations; five new stores were opened. On projections, a profit of over R1 million might have been expected. But the actual results were very different; pre-tax profit for financial 1983 was, at R600 000, dismally short of expectations. Yet market demand was strong, and the new store locations were good. The problem clearly lay not with the marketplace, but within the organisation itself. Koopman and his managers immediately began to thrash out the issues, to "re-evaluate the status quo". They realised quite quickly that the way they were managing Cashbuild would have to change. As Koopman writes in his book, *The Corporate Crusaders:*

102

"One of the things we had at the Cashbuild Head Office in those days was a picture of our hierarchical structure. It was something the 'boss' [Koopman himself] had seen to. Months later Cashbuilders would recognise that kind of thing as polishing the image, rather than greasing the wheels. Meanwhile, there it was, everyone nice and neat, each one in his own little box. No one going anywhere. No leaders moving up, no new leaders getting in. And no new ideas either. Just little 'boxed' ideas from boxed-in people.

Rigor mortis started to set in. People started politicking and pretty soon, individual goals and values were no longer congruent with management's goals and values, and neither of the two was in keeping with the company's philosophy. The organisation had lost the single-mindedness of its early days, and knew there was no 'cause' to fight for. There were a lot of trained men but no committed soldiers.

What was becoming clear was that our organisational structure was too autocratic. So was my own management style. Obviously we had to change to a more democratic approach — managing by consent of the people. We had to change gear — but how? Wouldn't the people see it as 'soft'?"

The Cashbuild management team were hearing a clear call for process innovation — not just for a new way of, say, handling merchandise or improving security, but for an entirely new approach to managing in the South African context. The challenge was colossal. Their response was both dogged and courageous: dogged because evolving and executing their solutions demanded sustained single-minded effort over a period of years. Even now in 1989 Gerald Haumant, Cashbuild's current Managing Director and Koopman's right-hand man from the start, candidly admits that the participative management system is working successfully in only about 40 per cent of their branches. And courageous because Cashbuild's management resolutely sailed the company into completely uncharted waters. The passage was often rough too. Gerald Haumant recalls that there was initially deep mistrust on the part of the workers of management's motives in offering life employment, involvement in decision-making and so on. He goes on:

"That was all promises — now we had to apply them. We had a few test cases — you know, we had to have a couple of managers losing their jobs on recommendation of staff members to really prove that we meant it. And we did that. There were a couple of guys who could have been worked on that we disposed of a little too quickly just to prove how strongly we felt about it. It was a matter of 'shape up or ship out' and things turned very, very quickly. We only had to do a few drastic actions like discharge three branch managers, basically siding with the workers on issues which in the normal South African environment would be looked at as political and not part of the business scene."

Cashbuild's participative management system (discussed in Chapters 4 and 10) may still have a way to go, but even in its present imperfect form it has palpably improved the company's organisational processes, and made a real contribution to the bottom line. It provides a fine example of the kind of tough-minded innovative approach to organisations that our country so desperately needs.

New Knowledge

Technological research is the source of innovation that comes most readily to mind. It would be the obvious first choice — at the head of most lists of innovation sources. Even though Drucker calls knowledge-based innovation the "super-star of entrepreneurship", he puts it at the bottom of the list and discusses it last. Drucker observes that knowledge-based innovation gets the publicity and the money, and that it has undoubtedly been the wellspring of many — if not most — important invention and discovery through the course of history, but he warns that "like most super-stars, knowledge-based innovation is temperamental, capricious and hard to manage."

You may be asking whether knowledge-based innovation, with its image of high-tech, big-budget research labs, happens in a country like South Africa. Don't we leave the pure research to the American, European and Japanese giants that are big enough to afford costly research programmes? Isn't it a little far-fetched to expect our small country with its limited financial and technological resources, with a dwindling corps of scientists and engineers, to be up there with the world's best when it comes to R&D? Well the answer that our own research provides is that you might be surprised. We were. And while we don't want to convey the impression that South Africa's top-performing companies are committed one-and-all to pure research and development, we will observe that there are companies in this country that spend very significant amounts of money on pure research and that have produced world-beating technological innovations. We will see that research of this nature is not the laid-back, blue-sky kind, but that it is organised and managed to deliver results without stifling the individual creativity that is essential to success.

Our list of super-performers included two high-tech companies: Plessey and Altech. In some superficial ways the two are similar — both are in the electronics business and both compete aggressively in several markets, particularly telecommunications. In more important ways, however, they differ — Altech is much larger than Plessey's South African operation; but Plessey is part of a worldwide electronics corporation, while Altech is home-grown South African; Altech's relative youth and the still very pervasive energy of Bill Venter give it a more entrepreneurial feel than the more mature Plessey; Plessey's style is quite formal, Altech's perhaps less so. Given these differences, we were surprised to find that Plessey and Altech have very similar approaches to technological research and development.

Dr John Temple, Plessey's Managing Director, explains his company's concept of technology development:

"There are different levels of technology development; pure research, applied research, and so on. But technology is like an arrow. You can't have one part without the other."

The spearhead of the arrow is pure research and invention, where the aim is to push forward the frontiers of the technology itself rather than of a product. Plessey's chosen niche for pure research has been electronic distance measurement and it's in this area that the company has for years supported pure research on the campuses of the Universities of Cape Town and Stellenbosch.

Plessey's Tellurometer, a state-of-the-art distance-measuring device developed in South Africa, now sells worldwide.

The second level of technology, or the front half of the shaft of Plessey's arrow, is applied research. Here the company takes pure research and applies it to the development or adaptation of existing products. Out of the Tellurometer programme came a very fine knowledge of microwave technology, which has now been applied to the production of microwave data-link devices that allow PABX's and computers to communicate by radio.

The third level of technology, or the backend of the arrow shaft, is transferred technology. This is probably how you would expect so-called high-tech South African companies to acquire most of their know-how. Temple agrees that it makes absolute sense to do it this way. He doesn't want to reinvent the wheel either. But he adds a critical rider: **in order to successfully transfer technology to South Africa a company needs to have skilled and experienced people to handle the local receipt of the know-how, and the only way to ensure that those skilled and experienced people are available to it, is to participate in pure and applied research.** Temple's view therefore is that technology transfer cannot be effected unless the company is also actively engaged in research itself.

The last level of technology — the feather of the arrow — is the one that Temple believes South Africans are not yet too clever at, namely manufacturing technology. He thinks that some of Plessey's competitors are not presently capable of pure or applied research. "So what they do is they go over to Europe or somewhere," he says, pointing at our tape recorder, "and they say 'Ah, I want to make that tape recorder. Can I have the technology?' And what they mean by that is 'Will you please supply me with a kit of parts and a screwdriver.'" It's local assembly as opposed to local content. "Lego technology," Temple calls it. Now it's not our intention to beat the export drum here, but what this country's economy needs very badly is much more *value added* exports. Lego technology is a step in the right direction — if we can do it competitively — but the real goal must be to develop our local capability to add real value to locally produced raw materials.

Dr David Jacobson is the Altron group's Director of Technology. He is responsible for the group's *technology development* — a term he prefers to call "industrial research and development". "It's terminology that sits easier on the ear. People tend to know what it means and in the business world it makes a lot of sense. It has a more active, market driven feel than research and development." Jacobson's grizzled bushy beard and round spectacles give him a professorial air — and fittingly so; he has been an honorary professor in Applied Mathematics at Wits since 1975. He is a serious and thoughtful man. He's thought a lot about transferring and developing technology.

"From the point of view of technology and product there are some quite clever aspects to the group. Firstly it's a group — and I refer to Altron here — that is wholly South African owned. It does not have a Head Office in Europe, or the United States, or the Far East or elsewhere. Its Head Office is here; Boksburg. And that has meant that the group has had to stand on its own two feet in sorting out its technological problems. Secondly, it has been able to access world technology from very many different sources. So it hasn't been tied to one mother company. It's been able to develop very strong bonds with companies in North America, Europe, Asia — where else is there that really matters? — and to draw from those contacts not only product but knowledge and understanding. Now I think that is a very important aspect in the group's success — that we do have what you can almost think of as a very comprehensive insurance policy. We have multiple, very successful principals overseas, and we are on very good terms with them, and have taken care to develop those relationships."

Jacobson goes on to stress that Altech, part of the Altron group, are not assemblers of product — they are manufacturers. The distinct difference between those, he says, is often not appreciated by people who don't know that the business is in the process of transferring the technology. Altech's transfer process is a gradual one; they begin by importing the principal's finished product and servicing it for some time. Then they import kits for local assembly. A while later they begin to break down kits of parts and source sub-assemblies locally. "That requires a very detailed understanding of the product, which by now we have built up through this familiarisation process and through the education of our people that we've sent overseas to our principals to transfer the technology." At this stage they are, for example, making their own circuit boards, sourcing their own components, doing all their own troubleshooting with their own test jigs and test software. It is a process of steadily increasing local content in terms of both material and, importantly, in terms of know-how.

Altech's fourth step is one in which, as a consequence of the intimate understanding that has been developed, they begin to see ways of improving the product for local conditions. Says Jacobson:

> *"I can give you many examples, but one example would be the Diginet product, the digital network for the country, which was specifically transferred from Marconi of Italy — it was known there as Kilostream — for local manufacture for the Post Office. You can think of Diginet in layman's terms as a communication system for computers and for data transfer, whereas the telephone network is a communication system for people. When we reached this Phase 4, which we reached rather quickly, we found that we could improve the design of the network terminator units — these are the units that come into the customers' premises. In that system there were three Marconi integrated circuits which we were not too happy about because they were single sourced from Marconi — there is always cost penalty in single sources — and as we were redesigning this network terminator unit we decided to design our modifications into three new chips which we had made by South African Micro-Electronic Systems, SAMES, in Pretoria."*

That redesign is an example of going further than technology transfer. It takes Altech into enhancement, adaptation and design. Jacobson confirms that principals are almost always happy to go along with the improvement process. In Marconi's case there is real interest in the modifications that Altech has made.

The final hue in Altech's spectrum of technology development is where they do their own design. Jacobson cites, as an example, transmitters and receivers for fibre-optic communications that were supplied once again to the Post Office. The know-how came from Standard Telephones and Cables (STC) — the United Kingdom based telecommunications giant whose South African subsidiary Altech bought in 1976. In the course of the transfer of that technology, Altech learnt a great deal about optical systems, about lasers, about light emitting and detecting diodes and about repeaters for boosting the light pulses when they begin to weaken after many kilometres of travel. Armed with this new knowledge, Altech labs set about designing a so-called shorthaul fibre optical system that can transmit massive volumes of data at lightning speed over distances of up to 50 kilometres. There is real pride in Jacobson's voice as he talks about it. It is state-of-the-art communications technology and it was totally locally developed.

How does Altech match these diverse and burgeoning capabilities with the needs of its almost equally diverse markets? Jacobson talks decentralisation:

"Because we don't have one single principal, one Head Office overseas, you can think of our worldwide sources of technology as decentralised. And obviously our marketplace is decentralised — we serve many different customers at all times. Our thinking then on technology development programmes is that, once again, they should not be centralised. In other words, we have not put up central technology development laboratories for the whole group. To give you perhaps the most outlandish example, the problems of Willard Batteries in Port Elizabeth, which is one of our Powertech companies, are simply not going to be solved by STC technology development laboratories, and vice versa."

Grouping the battery boffins with the telecoms boffins in one facility wouldn't make any sense, and besides it would divorce them from their respective colleagues in marketing and manufacturing. So they have identified technology development centres throughout the group; STC has one for telecommunications, Willard has one for energy storage, Punchline has one for LAN (local area network) design, and so on, and they have put them on a "lightly-structured" programme. In each centre there is a technology development task team, chaired by the host company's Managing Director, that identifies new project opportunities, motivates funding from group coffers and sets about the actual development work. Jacobson sits on each of these teams, not as Chairman but as an ordinary member. Aside from contributing directly from his personal fund of knowledge and experience, his role is to help the team make connections into other group companies that might have useful skills, and into outside bodies like the Council for Scientific and Industrial Research and the universities. Jacobson is by his own description a somewhat unusual animal in that he's lived in three worlds; he was an academic (and is still an honorary professor at Wits), he was a Deputy President of the CSIR and he is now in the world of industry. So if his teams need technological assistance he can usually point them in the right direction.

While much of the initiative for Altech's technology development comes bottom-up from these decentralised task teams, there is also a top-down component. Jacobson is in a position to put suggestions to the teams. He does a lot of scanning of literature, sending copies of articles and papers to the relevant companies. Bill Venter himself is still enormously influential here too. "He is continuously sending copies of interesting things that he has noted to various people and saying 'What are you doing about this?' and 'Shouldn't you be looking at that?'"

Altech's approach to technological innovation is a pragmatic one. Their decentralised approach encourages initiative to be taken at the very lowest levels in the group — furthest from head office and nearest the customer. There is a deal of freedom and autonomy within a light structure of co-ordination and control. And each company must be self-sufficient. "It's a philosophy of every tub on its own bottom," says Jacobson, using a phrase he learnt during his teaching and research days at Harvard where each university faculty must pay its own way without any cross subsidisation. It is an approach that is at the same time both sensible and sensitive, practical and venturous. While it doesn't have Plessey's pure research component it's a good South African approach, and it works.

110

Intuition, Experience and the Right-Brain Way

We've taken a few pages to examine how our super-performers innovate deliberately, and innovate on the basis of information. Does that mean that we should only try something new when we've done our homework and sorted out an innovative opportunity from a mass of data? Does the evidence suggest that new ideas that are not methodically derived from data should be rejected, that "off the wall" creative concepts should be stifled at birth? The answer of course, is *definitely not*.

Imagine the sequence: Sol Kerzner climbs back into his helicopter after tramping around the virgin Pilanesberg site that first day in 1978, his mind bursting with the possibilities. The moment he is back in his office he gathers his team to brief them of the research data that will be required for the exhaustive feasibility study he regards as essential. In a week or two they reconvene. The team has worked day and night co-ordinating research and building computer models — only to conclude that Sol's little Las Vegas is a huge no-no. The findings are conclusive; not nearly enough people will take the trouble to drive out beyond Rustenburg for the proposed complex to even remotely break even. Sol tilts back his chair, sighs resignedly and, before dismissing the group, laments; "Hell, it seemed like such a good idea." The fact of the matter is Sol Kerzner knew Sun City would work. He didn't have to research it. And if he had he wouldn't have got the answers he wanted anyway. By all accounts, the decision his board took to invest many millions in Sun City was largely founded on Kerzner's proven intuition.

How did Mike Benn, Managing Director of Willards Foods, know that Flanagan's would fly? Willards have a system for researching and rating new product innovations on a scale from 1 to 10. Only product ideas that score 7 or more are launched. But Benn didn't have time for research, and besides, he just knew Flanagan's would be a winner. We asked him how he knew. "You just can't keep a good product down," was his reply. When they did the follow-up research *after* the hugely successful launch, Willards found that Flanagan's would only have scored 6 on the new product prospects scale. The rational model would have rejected the idea. Benn's intuitive assessment was spot on.

Think of Lois Wagner, the Cadbury's Brand Manager, charged with co-ordinating the development of Tempo and Cabrio. We saw in Chapter 3 that an almost unbelievable amount of careful and deep research went into specifying how the two chocolate bars should taste and feel, but at the end of the day how did Lois know the taste and texture that the manufacturing people came up with was right? Research and rationale could only take her so far; beyond that point she had to use her intuition. How did you know that you'd got it right? we asked.

"You know I've been in this business a long time. I just know. You get to a point and its the old thing that everyone talks about and no one can define — gut feel. I believe that is actually just the most important thing. It's right or it's not right."

But take heed. The lesson is not "Trust your intuition". The lesson is "Trust your intuition if you should". Remember that intuition is insight without the intervention of reason, insight that springs subconsciously from experience.

Sol Kerzner has been a hotelier ever since he left the accounting profession in 1962; he knows what South African leisure seekers are looking for. Mike Benn is the guru of the South African snack market — he was at Simba before joining Willards. He eats and sleeps snack foods. Lois Wagner has been running confectionery brands almost her entire working life. Each of these people has long and deep experience in their field. So let Raymond Ackerman make intuitive decisions about supermarketing. Trust Peter Savory's gut feel when it comes to beer. And listen to your long-serving machine-minder when he says he's got a bright idea. **Trust your gut, go the right-brain way — but only if you can speak from experience.**

Don't Reinvent the Wheel

Strictly speaking, imitation is not really innovation. But imitation is an important source of innovation for less developed economies like South Africa's, where there isn't much spare cash for research and development. Japan, of course, built its industrial might on imitation, not just of American products but also American

112

manufacturing and management techniques that the Japanese subtly adapted to their own cultural peculiarities. The imitation strategy paid off; success has allowed the Japanese to shift from imitators to true innovators.

Our publisher, Jonathan Ball, has, over the years, developed close ties with the publishing fraternity in the United Kingdom. His publishing friends there call him, he tells us, "the biggest buccaneer in the business", because he is constantly on the lookout for English titles that can be readily transposed to the South African market. Not imported, mind you, but rewritten, adapted for local publication. As we write this book Jonathan is working on a host of titles, many of which are little more than South African variants of books previously produced abroad. Subjects range from cookery to travel, from winelands to battlefields, and each project has been commissioned by Jonathan to be researched, written, illustrated and produced locally. They promise to be glorious books – a promise that, for Jonathan at least, is in no way demeaned by the close resemblance they bear to already published volumes. Aspects of their style of presentation, design features and even subject matter, where appropriate, have been transposed from existing models and modified for the South African book buyer. Jonathan is unabashed. On one occasion he even commissioned an artist because her style so closely matches the illustrations of a book he particularly admires. Jonathan knows a good thing when he sees it and he knows the local book market like the back of his hand. Innovation by imitation makes absolute sense to him. He offers a few words of caution though: **don't imitate blindly. Adapt a good idea to the characteristic of your own customer profile — and beware of copyright infringement!**

Keep the Focus

When you have one of those off-the-wall, out-of-the-blue *really* bright ideas that isn't actually terribly close to the things your business does right now — beware! This is temptation time. And as the saying goes, temptation steps in through a door left open. Close that door. Channel your organisation's innovative effort to the areas you decide on beforehand. Keep the focus. Lots of perfectly good companies have wasted a great deal of money and effort chasing and developing bright ideas that had nothing to do with the business they were in, or should ever have got into.

Fostering Innovation

Some of our super-performers are more innovative than others, although almost all would rate highly in the innovation stakes. How do they foster innovation? What conditions do they create to encourage their people to see things afresh, to chase new rainbows? We'll see that, like almost everything else, innovation is about people. Our points here, then, link closely to Chapters 4 and 10, on liberating human potential and building corporate culture.

Build a Performance-based Culture

Probably the most fundamental attribute shared by our innovation champions is their commitment to performance. Several of the super-performers were consciously trying to build or enhance performance-based cultures in their organisations at the time we did the research. We'll look at corporate culture in much more depth in Chapter 10. Suffice it to say here that **innovation thrives in a competitive corporate environment where individuals are expected to perform, and to outperform.** Robin Hamilton, Executive Chairman of Suncrush, understands this principle. Hamilton regards the increased emphasis on innovation as the major change in the way his company has been managed in the last few years. Part of his innovation success formula is to expect performance at every level in the company. "Put the pressure on them," he says, "and encourage short cuts." This way, you'll create champions who have personal stakes in their new ideas.

Structure it Right

Current management thinking holds that the entrepreneurial pursuit doesn't co-exist too comfortably with the daily business of walloping the competition out there in the market place. The theory is that the two behaviours need different mindsets, different controls, different feedback systems — in short, different management styles. And since it is difficult to manage the same people in different ways at the same time, the usual advice is to structure entrepreneurial activity separately from the organisation's ongoing competitive operations. Plessey certainly does it this way; aside from an identified research and development function, itself clearly separate from manufacturing and marketing, the company also has a Market Development Director whose job it is to develop new ideas together with research and development, production and marketing people, and to hand each new idea (be it a new product or a new customer) over to operations as soon as the first order is confirmed. We saw earlier how Plessey's bigger competitor, Altech, has several decentralised technology development task teams that report through to group level quite separately from the day-to-day lines of reporting. When they develop new products, Cadbury's forms part-time task-teams that comprise production, engineering, research and development and marketing specialists. In each case creative endeavour has been encouraged by giving people freedom to operate unencumbered by the formal structure and pull in the skills they need from elsewhere in the organisation.

Shrug off Failure

Suncrush doesn't develop new products. It has been selling Coca-Cola, Sparletta and Schweppes soft drinks for years. Nevertheless, Suncrush is an extraordinarily innovative company. We heard earlier how Executive Chairman Robin Hamilton has been prodding his organisation in this direction for some time now. Hamilton knows that if people are to be encouraged to experiment, then they must also be allowed to fail. When Dennis Smit was running Suncrush's Rustenburg operation, he and his counterpart from Klerksdorp, Dave Jackson, spent much of the company's time and money redesigning delivery trailers. Smit recalls the outcome:

> *"When I think of it now — how stupid it really was. It was a new concept and it never worked. We were going to have a rigid horse that drew this trailer behind, so that when you get to the likes of Pick 'n Pay you just leave the trailer and off you go further down the road while they unload it. It never really got off the ground properly. We produced two bloody trailers. They cost us R100 000 and those things bombed out from day one. And both of us are still working for the company."*

In fact Dennis Smit was subsequently promoted to Divisional General Manager. Hamilton recalls Dennis's days in Rustenburg with a chuckle: "He was always sailing very close to the wind. I still don't know how he managed to stay out of trouble." Quite clearly, though, it's just that kind of behaviour that Hamilton values.

Break the Rules

Part of tolerating failure is allowing people to break the rules occasionally. We quote Robin Hamilton again:

> *"We've got a manual here which tells you what to do under every goddamn circumstance. I haven't looked at it for years. You're not looking for a robot, really, you're looking for a guy who's going to break a few rules, and he musn't get knifed in the back because he breaks a few small rules. We have encouraged — out in the field — the sort of maverick who'll break the rules."*

At Cadbury's breaking the rules is a deliberate exercise. Here though, by the rules they mean the accepted ways of doing things — industry-wide. Managing Director Piet Beyers tells how they thought up their new way of handling consumer complaints:

> *"This concept came out of a larger concept — the whole thinking of breaking the rules. How can we manage differently? How can we break the traditional thinking? What is everyone else in the industry doing and how can we break the rules by doing something differently and so get some form of competitive advantage?"*

David Ogilvy is now Chairman of the huge international advertising agency, Ogilvy and Mather. One of several jobs he had before finding his way into advertising was as a salesman for Aga Cookers. In 1935, at the age of 24, he wrote *The Theory and Practice of Selling the Aga Cooker.* Nearly 40 years later *Fortune* magazine called it "probably the best sales manual ever written". In it, and amongst much else, Ogilvy offered his fellow salesmen the following advice:

"Study the best time of day for calling; between twelve and

two p.m. you will not be welcome, whereas a call at an unortho-
dox time of day — after supper in the summer for instance — will
often succeed . . . In general, study the methods of your competitors and do the exact opposite."[3]

In his own eccentric way, Ogilvy has been breaking the rules
ever since.

Disturb the Routine

Every organisation needs routine. Routine is an essential part of
business life. It is central to the concepts of consistency and
momentum that are so dear to western business culture. It's part
of making the business day — and week, and year — predictable.
It is fundamental to the way that we measure and compare
business performance. But in business, as in marriage, routine is
deadly, a creeping killer. When routine becomes its own rationale, beware; you have taken a step towards bureaucracy.

**Routine brings on boredom, and just a touch of boredom is
enough to stifle creativity. Innovation drifts gently out of the
window. So introduce a little freshness, break the routine once in
a while. It'll do your organisation a power of good.**

Undo the Bureaucracy

Our super-performers evidence a pretty general abhorrence of
bureaucracy and red tape. In Chapter 4 we saw how companies
like SA Bias, Suncrush and SAB's Beer Division try to cut down
on bureaucracy by avoiding formal systems where they can, by
replacing formal systems with informal ones. In this way they
provide a more open working environment in which their people
become free to succeed. And one of the pursuits that succeeds
best in these conditions is innovation. Innovation needs freedom
from red tape.

Reward the Innovator

Remember the advice we were given in Chapter 2 by people like
Peter Searle of Volkswagen and Brand Pretorius of Toyota:
measure what you want to happen and reward it when it does? So

---

3 David Ogilvy, *The Unpublished David Ogilvy,* London, Sidgwick & Jackson, 1988.

too with innovation. Granted, innovation isn't going to be easy to measure; except in a formal R&D situation that will probably prove impossible. But while you may not be able to measure the innovation that is occurring in your company, you can surely identify the kind of innovative behaviour that the organisation needs and recognise it when it happens. Then you are in a position to reward that behaviour. In so doing, of course, you will be reinforcing peoples' understanding of what kind of innovative behaviour the organisation values.

Those rewards can take a number of forms. Money? Yes, but what we learn from our super-performers is that *recognition* is probably the most powerful form of reward for this kind of easy-to-spot-but-hard-to-measure achievement. Dr David Jacobson, for instance, told us how innovation is rewarded at Altech. There is a bonus system, but the emphasis, when it comes to rewarding innovation, is on the qualitative side of the equation. Firstly, the work itself is very exciting and very stimulating, says Jacobson. People derive enormous satisfaction from being a member of a successful development team. And secondly, an engineer who is largely responsible for a successful development project could go on to play a major role in an operation set up to exploit the new technology commercially.

Skunkworks — When it Starts to Happen

If you've read Peters and Waterman, (or Peters, or Waterman) you will have come across the word "skunkworks". Skunkworks are the small dingy workshops beyond the parking area behind the main workshops where time is stolen from the working day, and mugs of coffee are drunk deep into the evenings while new ideas are explored that will need bootlegged components to patch together a prototype.

Skunkworking starts to happen in an organisation when conditions favour innovative effort. It's a bit like spring. When the days begin to lengthen and the weather warms up a little, things suddenly start happening in the garden; bulbs shoot, trees start to bud, new leaf is everywhere. In the same way, when you start to value performance, tolerate failure and put in the right structures, innovation, almost of its own accord, will simply start to happen.

We have, we think, a superb skunkworks story to illustrate our point. We justify its inclusion in our South African book on the rather flimsy grounds that it features a car designer (more correctly "automotive stylist") called Keith Helfert who was born in Calvinia and educated in Cape Town. Aside from Keith, all the players are British and the setting is Coventry, England. It's the story of the development of Jaguar's new sportscar, the XJ220.

The car was unveiled at the British Motor Show in Birmingham in November 1988 — and stole the show. It is unmistakably a Jaguar. With feline form reminiscent of the famous E-Type, the XJ220 is immediately both classic and avant-garde. The curves are very sleek, very beautiful and very powerful.

"Aesthetically the XJ220 had to retain Jaguar's strong sports car identity, whilst maintaining an evolutionary link to the future", says Keith in *Car Magazine.* "The philosophy was to continue the feel of the Sir William Lyons and Malcolm Sayer designs in which visual appeal was created by beautifully sculptured flowing surfaces, in contrast to the current tendency to rely on feature lines and graphics."

Keith explains that this is part of a recent trend towards softer shapes, referred to in designer jargon as "bio". *Car Magazine*'s Dave Pollock describes the car's final shape as "beautiful — alive and breathtaking, its curves and forms breathtakingly pure". If you've seen a leopard crouching low on an anthill in the half-light of dawn you'll know what he means.

And the XJ220 isn't just good to look at either: if it went into production today it would outperform both the Ferrari F40 and the Porsche 959. With a top speed of over 320 km per hour, it would be the fastest production car in the world. That performance is powered by the awesome 6.2 litre 48 valve V12 engine that Jaguar developed for racing in the sixties and has now repackaged in state-of-the-art engineering — four-wheel-drive transmission, microprocessor controlled fuel injection, advanced-technology bonded-alloy chassis, anti-lock braking, viscous coupled differentials, and electronically controlled active shock absorbers. And there's luxury too. Under the huge space-age windscreen and in traditional Jaguar style the driver is closeted in fine Connolly hide.

Born as a sketch on the back of a Christmas card in 1984, the XJ220 took almost five years to be revealed to the light of photographers' flashguns in Birmingham. One can imagine the long process; a huge development team of designers, technicians and engineers working to a critical-path programme and backed by a multi-million pound budget. In fact, it didn't happen that way at all. Until April 1986 the project was entirely unofficial. Only at the end of that year was a small budget granted to the project. Almost unbelievably, Jaguar's world-beating supercar had been put together up to that point by volunteers in their spare time. Parts had been scrounged from other models and lines. Suppliers, about 40 in all, had contributed by developing components. In automotive terms the prototype had cost next to nothing. And although Jaguar is insisting that the car is still a prototype and that no orders are being taken, the project has been handed over to Jaguar Sport Ltd "to review public reaction and assess its commercial viability". Judging by the car's initial reception we might well see it on the road in a year or two's time. If we do, it will bear classic and beautiful testimony to making the right kind of innovation happen.

11 Steps to Winning Innovation

1. Look for clues in the information you collect on your own company, your customers, your competitors and the wider operating environment. Turn clues into cues.
2. Take your cues from South Africa's shifting demographics and the implications they have for your business.
3. Take your cues from changes in perception in your marketplaces.
4. Take your cues from incongruities between things as they are and things as they "ought to be".
5. Take your cues from process need, by evaluating the way things are done in your organisation.
6. Don't shy away from organisational innovation.
7. Deliberately pursue the new knowledge your business needs.
8. Trust your intuition — but only if you can speak from experience.
9. Imitate creatively. Don't reinvent the wheel. But don't imitate blindly — adapt a good idea to the needs of your own customer.
10. Keep the focus. Don't go off at a tangent unless you've really thought it through.

11. Foster innovation in your organisation:
   - Build a performance-based culture
   - Structure for innovation
   - Tolerate failure
   - Let people break the rules
   - Disturb the routine
   - Unravel bureaucracy
   - Reward the innovator

CHAPTER SIX

DO WHAT COMES LOGICALLY

"At the end of the day, if we are not good marketers, sellers, distributors and producers of beer, then what the hell are we trying to do?"

Graham Mackay, Managing Director,
SAB's Beer Division

THE WALTONS SUCCESS STORY

Waltons' real history began in 1969 when a cocky young representative from John Dickinson (the stationery arm of the fallen stationery and packaging giant DRG) approached Norman Walton, the owner of Waltons Stationery Company. The company then employed only eight people and was managing a steady monthly turnover of R9 000. Frankie Robarts must have fully employed his selling skills to get Walton to buy into the vision of a stationery giant that would surpass John Dickinson. Walton cut him in, and the rest is history.

The pace was frantic from the start. First they concentrated on opening branches in the Cape. They then followed the same pattern in Durban and later in the Transvaal. Backward integration into manufacture followed in 1980 with the acquisition of joint control of Pirie Appleton, and in 1983 with the DRG factory. The early 1980s saw some sizeable acquisitions, but throughout the expansion, acquisition was the predominant form of growth.

The formula was a bit like this: they would acquire a stationer which was not performing very well, and in no time turn it into a Waltons operation, spitting out profits and cash in the process. This they would do by putting a cracker under management;

rationalising their facilities; improving buying through skills development and providing access to their upstream facilities; improving their basic business disciplines, such as buying, selling, working capital management; adding an additional layer of business sophistication in, for example, information systems; but most important of all, the new company would be taught the meaning of margin.

People love to speculate on the reasons for Waltons' success. The favourite reason is that they dominate their markets. This is absolutely true. But the fact that they dominate their markets is an indication that they've excelled in other aspects too. Probably the most important reason for their success is that they are hard-nosed, hands-on and practical people, mindful always of the few important things they need to do well. As Managing Director, Frankie Robarts puts it:

"We are guys who know our business — we concentrate on profits — buy well, sell well and keep operating costs at a minimum."

Much of their business success is built on an extremely logical formula based on the variables of powerful capabilities in stationery, buying and selling, combined with a detailed understanding of where they make money and where they spend it, and managing it accordingly.

We all know how complicated organisational life can get — budgets, people problems, politics, foul-ups, procedures, strategic plans, head office requirements and so on and so on. The more scarce management skills become, the more we chase our tails with the chores of keeping the wheels from falling off.

It therefore stuck out like a sore thumb that **the super-performers have an ability to stand back and work out what is needed to succeed, given their strategy. If we don't get these things right, we will never get off home base.**

It all sounds so logical that one begins to wonder whether it even bears discussion. We have some experience of working in also-rans, and we are convinced that this ability to do what comes logically is most definitely a factor setting apart the super-performers from the also-rans.

There are three important elements to this. The first is building distinctive capabilities. That is, becoming superbly good at the things that logic suggests you should be superbly good at. We will show you the extraordinary lengths that super-performers go to to build distinctive capabilities. We will also illustrate how these capabilities are used to sort out the competition.

The second element we deal with comes from not doing what doesn't come logically. Here we will show that super-performers are as tight as anything when it comes to activities which don't create value for the customer.

The third element of doing what comes logically is that of picking on the few key measures that drive the success of the business. Here we will show the power of focusing on no more than a handful of measures that will allow you to keep your fingers on the pulses.

BUILDING DISTINCTIVE CAPABILITIES

Graham Mackay, Managing Director of the Beer Division of SA Breweries, personifies the corporate culture of his organisation; he is open, yet economical in his use of words. His direct, yet personable exterior belies a formidable mind and a ruthless ability to get things done. We caught him after his lunch hour game of squash. Mackay was clearly trying to get through the agenda quickly. When pressed on the standard question: "Could we talk a bit about some of the things you believe Beer Division is good at?" he sighed and replied:

> *"At the end of the day, if we are not good marketers, sellers, distributors and producers of beer, then what the hell are we trying to do?"*

Sounds logical, doesn't it? Yet in that one sentence he has shown that their management team have been able to stand back and work out what it is that they need to do well to succeed in the clear beer business in South Africa. The trick is then to devote organisational resource to building those capabilities. Beer Division has certainly got this part right too, and has in the process created a beer machine that is the ninth biggest in the world, with a brand, Castle Lager, that is the seventh biggest in the world. Its margins would surely put it in the Number One spot.

As we discussed above, super-performing companies are able to stand back and, by logical deduction, work out what sort of distinctive capabilities they need to build. What do we mean by distinctive capabilities? We saw in the super-performing companies no more than a handful of things they are able to do superbly well. Anglo American knows how to turn around multi-billion rand projects. It also knows how to mine. These are a few of its distinctive capabilities. It is also important to realise that these capabilities are not always obvious, even to the insiders. For example, the audit division of Deloitte Haskins & Sells, above anything else, is renowned for being superb at churning out Chartered Accountants. This becomes critically important if one considers that for most young accountants, the firm is a stepping stone into the commercial world. Only a small percentage of the annual intake will move on to become managers and partners of the firm. It has therefore become a first-rate CA factory first and foremost. Professional standards, the ability to recruit, to retain stars and the whole professional leadership of the firm depend more on this one distinctive capability than on anything else.

Recognising Your Capabilities

How, then, do the super-performers decide on their distinctive capabilities? More than any other way, they are built up over time, and often in a haphazard way. We think, though, that each of these super-performers is able to answer this one question: How is their organisation able to create value for the customer? As we discussed in Chapter 2, this is normally the basis of developing a strategy — offering the customer something that is different to a competitive offering and which creates value for the buyer. For a company like Mathieson & Ashley's Dashing, it is offering a high quality product, professionally sold and delivered on time. This has meant developing distinctive capabilities in manufacturing — they have factories which compare to the best in Europe. It has also meant developing distinctive capabilities in selling — those who have bought office furniture will know that they sell extremely well. Of course, within the distinctive capabilities of manufacturing and selling there are a number of capabilities on their own. But this is how the process starts.

Beer Division is big on distinctive capabilities. Above all else, however, it knows it has to be really good at producing, branding, selling and distributing beer if it is to retain its dominance in South Africa. Liberty Life knows that leadership in the life insurance industry will not come without exceptional capabilities in investment, product development, marketing and selling. Edgars knows that its future rests on its merchanting skills. Utico knows that its skill in branding is the only thing that will hold back the tide that is Rembrandt. Tollgate, with its massive capital investment in buses, knows that it needs to develop a capability in operations — keeping the buses busy — and finance. We could dwell on this, but suffice it to say that **the success of the super-performers depends on their ability to do certain things well. What these things are will depend primarily on the strategy by which they create value for their customers. This, in turn, will depend on the business environment in general, and the competition in particular.**

Building Your Capabilities

Having explained what we mean by distinctive capabilities and how they derive, by logical deduction, from the strategy followed by the organisation, we will go on to show how some of the super-performers have gone about building these capabilities.

As they have been demonstrated to us, they have two elements. The first is the capability of individuals in the organisation — the people themselves, their expertise and experience. The second element is what we call the support tools, which, through the support they provide to the individuals, provide the juice to turn them into something that is, collectively, special.

The initial phase of Edgars' growth came through selling to the working class on credit. An initial skill they developed was one of retail banking. They were better lenders of small amounts to the working class than anybody else — including the retail banks. It's interesting, too, that Vic Hammond started the lending operation at Edgars in its early days.

In the 1960s they were given good advice by one of their international consultants that the future of retailing lay in good merchandising. Then followed an incredible focus on developing their merchanting skills. As Hammond puts it:

126

"We really had to become serious about merchandise — we had to live, breath and eat merchanting."

The steps they went through to get there (in our view they have got there) make for interesting discussion.

1. They recruited extensively from overseas — particularly the United Kingdom — and brought in some of the best merchants in the world. Some may say that this was an option in the late 1960s, but not so now. Many of the leaders of super-performing companies disagree, says Winky Ringo, Executive Chairman of Mathieson & Ashley:

   "You've got to work harder to find them and pay more. The facts are that you need these people (the Germans) and they are available."

2. They put in programmes for developing the skills internally. They define the skill development as being a combination of inherent ability (which they know how to recognise), experience, overseas travel and time in the stores. The Merchandise Development Programme, which runs for a year, provides the young employee with a year of on-the-job training, which includes time in the stores and adoption by a buying department. Soon after this the overseas travel starts.

3. They developed a host of supporting tools to develop this organisational capability. Some of these were:

   - **Top management involvement** (remember Meyer Kahn's "shit rolls downhill"?). Nothing reinforces an organisational push more than top management involvement. Conversely, few organisational pushes survive top management apathy. The "Bellamy Reviews" started. Adrian Bellamy, former Chief Executive, set up a procedure whereby he and his senior management conducted a final critical review of all merchandise. Many of the buyers weren't able to deal with this and left. The superstars thrived on it. The word soon spread through the organisation that top management were serious about upgrading the standard of buying.
   - **Development of a merchandising culture.** Organisational

members began to understand that merchandising was the high ground and the place to be for people wanting to get ahead. The culture became enormously supportive of the idiosyncrasies that go hand-in-hand with a high level of creativity.

- **Keeping their people in touch with the international leading edge.** Edgars' buyers travel overseas regularly. They also have people in all the major centres whose sole job it is to follow trends and feed these back to Edgardale. Vic Hammond's shelf is full of bumf on overseas fashion. His top team talk about international fashion trends as if they were happening in the backyard.
- **Market feedback.** Remember the importance of feedback? Procedures were instituted to ensure that buyers receive timeous feedback on how their merchandise is featuring.
- **Systems support.** The information systems people played their part too by putting in place administrative systems to support the creative folk.

These are but a few examples of the support tools used to provide the juice for turning individual skills into a distinctive capability. There were many others, particularly in the area of human resources, where, over a period of time, they have become more sophisticated in their hiring and retention policies.

Organisations like Edgars show us that building distinctive capabilities requires time, effort, money, and above all else, a consistency in all of these. There will always be elements in the organisation calling an end to all this "madness". Super-performers like Edgars have a group of people at the top committed enough to making sure that time, effort and money are applied consistently.

The spin-off? Well, Edgars' results speak for themselves, and merchanting has been the foundation of these results. Stock turnover has improved, stock write-offs have been reduced and margins have improved. Above all else, Edgars is an organisation regarded as a world-class player in retailing.

The Story of Liberty Life and SAB

Our research material contains at least 20 descriptions of outstanding organisational capabilities. We will relate just two more, which shows how organisations in very different settings have gone about building competition-beating capabilities. They are Liberty Life and SAB, both in selling. That they are both in selling is a deliberate message: if there's one distinctive capability every organisation needs, then it has to be selling.

Liberty Life has an impressive list of distinctive capabilities. The one that interested us the most was the selling capability of their agency force. To put things in perspective, Life Insurers usually have two channels for their selling activities — an agency force who sell their policies only, and brokers, who sell pretty much anything. As with anything in life, there are pros and cons associated with each. The nub of it is, though, that with an agent, you have a fixed cost element and a lower commission and with a broker, no fixed cost element, but a higher commission. Traditionally the South African Life industry has relied mainly on brokers.

Liberty took an early decision to develop its agency force into a formidable machine. Comments Dorian Wharton-Hood, Joint Managing Director:

> *"As a competitor (referring to his days at Prudential) we respected the strength of Liberty's agency force. This respect has deepened since coming on board."*

On digging a bit, we found a machine that was so well developed and professionally run, that one begins to understand why it is that Liberty have been so successful. The man who heads it up is Mike Jackson, a trained industrial psychologist who entered the sales area at Liberty during the 1970s. Not surprising then is his opening comment on explaining the success of the agency force:

> *"One of the areas that Liberty Life has been very good at — and the industry would acknowledge this — is in the things like the application of the behavioural sciences to the whole sales process. Right from recruitment and selection, through training, management development, motivation."*

Jackson took us through some of the above processes, and they look a bit like this:

1. **Recruitment and selection.** They recruit about 200 agents per annum, and they have more than 15 years' experience in this. This not being enough, they carefully research the profile of the candidate. In fact this was Jackson's first assignment when he joined Liberty in 1974. He went abroad to the National Institute of Personnel Research and anywhere else where he might find research material. Finding 1: There is no personality profile of the typical insurance salesman. So much for the stereotypical salesman. Finding 2: There is no correlation with intelligence. Finding 3: There is no correlation with academic achievement (in fact, there is something of a negative correlation here). Finding 4: Most importantly, there is a fairly strong correlation with various interests. They then extended their research to the interest profile of someone suited to sales.

   The second major success on the recruitment and selection side was a biographical profiling. This science, which suggests that people with particular kinds of biographies are likely to be suited to various kinds of activities, was particularly well developed in the United States. They learnt the science there and developed a biographical profile of the sort of person that would succeed in life sales.

   After developing the technology, they set about systematising the procedures. They have taken it to the point where they are now developing an expert system. The aspirant agent will be able to sit in front of the PC for an hour and get a full report, concluding with whether he will make a successful life salesman.

2. **Training.** Having selected the right people, they set about training them in the arts and sciences of life insurance, selling and the running of their agencies. The initial formal training takes place over three years. As one would now expect, it includes a fair dose of courses in the behavioural sciences.

3. **Management processes.** The way in which they manage the agency force is loaded with lessons learned from the behavioural sciences — goal setting, performance measurement, counselling, feedback, motivation. The management of the agency force is taken very seriously indeed.

What they end up with, is an agency force that runs like a Swiss clock. What is regarded by the Life industry as being an expensive selling channel turns out to be an inexpensive one. Production rates are 4,5 times the industry average. The happiness index is high. This is a formidable competitive capability.

In numerous places in this book we deal with the successes of Beer Division — we really cannot but marvel at the achievement of this organisation. All things being equal, we have no doubt that they could have been a global player in beer. Let's just hope they get a chance to flex their muscles on the international scene at some stage in the future.

Some 18 months ago Graham Mackay and his team took stock of their organisational capabilities. Their brewing skills were certainly amongst the top in the world. Their marketing skills speak for themselves — they must surely be the best mass marketeers in South Africa. Their skill at branding is legendary.

As Peter Savory, Marketing Director and South Africa's doyen of mass marketing puts it:

> "A consumer goods company has only one asset, and that's its brands. If you don't have brands, you don't have a sale, and if you don't have a sale, you don't have the business. . . . A Mercedes-Benz is a marvellously engineered car, but it only becomes a Merc when you put that three-pointed star on it."

They also know that in a Third World environment, where markets are spread out and people have limited contact with mass media, distribution is paramount. Their distribution skills are what you would expect from what is probably the biggest mover of beer in the world.

Yet given all of this, they felt they were slipping in their selling skills. "We felt we were looking a bit 1970ish in the selling area," related Mackay. They set about addressing this in true Beer Division style. They took one of their best salesmen from the field, stuck him in Head Office for a year and told him to develop a sales course that was to become the "Guide to Extraordinary Achievement". It described in detail the 14 things that a salesman and sales manager must do. If he does all these things perfectly,

131

he scores five out of five. This is built into his assessment. Four out of five is good, three is acceptable. If it's less, they take action. "If all 14 things are done right, that is the route to the kingdom of heaven," says Savory.

So for a period in the history of Beer Division, the sales people will be getting a shot at the glory. The standards have been clearly set out, and this by someone who has excelled in the field — not some Head Office type. The sales people are further empowered by the additional training given in the Guide to Extraordinary Achievement. The incentive is given by giving them a shot at competing for the glory and getting to the high ground.

Now Beer Division are able to add a selling capability to their formidable arsenal of competitive weapons. Chink. Another gap closed. This is one mighty machine.

PROFIT = REVENUE – COSTS

Lee Iococca, in his book on his time at Ford, tells how on taking up the Chief Executive position he realised that they were looking at a soft market. So he went back to some very simple arithmetic: Profit = Revenue – Costs. So he diligently set about cutting costs where these costs did not result in customer value.

Hugh Mathew, Deputy Chairman of Foschini, gave us a lucid description of his thinking:

> "When the buyer has agreed the price of the merchandise, he can never pay less. And when the merchandise has been priced and put in the stores, it can never be sold for more. So when those two actions have taken place, you have circumscribed the potential gross profit and everything you do reduces that . . . even a sales drive . . . everything eats into that . . . you have to plan at a low level in order to maximise the success of realising that difference."

This is, then, the second leg of doing what comes logically. The point is that the super-performers have a clear understanding of which organisational activities add value. They are then ruthless about eliminating those activities which don't add value. The implications for the bottom line are clear.

The starting point lies in recognising how the organisation creates value for the customer. The other side of the coin lies in recognising where the organisation does not create value. The super-performers recognise that certain organisational activities consume costs without demonstrably adding value for the customer. So they don't mind spending big money on value-creating activities such as building distinctive capabilities, but they are as tight as hell when it comes to activities which don't add value.

In just the same way that each organisation has its own set of value-creating activities, each organisation will have its own activities which don't create value. However, there is one value destroyer that all organisations have in common, and this is most keenly felt by the decentralised structure. It's that hungry beast called Head Office.

The Story of the Lean Head Office

Waltons, the organisation which has led the way in creating shareholder wealth, doesn't have a Head Office — well, not one to speak of anyway. The Transvaal "Head Office" is situated on top of the warehouse in New Centre, just south of Johannesburg's city centre. You have to climb flights of stairs to get there, and the reception consists of a double seater and coffee table, on which there are a few "freebie" magazines.

The ladies behind the counter are kept so busy they are almost breathless. The offices consist of a row of boxes with plywood partitioning. Len Chimes, who heads up the Transvaal operation, has an office consumed by metal filing cabinets. Mark Davis, the Financial Director (who doesn't have a secretary to take calls) tells me that these are plush compared to Robarts's own offices in Cape Town.

Robarts spends much of his time there — he doubles up with Len. So when we did manage to pin him down in Johannesburg, Len's office was a hive of activity. Len was going about his daily business. This involves barking down the phone a lot, and calling for Joe when he heard him down the passage. We were trying to get questions in while all this was going on.

In Chapter 4, we touched on the preponderance of bloated middle management structures and found that most also-rans have Head Offices filled with bored middle managers. **In super-performer after super-performer, we found Head Offices to be lean and hungry. They consisted of no more than a few senior people with the appropriate supporting structure.**

For some super-performers this lean structure follows naturally from consideration given to the value created by organisational activities. For others, the lessons came the hard way.

Bruce Edmunds, Managing Director of Utico, remembers all too well his early days as Financial Director. They had been given a real hiding by Rembrandt. Remember the days when Utico ruled supreme — in market share terms, they were a bit like the Beer Division of today. Rembrandt launched an attack on this position of market dominance that was to prove to be almost fatal. Utico's market share went from close on 100 per cent to 20 per cent. There was red ink all over the place.

Edmunds was promoted to Managing Director and rapidly set things right. He implemented the Drive Policy, focusing organisational resources on four key brands which were superbly positioned in growth segments (see Chapter 2). He was ruthless with costs that didn't fall into this scheme of things. As he puts it:

> *"You find that when a company gets small, you don't get rid of people as quickly as you should. You don't realise that you don't actually need economists, highly qualified research people and so on. In actual fact, you can buy those services when you want them ... (This) got our fixed costs down, which meant our breakeven moved down."*

In this way, Utico went from a company with a 20 per cent market share and huge losses, to one with a 20 per cent share and whopping great profits.

Even the large, rich and highly institutionalised companies like SAB are tight as anything at Head Office. Meyer Kahn, talking about SAB at a group level, reckons, "We don't make any money here — that's the bad news — we tend to spend most of it." And, in talking about their absolute focus on the rand cost per hectalitre:

> *"At the end of the day, we don't judge production capacity by anything other than rand cost per hectalitre ... it's as simple*

as that. If the guys want snooker tables and snooker rooms, that doesn't add up to a row of beans unless we achieve our rand cost per hectalitre target."

Organisations like SAB have done two critical things:

- They have thought critically about the role of Head Office in the context of the organisation as a whole. Questions like "How do we add value? What is our role? How should we interact with the operating executives?" have all been answered.
- They have been able to harness the power of the computer to handle the information processing role of Head Office middle management. Before the advent of the computer, much of middle management's time had been spent in collecting and analysing information for top management. There is no longer a need for this.

FINGERS ON THE PULSES

The third leg of doing what comes logically is the ability to pick on the few key measures that drive the success of the organisation, to measure them and manage them. We call this the art of keeping fingers on the pulses.

Picking the Pulses

The lack of management information at Suncrush initially scared us. In getting to know the company better, however, we got to understand that they didn't need piles of printouts because firstly, they are an informally driven bunch and secondly, they have been able to pick on the few key measures that drive the success of their business, and monitor these accurately, timeously and frequently — mostly on a daily basis. As Robin Hamilton puts it:

> *"We've always tried to know more [than other bottlers] about the things that count — for instance the bottle breakages, raw material usage, capacity utilisation and labour efficiency. Going back 20 years we've spent a lot of time getting that right. You could say that we are consistently good at that. That's not to say that there are not some very peculiar and stupid things that happen, but we eventually get them right."*

135

The Suncrush information system is built around the few measures that they have of the pulses of the business. Derek Cook, Assistant Managing Director, sums up the logic of this well:

".. we've hammered away at those and got them right in all the places in which we operate. And really, the others tend to take care of themselves."

The stock of bottles is one such variable. Bottlers have millions tied up in bottles, which tend to get lost or broken easily. Cook thinks of bottles as a currency: "... if something goes out the back door and comes in the front door, we pay deposit value for it again."

Not surprisingly, then, Suncrush counts all of its stock (full and empty) at each of its 11 plants every single day. The result? Amongst other things, their breakages and losses are half those of the industry leader, Amalgamated Beverage Industries. Brian Thomas, Manufacturing Manager, has a set of hinged aluminium frames on the wall of his office in which he keeps the "stock graphs" — a graph for each plant showing targeted and actual closing stock for each day of the year. The figures are phoned through to Head Office daily. Robin Hamilton walks down to Brian's office at least once a day to check those graphs.

The focus on a few important figures means that the reports in Suncrush are brief. Cook explains that one of his jobs is to look after the contribution of each package, by make and size. He gets a one-page report which focuses on comparative package contributions from plants that are the most disadvantaged. If these are okay, he knows the rest will be okay. A one-page report.

We believe that the advantages of this focus extend beyond the rational. The danger with the "thick printout syndrome" is that managers get lulled into a mindset that says, "I've got all this information, I must actually understand what's going on." In fact, it n.ight be quite the reverse, i.e. "I've got all this information and it's actually preventing me from understanding what's going on." And some poor chap is having to produce it too.

Measuring the Pulses and Taking Action

The next trick the super-performers seem to get right is that they are able to measure these pulses, usually on a daily basis. It sounds easy, but the real problem is that it has to do with the computer!

We are constantly amazed at how organisations manage to get themselves in a cost bind with their investment in information systems. Meyer Kahn refers to it as the Salami Syndrome:

> *"Because when you get involved with information systems, right, you are dealing with experts that also have high egos, okay, and whenever you sign for something, that is never the end of the road. It's always the next step that you don't know about. So it is one of those few investment decisions that I have ever been in that worries me, because I never know the quo vadis. One, I don't have the intellect to understand what the guys are doing. Two, I am probably too lazy to get involved, as are most Chief Executives, because it is so dull and boring and three, the guys schlep you into more and more and bigger and bigger things."*

This sums it up pretty neatly! The interesting thing is, though, that most super-performers get a pay-off from this IS investment, simply by getting it to provide them with the information to keep the fingers on the pulses. Some examples: Len Chimes of Waltons will find on his desk when he arrives at the office at 08h00 printouts showing for each product, sales and gross margins by product category, by area, by branch, by representative, and by any number of variables. So after his morning ritual of "Where the bloody hell are my glasses!" he will pore through these printouts and phone through queries where appropriate (there are usually more than five of these per day). Then by 09h30 Len is ready to get down to the business of motivating people and selling stationery. His information system has given him the ability to feel the pulse, take the necessary action, and then get on with the business of making money.

Philip Coutts-Trotter, Managing Director of SA Bias, has also been able to put the punch into information systems. He is also able to gauge, day by day, how each line is selling, what margins they are making, which debtors are looking shaky. In other words, he also gets his fingers on the pulses on a daily basis.

We spent some time with Nigel Martindale, the Information Systems Executive of SA Bias. He looked exhausted, but then he doesn't really run the department — he *is* the department (well, except for a secretary and two Systems Analysts).

Just ponder this fact for a while: a manufacturing company which makes attributable earnings of around R10 million (it doesn't disclose turnover), has an information systems division, manned by three people, and most of the systems developed in-house. Its information systems costs run at about 0,8 per cent of turnover, which is about half the norm for a manufacturing company of similar size and complexity.

Yet the consensus that emerged from our discussions with information systems users at SA Bias was that information systems had enabled them to grow, at a compound rate of over 25 per cent, whilst at the same time maintaining tight control over the business. The managers have, throughout, been able to keep their fingers on the pulses.

Just one more example to clarify the point. Edgars is a very different company to Waltons and SA Bias, both of which definitely have the feel of owner-managed companies. Edgars is the epitome of the professionally managed company. We therefore expected to find some differences in its information systems set-up. Its investment in information systems is big. The sheer size of its debtors list — more than 1,7 million active accounts — combined with the competitive nature of its industry forced it to take a decision to lead the way in the use of information systems technology. Its initial drive focused on the basics — the things that would allow managers to keep their fingers on the pulses. The results were impressive. Vic Hammond, Chief Executive, rattled the measures of success off in staccato fashion. Stock-turn, debtors collection period, arrears — all these measures came down drastically. Furthermore, in its multi-branch set-up — it has 380 of them — and its multitude of product lines, it is able to pinpoint with accuracy and precision, and timeously, where it is that it is making or losing.

The next drive was directed at seeking competitive advantage. This they did by developing systems to ensure that it got the right merchandise into the right store at the right time. These included store gridding systems, distribution control systems, systems to analyse its debtors and sales data-bases. From there, its systems development activity has focused on extended value. This means, for example, that it is really going to get its debtors data-base working for it. The Club concept outlined in Chapter 5 is a good example. For R2 per month, Club members are offered access to a wide range of preferential offers and competitions. The incremental cost is minimal. The incremental revenue, if one assumes that 50 per cent of active account holders join the club, is R1,5 million per month. Now it's really got the computer working for it.

To recap then, the super-performers have, at the most basic level, allowed managers to keep their fingers on the pulses by liberating the computer. Much is written about the awesome power of the computer, but what really interested us was that the super-performers had got it to work for them. Our experience suggests that this is the exception rather than the rule.

So how did they get it right? Libraries are full of books on this subject. We would not claim to be familiar with this vast body of knowledge, but we will pass on some common-sense lessons taught to us by the super-performers:

1. In spite of all the bleating to the contrary, the information systems department should be managed in the same way as other critical functions. This means, *inter alia,* that the return on information systems should be measured.
2. The department head should ideally report to the Chief Executive. Traditionally, he reports to the Financial Director, who is likely to focus development activity on financial systems.
3. The Chief Executive needs to understand information systems in the same way as he understands other critical functional areas such as finance, marketing, human resources and operations. People like Vic Hammond recognise this and ensure that they fully understand what the computer can and can't do.
4. In the same way that it makes good sense to rotate people between, say, marketing and finance, rotate people between information systems and operations. It works wonders in helping them understand each other.

5. In managing the information systems department, get people to understand the concepts of customer service and how they need to support the other functions to enhance, organisation-wide, the customer service concept.

6. As with any area of the organisation, "Do it properly" principles should apply. That is, a "right first time" philosophy, coupled with the highest standards of professionalism.

7. As a general rule, go the in-house development route. Edgars, for example, have developed about 90 per cent of their systems internally.

8. Finally, even state-of-the-art organisations like Edgars believe that you should avoid the pioneering, state-of-the-art "bleeding" edge. Rather, follow tried and tested hardware and software options.

---

5 Steps to Doing What Comes Logically

1. Think clearly about the things your organisation needs to do superbly well if it is to beat the competition. If one of these isn't selling, think again.

2. Focus time, money, energy and attitude on developing distinctive capabilities in these things.

3. Remember the most logical equation in commercial life: Profit = Revenue − Costs. Whilst time, money, energy and attitude are lavished on developing distinctive capabilities, become ruthless in cutting out those activities which don't create customer value.

4. If Head Office is a big cost, rethink its role. The chances are that it consumes cost without adding value.

5. Work out the few key measures that drive the success of your organisation. Measure them frequently — and take action immediately.

CHAPTER SEVEN

DO IT PROPERLY

Aaron Searll is the archetypal self-made man, a role-model for any budding entrepreneur. Seardel, the group of companies that he built from scratch, has made him a millionaire many times over. He flies jets. He has a beautiful wife. He is a social lion. What is his secret of success?

Searll offers this advice:

> *"Having thought a lot about why some businesses are more successful than others, and having been in business for 30 years, I've come to one simple conclusion: Keep it simple and stick to the basics. I really think it's as simple as that. You can read millions of books and study all sorts of things but it all boils down to the basics of having a good product, doing the marketing and the selling aggressively well, producing the product to a high standard of efficiency, having a very good administration to monitor and report results and just to do things properly.*
>
> *A wonderful saying came out from the British Civil Aviation Authority, when they analysed hundreds of accidents that had taken place over the last 15 years. They came out with one statement to all student pilots and to everybody. It went something like*
>
> > *Do it properly*
> > *Be careful*
> > *And don't push your luck*
>
> *It's quite a good point in running a business."*

It's good advice. In this chapter we will look at how the

super-performers *do things properly*. We'll pick up on Searll's plea for simplicity. We'll see how the top companies plan the things they are going to do before they do them, how they get a fix on the probable consequences and risks of their decisions, and how, having decided to commit, they follow through with resolution. We'll see that they believe in doing things right the first time; that they believe in professionalism, in attention to detail, in discipline; and that all of these things are channelled by a commitment to the sort of quality and service they know their customers value. We'll see, in fact, that the super-performers accord quality such importance that it pervades their whole way of life, both on the job and after hours. We'll see too that they take great care to enhance the right kind of communication in their organisations by talking face to face, by cutting paper flows, by outlawing bureaucracy and by banning office politics. We'll see how they keep the size of their head offices to a minimum and focus their attention — and support — on what is happening in the field. And finally we'll look at a specific area of competence that our super-performers clearly demonstrate: the process of acquisition. Doing it properly is important to the super-performers. As SAB's Peter Savory says:

"The big ideas can get cocked up if you don't do it properly."

Simplicity — the Kiss of Life

No one would expect South Africa's top-performing companies to be anything but sophisticated. Indeed, they certainly are that. But the refreshing discovery is that sophistication doesn't necessarily imply complexity. "Keep it simple and stick to the basics," advocates Aaron Searll. His policy of absolute decentralisation and delegation makes running a group of 25 companies with consolidated turnover of R700 million look as easy as pie.

Suncrush is another of the super-performers that values simplicity. Brian Thomas is the Suncrush executive responsible for the supply chain — that sequence of transactions and activities that gets essential raw materials and packaging to each of the company's 10 bottling plants. Brian and his colleagues have set up amazingly simple procedures for ordering the right quantity of each ingredient, each crate size, package type, etc. For raw

142

material requirements, for instance, they have developed a formula for the quantity required in the month ahead based on projected production and current stock levels. The formula is simple but subtle — not the kind of thing they would like their competition to get hold of — and it enables a single head-office person to order the company's entire raw material requirement for the month ahead in about two hours. Such simplicity and clarity lets Suncrush commit to its input resources (raw materials, packs, etc) early — before others in the industry. Being first in line with suppliers, they usually get what they want when they want it. Plastic crates, for example, are as critical to the operation as bottles and cans. Thomas books time on his crate suppliers' injection moulding machines long in advance, only confirming the allocations much nearer the time if the all-important balance between crates and bottles warrants it.

Think Ahead. Make a Plan

In South African vernacular *maak 'n plan* has a very different meaning from planning ahead. *Ons sal 'n plan maak* means that we'll deal with the problem when it arises; cross that bridge when we come to it. It's an expression that has more to do with our native resourcefulness than with planning. Trouble is, though, we sometimes let our prided resourcefulness become a kind of substitute for thinking ahead; we feel we don't need to think ahead too much because we know we can "make a plan" if something crops up. We have seen in Chapter 2 that when it comes to strategy, some special companies can successfully avoid formal formulation and articulation of their strategies. What about the shorter term though? Are South Africa's super-performers good planners? The answer is unequivocally yes. At Cadbury-Schweppes and at Cashbuild, in SAB and SA Bias, and in many other top performers, we found that planning — old-fashioned everyday planning of the day-to-day activities that are important to the business — is alive and well. Hugh Mathew describes how Foschini approaches planning:

> *"I believe that Foschini has put its money on planning. Planning, measurement and replanning. We try to think up-front of all the issues that need to be taken into account. We*

put them into as logical an interactionary process as we can, and then we identify the way that progress will be recorded and the points at which a junction occurs — a change of direction. And then we try to identify what indicators would cause us to change so that when we come to the point and the indicators are present, firstly we know that our plan was good, and secondly we know what to do. We say, 'If we're going to be successful then this is what we're going to see at that point in time, and if we're unsuccessful then we should see that clearly too.' We try to plan that. And when we come to the point in time, if in fact that's the picture that we see then we know our plan was right. And then we take action."

The value of planning, of course, lies not only in the plan itself, but also in the process of considering the consequences of alternative courses of action.

Consider the Consequences. Know the Risks

Our super-performers think things through. They take the time to assess the consequences and impact of courses of action. They look at upside — what will success require of us? — and they look at downside — what are the risks here?

At SA Bias, for example, they believe that budgeting is important, not for itself, but because it causes people to focus on the right things and consider the consequences. The most obvious consequences of course are the financial ones. Financial modelling is part of life in all these companies. Patrick Fleming, Financial Director of Cadbury-Schweppes, uses as an example the proposal to launch Tempo, and tells how the financial consequences of that key strategic move were carefully modelled before a decision was taken on how to proceed. (Note that the necessitity of a new thrust into big-eat chocolate bars had already been identified. In this case the financial analysis was done to evaluate the *implementation* of the strategy, not to test the strategy itself. Fleming stresses that at Cadbury-Schweppes business strategy comes first and financial strategy follows.)

John Temple, MD of Plessey, personally built the first version of the financial model they use to assess the financial impact of their plans. As consultants, we routinely encourage clients that haven't yet taken to financial modelling to do so as soon as possible. With the off-the-shelf software now available, even the smallest company can easily build a model of its operations and begin to appreciate the consequences of tactical, day-to-day decisions as well as longer-term strategies. What is so handy about this clever new software is that it quickly allows one to understand the *range* of possible outcomes in financial terms, and understanding the range means understanding the risk, because risk is, after all, no more than a measure of the dispersion of probable outcomes.

Robin Hamilton has thought a lot about risk. He and most of the senior people at Suncrush went through the famous Kepner-Tregoe course a number of years ago. There they learnt that risk has two distinct components: probability and seriousness. Hamilton is frustrated by the generally poor understanding of this distinction. He had been talking to his Coca-Cola franchisors (and suppliers of concentrate syrup) about the risk of sanctions for a long time:

> *"Each time I talked about seriousness they came back with probability. It took years to resolve that issue. Extraordinary. When you ask a person 'If something happens how do we handle it? Will it be disastrous?' you can't answer him when he says: 'Look, you don't have to worry about it, it's unlikely.' That's been their consistent response."*

He goes on to say, incidentally, that Suncrush and the other large franchisees, together with the suppliers, have probably done as much as they can to reduce both probability and seriousness of the risk of Coke's withdrawal from the South African market. In his own company Hamilton has built a culture that is innovative and risk averse at the same time. So while a climate of innovation cannot thrive without tolerance of failure, it does not mean that risk should be ignored.

As Andrew Beggs, Suncrush's Marketing Director, puts it:

> *"You know some people think we're being a bit negative when we say 'Let's think about what can go wrong', but that's a very positive statement because you're looking at a programme or*

145

a plan and trying to anticipate what can go wrong with it. You may not always be right, but at least if you're thinking about it then you're going to get better at reducing the risk than if you're not thinking about it at all."

The key is to know the risk before you accept it. Hamilton is a horse-racing man. "If racing taught me anything," he says, talking about foreign exchange exposure, "it's that to take a bet when you don't know what the odds are is madness."

Aaron Searll refers again to the advice from the British Civil Aviation Authority:

"Be careful. Obviously you have to take risks but don't take a risk that can destabilise the whole company. And don't push your luck. If you see thunderstorms and you can circumvent them, then circumvent them. Don't fly through them. It applies to business: don't look for trouble."

Follow Through. Prove Your Breeding

Our smallest client, at the time of writing, is also one of our most interesting. K4TV News produces high-quality video material for television, and is increasingly involved in corporate video documentation and promotion. They are creative, talented people; hard working, ambitious and fun to be with. They are growing their business at around 100 per cent per year.

MD and controlling shareholder Russell Kay demands and gets high standards from his team. At a recent staff meeting we attended he talked about *pedigree.*

"When you come back from a shoot at 10 o'clock at night, you don't just put the damaged tripod back in its box and go home. You take it out, and leave it somewhere with a note where someone will find it the next morning and know what to do with it. Otherwise some other poor bastard's going to take it on the next shoot — probably to the middle of the Okavango Delta — and find that the bloody thing's maimed. No, even though it's late and you're tired, you do something about it. That's what I mean by showing your pedigree."

We like this concept of breeding, of pedigree. It describes a characteristic shared by the super-performers that has to do with relentlessly following through and meeting commitments. It's about running *through* the finish line and not *at it*. It's about thoroughness, about finishing off. It's a big part of doing things properly.

Bromor Foods manufactures Brookes cordials and Moirs Jellies. They were acquired by Cadbury-Schweppes in 1986 — a story told later in this chapter. When we asked Bromor MD, Mike Brownlee, to tell us what he thought had made Cadbury-Schweppes so successful, the first thing he talked about was Cadbury's inordinate concern for people. The second was their single-mindedness in seeing a project through to completion:

> *"There's this kind of endurance they have. The ability to lay out a programme over a hell of a long time and say — OK just chunk it, go through it till the project is finished. They make a programme and they live by that programme. In a sense it's single-minded. They have a very single-minded approach to things: 'We are going to succeed in this thing.'"*

Single-mindedness doesn't mean closed-mindedness. Cashbuild pursued their objective of a participative management system relentlessly, but the firmness of their resolve in no way limited their acceptance of new possibilities, or new ways of going about it.

Do the Right Thing Right First Time

Albert Koopman and Gerald Haumant candidly admit that developing the Cashbuild philosophy involved a fair amount of trial and error. They made mistakes. MBFA — Management By Fumbling Around — Koopman called it. The fact of the matter was that they didn't know quite what they were trying to do when they started doing it. Often, the situation is different. One knows, either intuitively or analytically, what the right thing is to do. Then, **the lesson from the super-performers is "Do it right first time." Of course, there's a rider to this: doing the thing right may be twice as expensive as doing the thing adequately. Doing it right may not be worthwhile or affordable at the time.**

Suncrush are trying to be the best bottlers in the business. They probably are the best soft drink bottlers in South Africa. They believe their filling lines must start well (quickly and without wasting product or breaking bottles) and run well (without stoppages). "That," says Divisional GM Dennis Smit, "means we must do the best installations." As an example he cites a line that was installed in their Ladysmith plant in 1975 and is still running today. "This is very unusual in this industry, considering that it's a single line plant supplying most of northern Natal, and it's running day and night. When you try to find out why, you'll find there have been no short cuts with the installation. The mechanical side was done properly first time round."

Professionalism — the Cut of the Coat

What is it that makes a company professional? In their business, Waltons are real professionals; they have a professional approach to running a branch operation. But what does "professional" mean in the stationery game? Len Chimes reckons you need to know what the area can cope with in terms of volume and product range, you need to know the business formula for pricing and stock control, and you need good representation. **Professionalism in stationery, and probably in every other business, is a combination of competence and presentation. You've got to have the distinctive capabilities that your industry requires, but beyond that you have to package and present that competence in a way that your market will appreciate.**

When we began working with one of our clients about two years ago, one of the seemingly small things we noted was that although they were undeniably outstanding at what they did, the company lacked a certain smartness and sharpness — in a word, professionalism. Together with them we worked out ways to encourage a more professional style of behaviour. Today the distinctive capabilities of the company haven't changed — they are still outstanding at what they do, but in many ways the company is unrecognisable. People dress better, speak better, present reports better, prepare for meetings and arrive promptly — and even keep their cars cleaner. Why did we focus on these seemingly trivial traits? Because those are the ones that their *customers regard as important.* And in the same strange way that clothes maketh the man, the organisation has found new pride and new self-respect that are apparent to the world at large. The company hasn't changed its products one jot, but its customers, now more than before, rest comfortably in the knowledge that they are in the hands of professionals.

FAD — an Enduring Doctrine

The Beer Division of SA Breweries astounded us. How did such a huge operation, one of the biggest brewers in the world, with an effectively monopolistic market position, keep as lean and stay so aggressive? On examination, we expected to find at least some evidence of complacency, just a little creeping bureaucracy. Not a bit of it. SAB is as close to its fighting weight as ever — and as ready as ever to bash likely contenders. And while it waits for another hapless challenger in the clear beer division, it keeps on its toes by competing with itself — shadow boxing, if you like. Its workout routine is regular and varied; it includes a few strenuous sets of strategy arm-bends, repetitive cycles of staying close to the customer, and lots and lots of FAD — Fanatical Attention to Detail. Meyer Kahn has strong views on this:

> *"It's all about FAD," he says, banging on the table. "FAD (thump) FAD (thump) FAD (thump)! OK?"*

SAB's obsession with FAD began with their strategic rethink in 1962. Recall that in those dark days beer accounted for only 13 per cent of the non-sorghum liquor market. That unhappy situation had been caused largely by poor product quality and consistency, and by lousy packaging and labelling. The product had to be upgraded, to be moved "from the kitchen to the living room". Ever since then SAB has been fanatically attentive to detail. As Meyer Kahn says, "If you have the best product in the world, how can you accept a label that is not on 100 per cent?" They brought twist-off caps back in 1977. The twist-off hadn't worked previously simply because it hadn't been dealt with in a sufficiently detailed way. The revised — and effective — version immediately made 40 per cent of the competitors' products obsolete. Peter Savory, SAB's marketing maestro, reckons that it is the little things that make a difference. As a result, says Savory, his people think he's a "bloody fusspot". "FAD needs a special kind of attitude coupled with a high ego," says Kahn. "Fortunately we have both of those."

Equally fanatical about attention to detail is Dr John Temple of Plessey. He was visibly upset when he learned that we hadn't been accorded the full VIP treatment at the front gate. There should have been printed name tags and low bows, but instead we got the courteous body search and the regular visitors' forms. Temple really is serious about detail, not only when it comes to products, but also in Plessey's marketing.

"We want to communicate in our marketing something of our own ethos, something of the excellence we practise in the company. We've positioned ourselves as being the best. We cannot be the biggest, we've no intention of being the biggest. We're not the cheapest, we're not the most expensive. We just want to be the best. Everything we do has got to be the best value for money. That means that things have got to be done properly and professionally. We take a great deal of pride and effort in the way we conduct our marketing. Every little detail has to be right."

When they host their on-site public relations luncheons, as they regularly do, they make sure, for example, that the menus are positioned so that each guest can read one without having to pick it up or turn it, and that the printing on name tags is large enough to be clearly legible from across the table. Nothing is too small to warrant detailed attention. "It's interesting that everybody thinks that way," says Temple. "We don't do things by halves. We don't do it in a sloppy or haphazard manner".

John Temple's main competitor is also a detail man. In fact Bill Venter's capacity for detail verges on the legendary. Neill Davies, the Altron Group's Financial Director, says that Venter is "very much a detail individual. If we do a deal he'll have gone through the document and he'll know what the hell's in it and he'll pick holes in it." He has, too, an uncanny ability to focus in on the *right* item of detail. Davies recalls how Altech swung their landmark deal in 1976:

"We were negotiating the STC deal, which — at that stage we were a small company — would really have taken us into the big time. It was a wonderful deal for us. It would have meant a quantum leap in technology and facilities and everything else. While we were negotiating the deal various things came up. One of them was that STC was at that stage doing a containerisation project for the Railways. Bill said he wanted a warranty on this project. Now there were many, many projects they were doing, but he wanted a warranty on this one particular project. We were taken to the Railways, introduced to the General Manager and the site guys. We visited various sites. Everybody told us how well the project was going and what a fabulous project it was. But Bill insisted that he wanted a warranty on the project. And it virtually broke the deal. Our own accountants and attorneys got hold of Bill and said 'Don't be stupid. What the hell could possibly go wrong? Even if it did go wrong what could it cost us? A few hundred thousand rand?' Eventually he was convinced. He sat down. The meeting started. He wanted a warranty. Big blow-up — he got the warranty. When we got into the company that project was an absolute mess. We were paid out several million on that warranty. It was a complete and utter disaster. There were probably a hundred other projects on the go that he could have asked for warranties on, but he wanted a warranty on that one. He can't explain why."

Stories about Bill Venter's extraordinary memory and uncanny capacity for detail abound. Another is told by Jacques Sellschop, the Group Executive: Corporate Relations. On his first day with the Group — it was a Friday, he recalls — Venter phoned him from California where he was winding up some business. He wanted to make sure Jacques was comfortably settled. Sellschop gratefully assured him that all was perfect. Venter returned over the weekend, and on the Monday popped into Sellschop's office to welcome him personally and to enquire once again about the arrangements in the office. Sellschop once again assured him that all was well. A minute or two after Venter had left, Sellschop heard his secretary take a call and converse briefly in subdued tones. She came through to Sellschop's office to say that Dr Venter had phoned to ask her to remove a dead leaf from Sellschop's planter. The leaf was removed. A few minutes later the service man arrived carrying his toolbox with the message that Venter had phoned to tell him that Sellschop's telephone cable was lying untidily on the floor and needed to be fixed to the skirting. "I got a very distinct message," says Sellschop, "that this guy doesn't miss a trick. Attention to detail is absolutely vital to his way of doing things, and it may start with seemingly silly trivialities like picking dead leaves out of planters and grow say to the checking of entertainment invoices, but ultimately when it comes to an acquisition and the guy says to him 'Our stock on hand is R1 million,' he says 'Come, let's go and count.'"

Delivering the Goodies

The title of this chapter begs the question "Do *what* properly?" **The super-performers seem to do most things properly, but the two specific areas that appear to benefit most from professionalism, follow-through and attention to detail are two that have a special place in the heart of almost every customer, no matter what he is buying: quality and service.**

At SAB they take the quality of their beer very, very seriously. Marketing Director Peter Savory isn't kidding when he leans back in his chair, looks you right in the eye and says "He who fucks up the beer is dead." This spirit of perfectionism restrained SAB from competing with South West Brewery's draught beer until they had perfected the tricky business of packaging unpasteurised product. Savory knows that the consumer's perception of quality is both objective and subjective; objective in the sense that the consumer actually experiences the physical taste, colour and clarity of his glass of lager, and subjective in the sense that an aura of perceptions surrounds the product, perceptions like the "front-office interaction" (the friendliness of the pub), whether the label is straight, the condition of the returnable bottle, etc. Savory believes that it is these subjective perceptions that to a large extent influence the consumer's overall perceptions of the quality of the product, and that the subjective can most easily be influenced by FAD, professionalism and follow through.

In Chapter 10 we'll see how Volkswagen have turned around on the quality of their product. It is an amazing success story. Like SAB, VW are able to measure the physical quality of their product — in this case cars. In the factory they can test welds, check assemblies and measure components against specification. They can compare their quality to other VW factories around the world — and they do; in 1985 the Uitenhage plant won VW's World Quality award, the first time by any plant outside Germany. In the field they can monitor the condition of any car any time it is brought into a VW dealership for service. VW, too, know that the perception of top quality is built from very many small building blocks, both in the factory where the cars are put together, and in the minds of their market where the consumer receives VW's image and advertising communication.

Dr John Temple knows that Plessey's customers place quality high on their scale of value.

> *"Our quality is the highest in the country. Nobody questions that, because we have the customer's inspectors on-site, the Post Office inspectors on site. They live here in Cape Town and they've got offices on our premises. They watch our quality like a hawk and they publish results. We come out with the top results every single month in the whole country. We've done that for years and years and years. Quality is just part of our way of life."*

Temple goes on to say that to have a quality product, the quality ethos must pervade the entire organisation. The factory, the offices and the facilities must all be high quality. It goes further than that too. As Peter Searle of VW says, how can you expect a person who lives in a tin shack with no electricity to switch on his commitment to quality the moment he walks through the factory gates? Fundamental to the production of quality at work is not just a correspondingly high quality of *work* life, but an at least reasonable quality of life *as a whole*.

Mathieson & Ashley's headquarters are in Dashing House, reflecting the importance of their focus on the Dashing brand name. For them, quality is an obsession. You can feel it the moment you walk into the smart new building in leafy Rosebank,

Johannesburg. The way people dress, answer the phone and speak to customers mirrors the quality of the beautiful modern furniture their company makes — the quality that Dashing customers pay extra for. Winky Ringo knows that alongside quality the other thing his customers value very highly is service; you want your new furniture the same day you move into your new offices. The logic could not be more elementary, yet still some of Dashing's competitors miss the boat with awesome regularity.

In mid-1988 Mathieson & Ashley, Dashing's holding company, acquired struggling competitors Anglo Dutch, who had experienced production problems for the previous two years. Market share had slid badly. Six months after being bought into the Mathieson & Ashley stable, where, incidentally, it must compete with Dashing, Anglo Dutch is back in shape. The Mathieson & Ashley production team, led by Ringo's technical director and long-time colleague Rudi Schmidt, has eliminated the order backlog and brought normal delivery time back in line to four weeks. Urgent orders can be delivered in half that time. "Slowly but surely," says Alan Green, the new MD, "old Anglo Dutch customers are coming back."

Service is a key deliverable, too, for buyers of garment accessories. As SA Bias's Philip Coutts-Trotter says, if service is so important make it part of the system. SA Bias steals a march on its smaller competitors by *guaranteeing* a 10-day service from day of order — and often delivering in five. They simply have a deep commitment to it. That means they make sure they've got the stock and the manufacturing capacity. The Charmfit service teams visit their retailers every few days to restock so that no lady shopper will suffer disappointment by not finding her size of bra in the colour and style she wants. Cashbuild go to extraordinary lengths to make sure that there is always stock of the 100 most popular lines of merchandise in each branch.

Service and quality may not be "the goodies" — the critical value factors — in every market, but the super-performers tell us that if they are you had better deliver them. It's not difficult, but it needs an attitude that says "Let's do it properly."

154

Opening the Lines

People think of communication only as a soft skill — something that takes time, talent, and needs practice. The super-performers demonstrate otherwise. They show us that communication has its soft and hard sides and that far from being all art, communication has much to do with science too. In many subtle ways they take great care to keep communication channels wide open. The super-performers are both great talkers and great listeners. They try to ensure that the right messages get to the right people in the right ways, by using suitable communications systems, by choosing the right communication media.

Suncrush is one of the least — probably *the* least — formal of our super-performers. There is virtually no formal reporting. But people stay closely in touch through frequent meetings. Divisional GM's don't wait for the branches to send reports or call for help, they visit them and talk to them several times a month, and they review their figures right there and then, across the desk in the Branch Manager's office.

At the Ridge Road headquarters on Durban's lush Berea, Executive Chairman Robin Hamilton spends all morning every Monday in a series of meetings with his key people. The morning's programme is tightly structured so that meetings don't drag on; each is no longer than one hour. "Mondays here are actually pretty terrible," says Hamilton with no hint of apology, "because I refuse to expand the time available. So you've just got to squeeze it in." Once a month, there is a more formal management meeting at which everyone has the opportunity to contribute. At Plessey too, John Temple encourages direct communication. He says he's happy to live with a high phone bill and a high travel bill because "face to face communication solves problems". SA Bias's Executive Chairman Chris Seabrooke talks to his Managing Director, Philip Coutts-Trotter, every day — no matter where each of them is.

Cadbury's is one company that has discovered the power of video as a medium of communication. MD Piet Beyers admits they're still in the very early stages; their first foray into the area began in March 1988 with a video series that explained the concept of profit and typical commercial transactions, and showed how the company's mission and objectives aimed to benefit — albeit in different ways — management, workers and shareholders alike. Since then the video idea has been extended to other forms of communication, which lets all employees know about recent company performance, new products that are due for launch, individuals whose achievement has been recognised, and anything else of topical interest that can conceivably improve employees' understanding of the workings of the company and help them identify with what is happening around them. Beyers explains the philosophy behind Cadbury's communication drive:

> *"The whole concept of increasing dramatically the communication flow with all employees, we're fully committed to that, and not only cascading through the various management structures but also communicating directly — myself and Malcolm [Personnel Director, Malcolm Ackhurst] and other managers. On the video news we speak to employees about our objectives, the training programme, and so on.*
>
> *And then we communicate directly with them by way of pamphlets or posters, so that we know we get a message across in a uniform way and we get it across to everybody — and we get it across in a certain time frame so that it's not watered down in different interpretations over a long period of time."*

The super-performers abhor bureaucracy, red tape and office politics — all cancers that invade the company's internal communication system, rendering it ineffective — or worse. In these companies the memo (that quintessential bureaucratic artefact!) is on the endangered list. When John Temple joined Plessey in early 1985 he found the level of red tape horrifying. "Communication by memo" was the order of the day. "Backside protection" was rife. He immediately did three things: firstly he required that a copy of every memo typed throughout the company be sent to him personally. The volume of typed memos dropped to virtually zero. Secondly he introduced a pad for handwritten memos — but a pad with a difference, because it is only 9 x 12 cm, and has space for only 10 short lines of handwriting, enough to write about 50 words at most. Thirdly, he outlawed "backside protection". "A mistake made in good faith isn't a problem, but you can get fired for backside protection."

Perhaps these things go together. If you provide a supportive, risk-accepting, failure-tolerating environment for people to work in, the level of bureaucracy will automatically decrease, because people don't have to "cover their arses" the whole time. And less bureaucracy means better communication.

Robin Hamilton is another anti-bureaucrat, perhaps even more radically so than Temple. We heard earlier that in Suncrush there is an almost complete absence of formal reports. When reports do have to be written they must be short. Hamilton, who according to one of his managers is himself attributed with an uncanny ability to economise on words, requires that reports sent to him must be condensed to two or three pages, or better still, presented in diagrammatic form. As Divisional General Manager Dennis Smit says, "There's method in the madness — condensing something like that ensures that you get to the crux of it."

At Suncrush office politics is non-existent too, not because it is banned, but because it has simply never been there. Hamilton, like many of our super-performing CE's, has an open-door policy that really works. "You just go and talk to him," says Brian Thomas, one of Suncrush's executives. We'll say more about Suncrush's uniquely anti-bureaucratic culture and the power it brings in Chapter 10 but suffice it to say here that there are aspects of their culture that stimulate free and open communication throughout the organisation. And organisations thrive on free and open communication.

Do it in the Field

We recently met the Chief Executive of a fairly large group of companies, several of which are listed (but none of which qualified for the "super-performer" label). With evident pride he told us how thoroughly he had decentralised his group and delegated authority so that it was now hardly necessary for him ever to leave his Johannesburg Head Office. In fact, he told us, he had visited a Natal-based subsidiary only twice since its acquisition several years ago. While we admired his approach to

157

decentralisation, we couldn't help comparing his management style to what we had seen in our top organisations.

You will find no ivory towers in the super-performing companies. By that of course we mean that although some of the super-performers may operate from beautiful offices — Seardel comes immediately to mind — there is amongst these companies a quite general attitude that Head Office is there only to support operations.

To begin with their Head Offices are as small as possible. Staffing is lean. Pretoria Portland Cement's Parktown Head Office couldn't be called small, but as MD Guy Luyt puts it:

"There's no cement or lime coming out of Parktown — only Mercs."

It's his way of saying that Head Office has to earn its keep. At Suncrush too, the function of Head Office is seen to be "service and monitoring". Everyone there knows those words. And, as Robin Hamilton says, "you won't find anyone here who isn't working". Even secretaries have additional responsibilities; Hamilton's secretary, Sheila McCallum, for example, is responsible for placing all orders for beverage cans.

Small and lean as their Head Offices may be, however, our super-performing managers don't sit around inside them more than they have to. As Chapters 9 and 10 on leadership and culture show, there's plenty for them to do out there.

Lord Wellington, that most successful of British Generals, was well known for his meticulous attention to campaign detail — from the disposition of his enemy to the welfare of his troops. In the autumn of 1809, while awaiting the attack on Portugal of Napoleon's huge southern army, he rode for weeks, till all hours and in all weather, over the hills of the Lisbon peninsular, unobtrusively building an intimate personal knowledge of the terrain he would soon so successfully defend. It was typical of Wellington's management style; before dealing with a situation he would very often remark:

"I will get upon my horse and take a look; and then tell you!"[1]

Aaron Searll would agree with this approach. Despite the beauty and comfort of his headquarters, Searll visits his subsidiaries frequently. In fact, all of our top CE's and their management teams wander around a fair bit. "Doing it in the field" is an essential part of their working life.

Acquisitions — the Tough Go Shopping

Chapter 1 recounts how one of the conclusions that flowed from Cadbury-Schweppes' 1985 strategic rethink was to reduce the group's dependence on high import-content chocolate confectionery. They already had a minority stake in the huge Coca-Cola bottler Amalgamated Beverage Industries and of course they owned the Schweppes franchise business. Where to next? Time was pressing, and the cocoa price was rocketing: R2 700 per ton in 1983, through R3 700 per ton in 1984, R5 600 per ton in 1985 and heading for a staggering R8 000 per ton in 1986. Clearly an acquisition was called for, but in which direction should they diversify to better balance their portfolio of businesses? Group MD Peter Bester explains how they defined the acquisition they were looking for:

> *"First of all it had to be within our general defined scope — fast-moving consumer goods, oriented towards confectionery or drinks, something that was in the impulse area — we saw that as being an area of skills in our business. It had to have low import dependency and it had to have a low capital intensity. So we set out with a little shopping list."*

Bester and his team then began approaching their prospects. It was a frustrating time. No one seemed keen to sell. However, they did make one small acquisition before 1985 was out: Sodastream, seller of in-home carbonated soft drink systems, fitted their criteria very nicely, but wasn't large enough to stand

---

1 This was reported by one of his officers, Sir Harry Smith, later a governor of the Cape and after whom the South African town of Harrismith was named. His beautiful Spanish wife Juana Maria, rescued by the British from the siege of Badajoz, gave her name to the towns of Ladysmith in Natal and Ladismith in the Cape.

on its own. They kept looking. Very near the top of their list was Bromor Foods. Bromor simply wasn't on the market in 1985, but one Friday evening early in 1986 Bester heard that Bromor's owners, Murray & Roberts, wanting to get back to their core business, might have reason to sell. Says Bester:

"Quarter to eight on Monday morning we were actually sitting in their office saying, 'Well now's the time to really talk about it.'"

M&R had bought into "countercyclical" companies in the late seventies as a strategy to even out the wild peaks and valleys to which their traditional construction business was prone. Mike Brownlee, Bromor's MD, recalls having "nothing in common at all" with his M&R shareholders. They didn't understand Bromor's business. "It's just not their world," says Brownlee. "So when we got in tow with Cadbury's, that was a pleasure, that really was a positive step. When I talked to Peter Bester, we talked the same language. That was tremendous." And were the synergies really there? "Absolutely," replies Mike.

There was good fit between Cadbury-Schweppes' carbonated drinks and Bromor's non-carbonated drinks businesses; Cadbury's had Roses cordials and preserves which would fit perfectly into Bromor's line-up, as would newly acquired Sodastream.

Peter Bester and his Group Finance Director Patrick Fleming did their homework. "We did the product/market analysis, we did the financial analysis, we confirmed the strategic fit," says Fleming, "and we put a price on it." Negotiations took a long time because there was "quite a wide gap," Fleming laughs, but Cadbury-Schweppes knew how far they were prepared to go. The deal began to look promising. But how to finance it?

Politically 1986 was not a good year for South Africa, with internal strife and mounting disinvestment pressure. Cadbury Plc were not excited by the suggestion of a rights issue. The local company didn't want to issue debt — their debt/equity ratio would move far beyond their target level — which left two options: to issue shares to M&R which M&R would renounce in favour of institutions (because they wanted cash), or to place those shares with a single party who might want to increase their investment in food and, at the same time, get their foot in the door in case Cadbury Plc did decide to disinvest. Bester and Fleming looked around for someone they could feel comfortable with, and settled on one of South Africa's large industrial conglomerates. But now what about the price? Cadbury-Schweppes shares were then trading around R17,00. Their merchant bankers advised that a discount would have to be accepted if the shares were placed with institutions. The best they could hope for was about R16,00. Bester and Fleming rethought it — without the help of the merchant bank. Surely, they reasoned, any buyer of such a large and attractive parcel — between 17 and 20 per cent of the company — should be prepared to pay a premium. They offered the shares to the potential investor at R20,00 each. After some negotiation the deal was concluded — at R20,00 per share! Which only goes to show, that whether it be chocolate bars or their own shares, Cadbury-Schweppes are superb marketers!

Since the acquisition, Bromor has gone from strength to strength. There was substantial rationalisation of the product range. Probably most important, though, is the emphasis on the people involved in the merging of two companies, and the often overlooked similarities and differences between their two corporate cultures. The effort has been worthwhile; Bromor now makes a significant contribution to Cadbury-Schweppes' results.

Of the super-performers SA Bias must be a strong contender for the Frequent Shopper Award. They have acquired 17 companies. But this was no Saturday morning spree — with hardly an exception each company is successfully playing its role in the industry that SA Bias so deliberately restructured. Executive Chairman Chris Seabrooke attributes much of that success to their acquisition strategy and process. He offered three Golden Rules for successful acquisitions.

People

Seabrooke's first Golden Rule is about people. As regards SA Bias's own acquisition, he states :

> *"The key to the whole thing was the people — which was why we chose the acquisitions. All of them at that stage had the*

161

same outdated technology, in particular a company called Narrowtex which we bought in Estcourt which had exceptionally good management. The choice really started with the management and we spent a lot of time with the management before we actually did the acquisitions to make sure they would fit into our way of thinking."

Assessing the people that they are going to be working with is the first step. Seabrooke recalls that there was a superb prospect in the metal fittings industry that they wanted to buy, but in the end they decided they could not have operated with the existing management and terminated negotiations. However, on one occasion SA Bias did succumb to temptation — and paid the price:

"We decided to go into buttons. We had always bought the buttons and sold them. We looked at the various companies in the industry and bought the one we thought was the best. It was called Fashion Buttons. And I want to tell you for three years we sweated ourselves silly to get this business operating correctly. And going back to see where we went wrong we waived one of the golden rules — we had the wrong people in the business. It was the only one of the button companies we could buy at the right price — we'd bought quite a lot in the year concerned and we were a bit short of cash at the time — and I remember our discussion was 'Well the people aren't that great but we'll make it work.' It was a grave error. It took us three years to get it right."

SA Bias has preferred to take full control of their acquisitions to allow rationalisation. Original management is kept on — and motivated by a healthy share of the profits.

Plan Ahead

Seabrooke's second Golden Rule advises against impetuosity — a personal trait of his own that he has sometimes had to check:

"Ferret out all the difficulties before you start and beware of them. I think a lot of people say 'We think this business is good for us, they're making good money, we like the people,' and

162

they never actually go into the next stage of the planning. We always have a 12-month plan for the rationalisation of the business in writing before we actually do the merger, or the takeover."

That planned approach has in fact put SA Bias off a number of acquisitions that looked quite attractive at first glance. Seabrooke cites as a case in point a factory that looked perfect from the point of view of product range, people, profits and price. But the plan for the business involved moving it lock, stock and barrel up to the Reef to merge it with another SA Bias operation. When the detailed planning was done they found that to move the specially set-up machinery from the existing premises would have cost about double the purchase price. "If we hadn't done that study up front," says Seabrooke, "we would have bought it and then found we had a problem."

Don't Be Shy

On the other hand, and it is Seabrooke's third Golden Rule, don't be shy:

"It may not be the right time for you to make acquisitions from a financial point of view, you may have too much on your plate, or whatever. But opportunities arise and it's timing — you've just got to go in and do the deal. You can't actually suit yourself. You've got to suit the seller to an extent. A couple of times we really didn't have the money to buy the business concerned, but the timing was right; we were smack in the bottom of a recession, but the price was right and one or two of the guys were obviously looking to get out with cash in the wallet. So we just borrowed and we bought."

Of course that meant putting detailed feasibility studies in front of their bankers. And temporarily their gearing ratios had to "go through the window". Conversely though, you mustn't be shy to walk away. "It's your money and it's your business," says Seabrooke, who learnt that lesson from Bennie Lubotzky, the low-profile owner of Trump and Springbok Clothing, in Seabrooke's opinion the best clothing business in South Africa.

163

Lubotzky bought many businesses in his day and wasn't shy to withdraw from a deal at the eleventh hour if it didn't feel right. Even when the lawyers had done their work and the papers were on the table, Bennie wouldn't shrink from saying "No boys, this isn't right."

What Price?

How do you decide what to pay? Robin Hamilton of Suncrush has this quite clear:

"A good rule of thumb is to pay half price."

Seabrooke sees it a little differently. He's often happy to overpay. "If everything is right the price is irrelevant because you actually print the money when you've got it running."

---

12 Winning Ways to Do Things Properly

1. Keep it simple.
2. Think ahead. Plan.
3. Consider the consequences. Know the risks.
4. Follow through. Prove your breeding.
5. Do the right thing right first time.
6. Define "professionalism" in your business and do things that way.
7. Convert to FAD — Fanatical Attention to Detail.
8. Identify the "goodies" — the critical value factors that your customers want — and deliver them.
9. If the goodies include quality and service, make those things part of your culture.
10. Improve communication by using the tools and techniques that will suit your people. And cut bureaucracy wherever you can.
11. Do it in the field. Head offices are expensive.
12. When it comes to acquisitions:
    - know clearly what you are looking for — and why
    - look hard at the cultural and human fit of the prospect with your own business
    - plan ahead — and beyond merger date
    - if the prospect passes the test, don't be shy.

164

CHAPTER EIGHT

BEYOND 15-MAN RUGBY

DANIE THE EXEMPLAR

Rugby is big in the Eastern Cape. This big following noted with interest the development of the Watson brothers, who became legends in schoolboy rugby in Grahamstown before moving on to the Currie Cup game. Then came their dispute with the South African Rugby Board over the participation of black players, and their subsequent expulsion. Valence and Cheeky dedicated their considerable talent to developing black rugby in the Eastern Cape. Craven was adamant that rugby should not be integrated. He was also adamant that sport and politics should not mix. Pardon the confusion, please.

It was therefore with surprise that we read about Craven's Indaba with the ANC in Zimbabwe in October 1988. What Craven had learnt in just over a decade was that there are things other than spectators and 15 players that determine the success of rugby. In fact, some of the most important elements of the game are played off the field. We call this moving beyond 15-man rugby. Just as in the game of rugby, business leaders the world over — and in South Africa in particular — are learning that there are players other than customers (spectators) and organisational members (15 players) that determine the success of the organisation (the side). We found that the super-performers have become adept at moving beyond 15-man rugby.

The Concept of Moving Beyond 15-Man Rugby

Business has, of course, changed drastically since the Industrial Revolution. In the early days of the Industrial Revolution much manufacturing was done in cottages and co-ordinated by a merchant manufacturer who supplied the raw material and sold the end product. Efficient but costly production equipment subsequently tipped competitive advantage in favour of large organisations capable of achieving economies of scale. In the process, co-operation between suppliers,manufacturers and distributors gave way to a system of adversarial relationships. Squeeze your suppliers until the pips squeak. Strangle your distributors. Go even further: disclose the barest minimum to your shareholders and bankers. Vertical integration was one of the natural extensions of this business system. You want to control your distribution channels? Buy them. You want to control your suppliers? Buy them too. The world over, these vertically integrated businesses have been broken down. If one looks at the auto companies of the world, it can be seen that Toyota now produces only about 20 per cent of the value of its cars; Chrysler 30 per cent; Ford 50 per cent. Whilst slightly behind, the trend in South Africa is also noticeable.

There is also a very clear message from the super-performers: there are players out there that vitally affect the fortunes of your company. The previous paradigm of controlling them through ownership doesn't work. Nor does the system of adversarial relationships. Here we can learn something from the Japanese model of harmonious relationships.

They see the business enterprise as the hub in a network of relationships. In that network there are multiple players that have a real interest in the success of the organisation, whose livelihoods depends on your success. We'll call these stakeholders and they include employees, customers, suppliers, distributors, the community at large, the financial markets, your bankers and, of course, government. Then your own organisation will be seen to fit into their own network, and your success to depend on the success of other players in the network.

The lesson we have been taught is a powerful one: **Find out who your stakeholders are, and work like hell to develop mutually beneficial, harmonious relationships. That is, move beyond 15-man rugby.**

In this chapter we'll show how super-performers play the game, first by showing you the VW way — it's become a fundamental in

166

the way they do business. We'll show you that the community itself is the starting point. We'll then examine some of the important relationships in the business's value-added chain. You will see that you cannot ignore what people up and down the chain are doing — they vitally affect your business. We'll show the importance of engaging the equity market, which is, after all, what prices your shares. We'll deal also with relationships with bankers and the government. We'll also show that super-performers appeal to the emotions — a key ingredient in any deep relationship. Whilst employees and customers are quite obviously the most important players in the team, we deal with them elsewhere in the book. This chapter is really about off-the-field players.

VOLKSWAGEN LEADS THE WAY ON 16 VALVES

Volkswagen got themselves into trouble during 1982 by churning out poor quality product — they are the first to admit it. The first step in their turnaround was to sort out their quality problems. In analysing the task, they realised that they could only do this by looking at quality throughout their value chain. How could they produce a quality car if they had quality problems with components? And what would be the point in producing quality cars if their dealers couldn't sell and service them according to the same quality standards? Also, even if they got these things right, it wouldn't matter a damn if the motoring press continued to whip them. This led them to study carefully the Japanese system of harmonious relationships. Out of this was born the Volkswagen family concept. In short, it recognises the symbiotic nature of the relationship between all who have a stake in the success of VW.

Few people could have failed to notice the powerful television advertisements run by Volkswagen over the last 18 months. It began with the "Puppy Love" ad with the young girl with flowing locks carrying a cuddly golden labrador puppy. Then there was the ad of a typical family car-washing scene, again with the young girl and the puppy. Then David Kramer and the "Diepkloof Pas". These prepared the ground for "You're Our Kind of People", with all the VW's in the VW badge formation, with Sarel van der Merwe, Senior and Junior, David Kramer, girl and puppy again.

167

Then, more recently, the workers of VW singing the company song in the VW badge formation. These ads are not only targeted at car-buyers, but at all people in the Volkswagen family — customers, suppliers, the motoring press, the community — and make them feel proud of being part of the Volkswagen family. This positive pride is the starting point for the building of harmonious relationships for all people in the Volkswagen family. This is the concept of moving beyond 15-man rugby in action.

THE COMMUNITY – WINNING HEARTS AND MINDS

Johan Barnard, the outgoing Managing Director of Tollgate, is the epitome of the Cape Afrikaner — polite, astute, direct and formal. He told me:

> *"To successfully run a public utility you need a good dose of common sense."*

To illustrate this point, he related to us the story of Tollgate's 1986 125-year celebration — quite an achievement for any business. They decided to celebrate with fanfare, focusing on staff, but also involving, for example, suppliers, transport officials and community leaders.

> *"We asked ourselves: 'Now what can we do for the public?' So we traced to the nearest day the founding of the company. This was found to be 9 July 1861. So on 9 July 1986, we decided that everyone could travel wherever they wanted to go for 20 cents. To get the message across, we advertised on Radio Good Hope. This was one of the best decisions we ever made — advertising and getting the message to our public that we were part of their community and that we cared about them."*

So successful has this been that they have followed up. Every second month or so they now advertise a special. This may be, for example, a 20 cent fare for a return trip to the harbour in off-peak hours. This has become something of an institution in Cape Town.

Our interest in Tollgate stemmed not so much from its absolute ranking (75th, with an all-in-return of 37,1 per cent), but from intrigue. The passenger transport industry has been hammered over the last five years. With the introduction of Kombi-taxis and the rampant SABTA, increasing unemployment, political unrest and horrific increases in vehicle costs, most operators are surviving only because they are being propped up by the Department of Transport. Yet during this period Tollgate has been able to provide its shareholders with a substantial real return.

Not surprisingly, therefore, we found Tollgate to be a company rich with lessons. Most importantly, they would tell you, is that particularly for a public utility, you need to move beyond 15-man rugby. Not only are you answerable to shareholders, but also to the community and government.

Management has spent an extraordinary amount of time and money demonstrating its commitment to the community and projecting an image of a caring, indispensable part of that community. Apart from the usual methods, such as public relations events and community newsletters, they have adopted some innovative activities like the 20 cent trip. Any research into lower income communities will show that the two things they value most highly are education and children. It is not surprising to find that Tollgate has directed its budget at both of these. For example, they have an Adventure Bus scheme in Cape Town which takes children on mind-broadening trips to places like the harbour, the zoo, Rhodes Memorial and the Tokai Forest. They also participate in the Teacher's Opportunity Programme by providing discounted fares to students.

What has been the spin-off from all this time and effort? Barnard will tell you that it has been manifestly lower rates of vandalisation and "bilking". Most importantly, it has changed the whole dynamic of the fare increase procedure. Whereas in the past community objections had manifested themselves in public hearings, court cases and considerable ill will, recent fare increases have not met with community resistance. How sharply this contrasts with Putco!

In explaining this, Johan Barnard made it sound like pure common sense. That is, if you are a public utility, the emphasis is on the public and you need to market yourself to the public. We have a soft spot for this business philosophy. Barnard could develop a growth industry second to none if he managed to get this philosophy going in our own public service.

In any case, the super-performers have shown us that public utility or not, **time and effort channelled into marketing to the community yields immeasurable returns. The fact is that the composition of consumer markets has changed and will continue to change to reflect the greater purchasing power of blacks.** South African managers don't need reminding of the prevalent view held by black consumers of the linkage between business and apartheid. Brand advertising, no matter how intense and smart, is unlikely to be enough. SAB, in our view the most experienced and sophisticated mass marketeers, learnt this years ago. Their situation certainly required some novel thinking — Beer Division sells more than 80 per cent of its product to blacks. It is also a "sole supplier", and a highly visible one. These factors got them to pioneer the Public Affairs concept in South Africa. Like most things they do, they have applied a rigorous scientific process to the fuzzy area of public perceptions. They have defined quite clearly what sort of perception they desire of Beer Division in the target public. They are able to measure it and to assess the impact of Public Affairs programmes on the perceived image. They are particularly big in sports sponsorship, and it's interesting to see their switch from sports such as rugby to soccer. Their econometric model must have given this strong message.

Pick 'n Pay is another company that pays attention to its community — Executive Chairman Raymond Ackerman sees this as a natural extension of the concept of consumer sovereignty. Here, unfortunately, lies the rub. In projecting an image of an equal opportunity employer (which is surely a starting point for an organisation selling to black customers), you then have to *really* be an equal opportunity employer. It will mean, for example, getting involved with the Group Areas Act, and any other Act that affects the dignity of black employees. This is going to obviously affect relations with government. It will also upset some of those folk on the right. Forget about them, some might say. But Ackerman, as one would expect, sees the dilemma somewhat differently and gave us a good illustration:

"Some uniformed AWB shoppers at the Hypermarket north of Pretoria are refusing to be served by black checkout staff, producing a conflict between the non-discriminatory princi-

ples that we uphold and the recognition of consumer sovereignty. So do we say that the consumer is Queen except when in an AWB uniform?"

Cashbuild is one of the super-performers that is very mindful of its black customer base. They would like to see their image as being an organisation with no discrimination, in touch with the Third World, in touch with the people and in touch with their employees. They see their employees as being the communicators of this image to their community. Their research shows this to be very much the case. Said one of their employees in an interview:

"You know, it's actually a disappointment to have to leave Cashbuild and go home to South Africa!"

THE VALUE-ADDED CHAIN

The term value-added chain comes from microeconomics, where it is used to describe the steps a product goes through from raw material to consumption. For the cotton labelling part of SA Bias, this might be:

Farmer (cotton) — Miller — Spinner — Distributor — SA Bias — Apparel Manufacturer — Wholesaler — Retailer — Consumer.

As we know, microeconomic theory is based on a rational model of man. In this framework, all dealings through the chain are completely arms-length. In line with a worldwide trend, the super-performing companies are redefining the nature of these relationships and their levels of understanding of operations throughout the valued-added chain.

We are talking here about a category of stakeholders in the network who are nothing more than parts of one big system. We will take you through some of these relationships, showing you how they operate and why they are important. We will concentrate on suppliers, distributors and will take a look beyond distributors, to your customer's customer.

Suppliers

Just a point on relationships. Peter Searle makes a point of stressing that a system of harmonious relationships shouldn't be taken to mean that you are soft or easy going.

171

Robin Hamilton told us a good story to support this point. The people at Suncrush also consider it important to develop harmonious relationships with suppliers, but believe that this relationship should work both ways. They were concerned about their dependence on the major CO_2 supplier. As Hamilton puts it, "We lined up a supplier and they said to us 'If you take one (plant) away, you take 'em all.'" Hamilton phoned the supplier's managing director. He was told he was in a meeting.

"I said 'Call them to get him out.' I asked him if he meant what he said, and he said 'Yes,' so we took the business away. It was quite a risk, but you can't let people treat you like that."

Peter Searle, Managing Director of VW, has become something of an expert at developing harmonious relationships. The first bit of advice he gives is that it's not enough to just talk. As they say, action speaks louder than words. VW senior management began visiting their suppliers, understanding their operations and the problems they faced. They then got their suppliers into the Volkswagen plant to show them how they operated. The results of this approach are threefold. Firstly, when the supplier has a problem, you will know whether the problem is real or not. If it is real, you are in an informed position to resolve it. Secondly, if you have a problem, supplier and manufacturer are better placed to work towards a solution, and thirdly, suppliers quickly realise that product quality and customer care aren't just catchy slogans, but rather something of a religion. It sounds so logical, but our experience is that the adversarial mode of doing business is deeply ingrained in the South African manager. It also sounds easy, but Peter Searle would be the first to tell you that, like any relationship dependent on mutual trust, it takes time and constant effort to develop. VW people swear by it. Apart from making for better business dealings, they will convince you that it makes economic sense. It would be interesting to see whom component suppliers would favour when faced with one of the all too common capacity problems in a booming vehicle market.

It's interesting to note how sharply this contrasts with Samcor's approach. Soon after Spencer Sterling assumed office, he travelled to all the major centres and gathered together all their suppliers — most of whom he had never met. He summoned them to the local five-star hotel and gave them the message: "The company is losing a million a day. We can't continue like this. I want a commitment from each and every one of you to hold your prices for a year." Quipped one beleaguered supplier, "Sure — we would be only too happy to. That is, if you'll give us a commitment to hold your prices for a year." What Sterling failed to grasp is that true co-operation comes only when there is a true relationship involved; that you can't ask for commitment without giving yourself. That is a fundamental in relationship building.

Cashbuild is another company that swears by the system of harmonious supplier relationships. In fact, they will tell you that they would never have got the business off the ground had certain key suppliers not decided to support them from the word go. Right at the planning stage of Cashbuild, management identified key suppliers. They discussed in detail the concept they had developed for their building material Cash & Carry operation. As Gerald Haumant, Managing Director, puts it: " . . . we told them of our ambitions and asked them to share the same dream."

Those that gave their support became part of an élite club called "Royal Suppliers". Says Haumant, "It's very much a sort of Japanese approach where you go to bed with one guy and commit yourself to maximising the joint opportunity. We commit ourselves to a certain target. If we get feedback that we can buy better on the open market, we go back to our Royal Supplier and say 'Look, this is the price we can get in Queenstown. Are you prepared to meet it? Not beat it, because we expect you to make a living, but if you meet the best price offered that's fine and you get the order.'

Cashbuild, then, get their planned volumes at the keenest prices in what is essentially a commodity product. The Royal Supplier gets enough throughput to at least cover overheads. Other reciprocal benefits? The relationship reaches the point where they share market intelligence. Two minds (and sources of information) are a powerful combination.

Toyota South Africa is one of the country's success stories. It was started from scratch by Dr Albert Wessels. He learns quickly, and identified from the start with Toyota's system of harmonious relationships. His son, Bert, now Managing Director, spent a year working on the plant floor in Japan. He speaks Japanese fluently, as does Brand Pretorius, Managing Director of Toyota Marketing. Recently, the pressure to reduce exports to South Africa has been intense. Somehow, we are less concerned about this than we are about reduced imports of Hondas, Mazdas and Nissans.

Distributors

Most of the super-performers don't sell directly to the end-user. The messages they give us are: **firstly, get to understand the end-user at least as well as your distributor. Secondly, start doing things in your business that will pull more product through your distributor and help him beat the competition. Thirdly, going back to our earlier point, ownership is not a powerful form of control — rather "control" your distribution by helping them to be better, more profitable and more dependent on a symbiotic relationship with the supplier.** As Philip Coutts-Trotter, Managing Director of SA Bias, puts it:

> *"Sure, it's an important strategy of ours to control our markets. We get this control by market dominance, which itself is more than anything a result of customer service and innovation. Not through ownership. In fact, it's a critically important leg of our policy not to involve ourselves in downstream operations."*

Our discussion with Graham Mackay, Managing Director of Beer Division, meandered through their recent history. We pressed him on the Rembrandt Beer War. We asked him how he had felt about losing their retail outlets. The feeling at the time was that Rembrandt, which was much better networked to government, had managed to engineer an order on SAB from the Competitions Board to divest of its retail outlets. In talking about this, Mackay stressed the point that if you are a branding company, such as Beer Division, it doesn't pay you to own your outlets. In their case, of course, it brings with it all the negative perception baggage associated with monopolistic power. Far more powerful, he believes, is their philosophy of "Partners for Profit". To support this philosophy, they have implemented a number of programmes. For example, the budding entrepreneur can avail himself of training programmes freely supplied by Beer Division. Or of their full-time architect. They even have employees who will freely dispense retail and business advice. Looked at in cold commercial terms, this fits in neatly with Beer Division's overall philosophy of "closing the gaps". Anyone wanting to compete will have to go through the time, expense and learning curve of developing these symbiotic relationships. And it can't be legislated away as was the case with Solly Kramers.

Few of the super-performers are as dependent on their distributors as the motor companies — VW and Toyota. Brand Pretorius, Managing Director of Toyota Marketing, summed it up neatly:

"We came to realise that in marketing terms, we had focused heavily on promotion, pricing and product, only to find that we became constipated at our distribution. Even if you have the best product, well promoted and appropriately priced, it's not going to matter unless your distribution is superb."

So what did they do? The people at Toyota Marketing are an analytical bunch. They began by doing an exercise to determine the optimum positioning of dealers throughout the country. This was followed by a dealer development programme in which they filled the obvious gaps and rationalised the overtraded areas. Over a three-year period, they moved from 200 to 320 dealers. They then looked at the obstacles to improved profitability of their dealers. The most urgent need was identified as a basic accounting one. They recruited accountants to implement a standard accounting system — all the dealer has to do is supply the information on a monthly basis. In return, they are supplied with monthly income statements, balance sheets and an array of ratios, together with appropriate comparatives. Pretorius pores through the thick printouts and shoots off telexes to the top 10 (the 10 most profitable) and the 10 problem children (the 10 least profitable).

They then focused their attention on the cash constraints which apply to most owner-managed businesses. They found numerous ways of decreasing their working capital commitments. This includes an on-line stock order system. All the dealer has to do is punch in the required stock items and these will be delivered within 24 hours. The chances are that he will be paid long before he receives an invoice from Toyota.

They also offer their dealers, free of charge, a dealer management consulting service. The objective: more profitable dealers. They know that the more money the dealer makes, the better will be the relationship. And the more Toyota will make.

Again, being the analytical types they are, they've come to realise that these areas of "hard" support are great, but that attitudes need to be changed. Super-performers show time and time again that attitudes count. Not surprisingly, we found Toyota's training machine pulling through dealer employees at a phenomenal rate. Their Toyota Touch campaign, which instills the value of service excellence, extends naturally to their dealer network. Pretorius's regular video features stories of dealers who have excelled at customer service or who have run a Toketsu (Quality Circle), how it has worked and what it has delivered.

VW has nurtured its dealers in a similar fashion. While Toyota has been analytical, VW has been emotional. Peter Searle remembers only too well the days when Beetle owners used to flick their lights at each other. They have attempted to capture this sense of pride and belonging with their dealer network. We recently attended a presentation Searle gave to a group of Lindsay Saker managers. The presentation centred around the culture change programme that had led VW through the past seven years. It was punctuated with bursts of audio visual display, which traced the development of VW in South Africa from the day the first Beetle came off the production line. The audio was gut-wrenching stuff, moving from *I See Skies of Blue* to the VW company song. Were it not for the absolute sincerity, it might have been stage managed. The climax came with Searle relating the story of the ad featuring VW workers in the company logo formation. He had been sent a photograph from a section of the plant with the workers standing in the logo formation, autographed by all in the photo. This had sparked off the idea, wham! On came that powerful ad. When the lights came on grown men (with beards nogal!) had tears streaming down their cheeks. These people were imbued with a deep sense of pride and belonging and all were ready to preach the gospel of customer service. This was the concept of moving beyond 15-man rugby at its highest level of finesse.

... and Beyond: the Customer's Customers

There is something about the average factory that suggests it is far removed from the marketplace. Certainly, most manufacturers of consumer goods are at least two steps away from the end-user. Take the example of SA Bias. It makes bits and pieces that apparel manufacturers incorporate in their garments. These garments might be sold to a distributor, who then on-sells to a retailer. Yet Menashe Zaroozny, Group Marketing Director of SA Bias, if you can understand his thick Israeli accent, demonstrates an intimate knowledge of world fashion trends. One of his objectives is to ensure that his organisation is not just in touch with design concepts in the marketplace, but is actually ahead of them. As related in Chapter 5, when they detected a trend towards the display of labels on the outside of garments they began to work closely with their customers to produce the right sort of labels. Their sales of labels boomed. **The message that emerges from super-performing manufacturers is that it's not enough to enlist your customer. You need to enlist *his* customer, all the way down the chain to the end-user.**

THE EQUITY MARKET — YOUR SHAREHOLDERS: VOTING WITH THEIR WALLETS

We chose as our measure of super-performance that acid test of performance in a market economy — return to shareholders. Whichever way you look at it, a company's share price is an important variable in the return equation. What determines share price? Well, that depends on whom you talk to. Some will tell you that it's dividends, others that it's earnings. Or cash flow. Or return on assets. Others will tell you that accounting measures bear little relation to the true worth of a company.

177

We got bogged down in this mine of theory for some time. What could the super-performers teach us about the determinants of share price? Back to the research material.

What emerged is that **super-performing companies understand that there is a player out there that determines the worth of their company. They actually get out and engage this player. The player is the shareholder body and the forum is the equity market.**

There seem to be three levers for increasing share price:

- **The Real Economy**, i.e. what is actually happening within the company — the business in which it operates, its products, how it produces and sells the products, how people are managed, and how the company deals with its product market. This is the primary lever for wealth creation. In essence, this book is about the Real Economy.
- **Financial Engineering**, i.e. the way in which the company makes use of finance, how it structures itself financially, its financial and accounting policies and the way in which it navigates its way through financial legislation and regulation. These factors are unlikely to affect a company's ability to compete in a product market, but impact upon share price due to their impact on actual earnings and the visibility (or disguise) of these earnings. This is a secondary lever for wealth creation.
- **Hype**, i.e. the image the company projects in the investment community. It is unlikely to affect a company's ability to compete or its earnings stream, but will affect the price/earnings ratio, and consequently the share price. This is a tertiary lever for wealth creation.

Our observation is that the relative importance of these levers changes with the run of the equity market. It seems to work a bit like this: bull markets tend to attract less sophisticated investors and it is these investors who tend to price the shares. It would seem that what is happening in the Real Economy is less important than the amount of creative Financial Engineering and Hype that takes place. In a bear market, the less sophisticated investors are either out or locked-in — certainly they are less active. This, coupled with generally quieter trading, means that the happenings in the Real Economy (happily) become more important. Nevertheless, Financial Engineering and Hype remain important levers.

Columbia Consulting is a good example. A careful analysis of their earnings on listing in September 1986 shows that they were a mixture of bits and bobs, including Bernard Herbert's course for aspirant chartered accountants, travel agency commissions, insurance broking commissions and a few financial training courses. Nothing of real consequence. The net asset value on listing was 25 cents per share, and this was made up largely of the proceeds of the listing. The issue price was 75 cents. Not that the Real Economy was too important at the time. In any case, Gordon Polovin and Co. engaged the Hype lever. To give you an indication of this, they collected two full files of newspaper clippings in 18 months. It took a blue chip like Barlow Rand five years to fill one file! Another important Hype component was added by Columbia's association with Arnie Witkin's New Bernica. The message came through consistently and strongly that this was a share to invest in.

Then they engaged the Financial Engineering lever with a spectacular acquisition spree using hugely over-rated shares. For example, 50 per cent of TOCO, using shares valued at 230 cents; 31,2 per cent of Swift Foods, using shares valued at 460 cents; 33,3 per cent of Milston, using shares valued at 500 cents. All these within six months of coming onto the JSE at 75 cents.

The net effect was that even after the crash, Columbia's shares stood at four times its issue price. After only 20 months, its cash balances had advanced from R1 million on listing to R22 million. Even more importantly, however, was that it entered the bear market with meaningful stakes in companies with substantial Real Economies.

We use this as an illustration, not as a role model. The lesson to be learnt is that to be a super-performer, having a super-performing real economy is not enough. The other two levers need to be engaged as well.

The SA Bias group is an excellent example of a group which respects the power of these levers. SA Bias Binding Manufacturers (SABBM), the subsidiary we studied, has a financial structure which we find difficult to understand. The way in which the 17 acquisitions have been structured could provide a few lessons for world class financial engineers. They don't pay an awful lot of tax either. Comments Executive Chairman Chris Seabrooke:

> *"Tax is an expense . . . it's our job to run the business at the lowest possible expense level. My first expense is tax, my second expense is salary and my third expense is rent."*

Needless to say, Seabrooke is a genius when it comes to Financial Engineering.

SABBM hasn't been listed long enough to know how it will employ the Hype lever. Clearly, however, Seabrooke will follow the path he trod with SA Bias. Here the level and quality of shareholder communication is outstanding. Corporate PR is as good as you will find anywhere in South Africa and they have regular sessions with analysts and others who influence the market. Says Seabrooke:

> *"We are not actually sellers of shares, but we like our shareholders to be able to sell well if they want to. To do this, you need to work hard at a quality image."*

It's often the small things that count. What does it cost to send a letter to a new shareholder? Not a lot — it's easy to standardise. Someone just needs to check through the share register on a daily basis and push a few buttons on the word processor, then take it off to the Chairman to sign. Just think of the impact it makes when you receive a short, polite welcoming letter to the share-holding group of SA Bias. They do it, and it works.

BANKERS: YOUR FRIEND IN NEED

There are, arguably, more jokes about bankers than there are about consultants. Yet leaders of super-performing companies take their relationship with bankers extremely seriously. And not just because of the leverage the bank holds over them, but more because of a belief in the principle of harmonious relationships. Very few companies that achieve super-performer status will have circumvented a patch of being over-borrowed. They therefore keenly appreciate the value of this relationship. The lessons they gave us probably apply to any relationship dependent on mutual trust. They are:

- Provide the bank with full information.
- Deal as closely as possible to the point of decision-making (i.e. as high up as possible).
- Understand how the bank works, i.e. their own internal procedures for approving loans and reviewing loan performance.
- Make sure you are short on promises (i.e. a gentle upward curve rather than a hockey stick) and long on action.

GOVERNMENT — LAST, BUT NOT LEAST

The rationale for developing relationships with government is compelling: government is a big spender, it passes the laws and it frequently subsidises. We will not dwell on the importance which super-performers attach to their relationships with government. Many would find it embarrassing. We will just relate one story, which has a powerful message.

The passenger transport industry is even more dependent on government than most. Half the turnover of the typical operator is made up of subsidy and the whole transport industry is tightly regulated. We have commented already on the difference between Tollgate and Putco. One is forever reading about Putco's battles with government. Putco gives the impression that it feels it is getting a poor deal from government. Government, you can bet, finds Putco something of an embarrassment. Contrast this with Tollgate. Its board composition tells you a lot. Its senior directors are known to be comfortable in political circles at the highest level. Whilst its corporate PR is tops, one never reads about its relationship with government in the press. Everything smacks of a healthy relationship. As we've said before, Tollgate is a master at moving beyond 15-man rugby.

THE FAMILY — A NEGLECTED POST-SCRIPT

One thing we've all had to come to terms with is that super-performance, at the individual level, cannot be accomplished without a great deal of after-hours work. How many times, in the course of a normal working day, do you hear the comment "Well,

I looked over this last night," or "We met late on Monday evening," or "I'll read it over the weekend"?

We also know that all this super-performance is emotionally draining stuff. The surprise to us is how few companies tie all of this to the importance of the employee's family. These are the people who bear the brunt of all the after-hours commitment and on whom the employee depends so critically as a support system.

Once again, super-performers like Volkswagen, Cashbuild and Pick 'n Pay explicitly recognise this. As with many things in life, it is the small things that count. They make a point of remembering to invite wives to functions, of remembering wives' and children's birthdays, and of giving family weekends away when someone has really put in a special effort.

Moving beyond 15-man rugby is about attention to these sorts of things.

TOUCHING BOTH THE HEAD AND THE HEART

A lesson that comes through strongly from our study of the relationships developed by super-performing companies is that as with all meaningful relationships one needs to touch not only the head, but also the heart. While it is important to constantly reinforce the commercial logic of the relationship by selling the benefits, it is also important that the relationship has an emotional dimension to it. The effect this has is that when the partner behaves in a supportive way of the relationship, he feels good not only because of the commercial logic of this behaviour but also because it "just feels so damn good".

Clive Warrilow, Marketing Director of VW, tells with real feeling the story about Volkswagen's 1988 Worldwagon exercise:

> *"We felt we'd got the message across well enough to start embracing the family. So we invited the Volkswagen family to a venue in Johannesburg where we staged the VW story. We brought Ferdinand Porsche back to life (well, not literally, but the actor they used looked and talked like him). We told the family that story of how VW had pulled itself together. The story was punctuated by commentary from Porsche, showing how he became progressively more proud of VW's fine achievements. You know, there were grown men crying at the end of it."*

7 Steps to Moving Beyond 15-Man Rugby

1. There are players out there who vitally affect the performance of your business. Super-performing companies have redefined the nature of their relationships with these players. Whereas in times gone by these relationships were of an adversarial nature, they are now characterised by influence and harmony. Find out who these players are, and get close to them.
2. Now, more than ever, businesses operating in mass markets need to win the hearts and minds of the community.
3. Get close to your suppliers. It makes for far better business dealings.
4. Control your distribution, not through ownership, but by doing things that make it profitable for them to do business with you.
5. Understand the end-user — everything else in the value-added chain depends on this.
6. It's not enough to simply have a "super-performing" company. To really get into the super-performing category, you need to engage the equity market. Otherwise the translation of "super-performance" will not be immediate or optimal.
7. As with all meaningful relationships, you need to touch the heart as well as the head. Symbols and emotions need to play their part in these relationships.

THE BEST IN YOUR INDUSTRY ARE DOING IT. THEY ARE TAKING OVER YOUR NETWORK, NOT BY BUYING THE NETWORK, BUT THROUGH A MUCH MORE POWERFUL FORM OF INFLUENCE: BY RELATIONSHIP DEVELOPMENT.

CHAPTER NINE

INSPIRED LEADERSHIP

"The problem with many organisations, and especially the ones that are failing, is that they tend to be overmanaged and underled. There is a profound difference between management and leadership, and both are important. Managers are people who do things right and leaders are people who do the right things."

Warren Bennis and Burt Nanus, *Leaders: The Strategies for Taking Charge*, 1985

The young Raymond Ackerman, as General Manager of Checkers, had been having a running battle with Norman Herber, the Greaterman's Chairman. Ackerman felt that Checkers was doing little more than acting as a poor imitation of Woolworths, selling mainly soft goods, with a limited range of food. He had a vision of turning it into a classic supermarket operation, mass selling mainly food, but also allied lines, with fewer, but larger stores, with space for a full range of perishables, and a wide range of branded goods. He had also become a disciple of the principle of consumer sovereignty and much of this didn't wash with Herber. In 1966 Ackerman was fired, and in the following year he bought three stores in the Cape that carried the name Pick 'n Pay. The rest is history (well, for Checkers almost).

The achievements are quite astounding by any numeric measure. In 21 years the company went from three small outlets to 86 supermarkets and 12 hypermarkets; a turnover of R5 million to R3 billion; pre-tax earnings of R310 000 to R91 million; a handful of employees to 24 072; market capitalisation of R620 000 to R800 million.

The less quantifiable measures are, we believe, even more astounding. Pick 'n Pay has unquestionably shaped the landscape of mass retailing in South Africa by setting a world class standard. Pick 'n Pay, more than anything else, is why the retail sector is one of the few truly competitive sectors in the South African economy. It has also shaped the landscape of employee relations, public affairs, social responsibility and a lot more besides.

Our study of Pick 'n Pay is in a way a study of all nine vital ingredients of a super-performer in action. Yet the more we dug, the more we came back to the font of success: the inspired leadership of Raymond Ackerman. For this reason, we have centred much of this chapter around Raymond Ackerman.

THE CONCEPT OF LEADERSHIP

The concept of leadership has something of a mystical ring to it. In the course of our research, we asked countless friends and colleagues what they believed to be the factors behind super-performance. Nine times out of ten their responses could be summed up in one word: leadership. We would agree, in the sense that leadership is about mastering your corporate destiny; giving the lady what she wants; liberating human potential; ringing in the new; doing what comes logically; doing it properly; moving beyond 15-man rugby; and building strong cultures.

So, the chances are that if you ask someone why Pick 'n Pay, Sun International, Altech or Toyota are successful, they will tell you it's because of Raymond Ackerman, Sol Kerzner, Bill Venter or Albert Wessels.

What we've tried to do in this chapter is to get behind the leadership concept as it operates in South Africa. To set out some of the practical lessons we have learnt from business leaders of this calibre — the sort of things they do to put their organisations into the super-performer league and the sort of people they are.

We will show that leaders *drive* their organisations; they are intrepid inspectors, relying as much on inspection as expectation; they fire-up people with excitement; they get their hands grubby down at the coalface; they blaze the trail in sniffing out business opportunities; they push their people like hell; they focus people's attention on what they want; they unite the organisation

185

around a vision of the future; they make meaning; they communicate constantly; they draw people around them.

We have tried to draw a distinction between the things they do and the people they are. The sort of people they are is really a deduction from the sorts of things they do. We will show that they are strong-charactered; ambitious, experts in their field; that they gravitate towards people; they are obsessive; they have a bold attitude to risk and most importantly, we believe, they know how to touch both the heart and the head.

The leaders of our super-performing companies are consumed by something that puts them into a category called "something special". A leader in this category is a vital ingredient in the super-performer recipe. We have therefore called this sort of leadership "Inspired Leadership".

LEADERS DRIVE THEIR ORGANISATIONS

At the start of each year Willards Managing Director Mike Benn sets the dates, times and duration of all formal meetings for the year. These include the weekly executive meetings, operations meetings, finance meetings, discount meetings, etc. A chairman is appointed for each meeting, and he must minute the meeting (by dictaphone) in front of attendants. These minutes must be published within 24 hours. Mike will get a copy. He reckons:

". . . It's bullshit that anyone believes you can run a company on a laissez-faire, open ended basis. A company must be driven — every successful company is driven . . . the guy at the top must get in there and set the energy level and the direction. He must demand performance."

What he touches on here is that when participative management came into vogue, many managers applied it incorrectly. Participative management was interpreted as allowing people to get on and do their own thing. What the super-performers have taught us is that yes, it's right to get people involved in decision making, to shove responsibility down the line, to give people autonomy and freedom, to allow the soft people issues to be legitimate data of the organisation. But that doesn't mean that you abdicate responsibility for setting the pace and energy level of the organisation or that you cease to drive it.

186

Some of the leaders of the super-performers which are the most participative in style are the most adept at driving their organisations. In Edgars, for example, one shouldn't be fooled by Chief Executive Vic Hammond's seemingly laid-back approach. All merchandise is subjected to a "Hammond Review" before the merchandising programme is approved. We found it interesting, however, that Farrel Ratner, the man responsible for purchasing all men's and children's wear claims to be "the supreme God in merchandise". Further down the line the buyers will tell you that they are entirely responsible. Why is this? This is participative management as it should be. The leader drives, but people down the line take ownership.

Pick 'n Pay is another excellent example of this principle. This company is widely regarded as a success story in participative management, yet Raymond Ackerman personally conducts much of the purchasing. And hordes of people take ownership of all the purchasing decisions. This is the driving concept in action.

Suncrush, a consistent super-performer, surprised us with its level of informality, participation and flexibility. Yet Executive Chairman Robin Hamilton gets very involved in much of the detailed decision making. For example, he walks around the sites of proposed bottling plants, inspects the plans, and sometimes even revises them himself. He even does the sales budget himself.

The driving leader of the super-performing company is fundamentally different to the driving autocrat. The autocrat doesn't understand delegation — he drives and hauls people along with him. The driving leader as we saw him is more like the shepherd — clearly in control, setting the pace, energy and direction, nudging his flock along with him. It is absolutely clear who is in charge, but people follow because they have been put in a position where they *want* to go along. It doesn't come easily, but we've seen it in action and it's powerful.

LEADERS INSPECT

Mike Benn spends every Tuesday pounding the streets, walking from café to café. He always looks for the same things and asks the same questions: Are you being well served? Are you properly stocked? Do we have the best positioning and frontage? Is the shelf mix right? In short, has the café been served in the Willards Way? On the way to the next café he shoots off a memo congratulating (or chastising) the representative responsible.

Leaders like Benn aren't scared to inspect or fearful of treading on toes. They see it as part of the job, and a very important part at that. How else can they give feedback to their supercharged people? There is something wrong with a company that resents the legitimate right the leader has to tread his own turf. It follows closely from the driving concept, and many of the leaders of the super-performers do it relentlessly.

Bill Venter, Executive Chairman of Altron, is an intrepid inspector with a fearsome eye for detail. Neill Davies, his Deputy Chairman, tells the story of their mid-morning return from a business trip. At the airport they bumped into one of their senior executives, who mumbled something about waiting for a customer from Durban. Venter thought this strange — he knew there weren't any planes due from Durban at that time. Back at the office, with a hundred and one other things to do, he followed up. As it turned out, the employee was running a contract at the airport in his private capacity.

We both enjoy shopping at Edgars. Antony has seen Vic Hammond on Saturday morning on two occasions. He watched him with interest on both occasions. He strides around greeting Edgars people and asking them about their displays and assortments. "How are those shirts selling? Have you thought of changing the display? Try putting them there. That looks great. Well done kids." And then he moves on.

Inspection makes sense for a number of reasons. First, it is demonstrable proof that the leader is in the driving seat. Second, it shows that he's in touch with the coalface (we pick up on this later). Third, he is demonstrating to the whole organisation what to do and how to do it — not through words, but through behaviour. Fourth, and very importantly, it provides the leader with the opportunity to give feedback. Raymond Ackerman explains:

"When I go round stores [which he seems to do all the time] I don't just go round stores. I come back to my hotel room and I dictate letters — about 10 letters per store, to key people

saying, 'It was lovely seeing you. Hell, your produce department was great!' My poor secretary! When I go round on trips now she'll probably have about 60 or 70 letters a day of that type."

This sort of rapid instantaneous feedback is the breakfast of champions.

LEADERS GENERATE EXCITEMENT

Aaron Searll, Executive Chairman of Seardel, has a laid-back air about him that belies his bone-deep attachment to his company, its product and his people. His eyes light up when you talk about these things. He is a leader who generates excitement.

"Being emotionally involved in my business, I think that's an important thing. I get upset if things go wrong, I get very excited if I see my products being bought or worn by people. I love to see Sharp electronics products in various places. I love to see my outwear and underwear being purchased. I get a kick out of that, I think that's important, that seems to rub off. In a bureaucracy or a municipality or in government departments, nobody really gets emotionally involved or excited about the good things that happen, the exciting things — the results — good results."

By their own admission, the leaders we spoke to tend not to be an animated bunch. Yet they show an enthusiasm and emotional attachment to their organisation, its people and products that borders on the boyish. And it's infectious. People pick it up like a fever.

Mike Benn is not the most animated person you'll meet. But when you start talking to him about Willards or snack food, there's no stopping him. His hobby is snacks. He reads voraciously everything that is written about snacks and he has personally tested almost every brand of snack food worldwide. Raymond Ackerman gets misty-eyed when he sees the 100th fresh product display, check-out configuration, or when he shakes hands with the 15 000th employee of the year. Winky Ringo, Executive Chairman of Mathieson & Ashley, takes on a mystical look when he starts talking about office furniture. Ken Rosevear, Managing Director of Sun International, bubbles with enthusiasm over the prospect of opening another day-trip hotel somewhere God knows where.

The fact of the matter is that a leader cannot expect his company to be any more enthusiastic or emotionally involved than he is. He sets the level of excitement, and the most he can hope for is that the people around him will match it.

It should be remembered that if enthusiasm is infectious, then so is apathy. Few things kill employee enthusiasm and excitement more than apathetic leadership. No excitement means boredom and organisational life becomes a slow slog.

LEADERS GET DOWN TO THE COALFACE

A leader doesn't drive a company by remote control. He doesn't generate excitement by sitting on his arse. He gets down to the coalface and gets involved. He finds out, first hand, what the problems are in the office, the plant and at the point of customer interface.

We had a lot of trouble pinning Peter Searle down to ask him if VW would participate in the project. He was either visiting dealers or giving them a guided tour of the plant. Or walking around the factory on his own — looking and asking questions. He's been known to arrive on a dealer's forecourt, unannounced, at 07h30 asking customers about their cars, their problems and the service. It's not surprising that very soon the dealer principals start doing the same thing themselves.

It was just as impossible to pin down Raymond Ackerman, Vic Hammond, Bill Venter, Ken Rosevear and Winky Ringo. The chances are that these people were out in the field, at the coalface, learning, driving and generating excitement.

The effect that this has on people down the line is astounding. It cannot be explained within the framework of rational man. It has more to do with the emotions. That a leader can descend from his elevated position and ask, "How's it going? What problems are you having with your job? Have you tried doing it this way?" It makes the guy feel so damn important he just wants to burst with pride and do it so much better next time.

Raymond Ackerman loves spending time at the coalface. One of the tenets of his philosophy of motivating people is getting around.

"Motivating people is more than salary; it's getting around. Yesterday I sat with three trainees from Cape Town for lunch. When I'm in Johannesburg I try and do the same — and Durban and PE. Out of the blue I'll say to the local GM 'Get three of your bright guys around' and I'll sit with them from 13h00 until 14h30, and just let them talk about the company and ask questions.

In fact this one guy from [Competitor X] — don't quote me on X — said 'You know, Mr Ackerman, X is a great company, but it's so structured and everybody does things by the book. In all the years I've been at X [he'd been there seven years] I've never even met Mr X [MD], and here I am having lunch with you. I'm just going to go bursting back to Pick 'n Pay and say "Wow!" you not only say hello to me but actually take me to lunch.'"

LEADERS BLAZE THE TRAIL

Winky Ringo, Executive Chairman of Mathieson & Ashley, gave us the time to chat about a wide range of business topics. We spent some time talking about the role of the Chief Executive. He sees the Chief Executive of a super-performing company as an entrepreneur — he must be the entrepreneur in that organisation. He thinks about it like this:

"There are opportunity waves in the air. They are going on all the time. They are very faint. The Chief Executive's job is to tune into these waves, then amplify the opportunity, select it and turn it into a reality."

We think the analogy is apt. It's a truism that the higher a person rises in an organisation, the more conservative he becomes. The more he becomes a custodian of the status quo, the more he can think of reasons not to do something than to do something, and the greater the noise level becomes of competing priorities, competitive threats, reactive requirements, time pressure, shareholder restraint, preventing him from focusing on these opportu-

191

nity waves that go on all the time, amplifying them and turning them into a reality.

In the super-performing companies the Chief Executive is the person who pushes the company into new opportunities. The people around him don't grumble about their risk-averse Chief Executive — as is the case with poor performers — but rather about him running ahead of them. "The guy needs to be restrained," they say.

When Sun City opened in 1979, the news was generally received with interest, but also with a hint of derision. Who was actually going to drive 160 km to some place in Bophawheresit to visit a casino? Many thought that Sol had overstretched his vivid imagination with this one.

It's probably just as well Sol Kerzner kept the ultimate vision he had of Sun City to himself. His initial plan of a casino with 340 rooms and a few attractions was enough to make one gasp. Today it stands with close to 1 000 rooms, neon-lit fantasy buildings, a golf course designed by Gary Player, a man-made lake, an entertainment centre, a superbowl and a whole lot more. Sun International is now talking of putting another R30 million into it.

Kerzner just knew that there was a market for this sort of concept — he didn't need piles of market research to support it. He came up with the concept and brought it to reality. The result? Apart from the unique concept, shareholders have never had cause to grumble at the returns.

LEADERS MAKE EXPLICIT AND HIGH DEMANDS

We have studied the subject of leadership *ad nauseam*. That is because the subject has been researched *ad nauseam*. This has a lot to do with the mystical air, discussed earlier.

During the course of our research we came across a short article written by an American academic, Warren Bennis, that made more sense in four pages than the wads of stuff we had read. In the article, he tells the story of his many futile attempts to interview Leon Fleischer, a prominent pianist, conductor and musicologist. Fleischer kept turning him down for an interview, refusing even to answer his letters or phone calls. He finally gave up.

A couple of summers later Bennis happened to be in Aspen, Colorado, while Fleischer was conducting the Aspen Music Festival. He tried to reach him again, even leaving a note on his dressing room door (pushy, these Americans). He got no answer.

One day in downtown Aspen, he gave a lift to two perspiring young cellists who were taking part in the Festival and offered them a lift. On the way, he questioned them about Fleischer. "I'll tell you why he's so great," said one. "He doesn't waste our time."

Bennis eventually got his interview, and was even allowed to watch Fleischer in rehearsal. He linked the way he saw him with that one sentence, "He doesn't waste our time." The fact was that every moment Fleischer was in front of the orchestra, he knew exactly what sound he wanted. He didn't waste time because his intentions were always evident. And what united him with the other musicians was their concern with intention and outcome.

This explains very well something we found the leaders of super-performing companies to be adept at. That is, being so explicit in their expectations that intention is linked directly to outcome. If you walk into a hotel you'll know it's a Sun International hotel by the time you get to the lobby. It has to do with design, excitement and service. So when Sol Kerzner sees to the development of a new hotel, everyone from the architect onwards know *exactly* what sort of hotel he is out to build, because Kerzner knows exactly what sort of hotel he wants and is able to focus expectations on that. There's nothing vague about it. When Raymond Ackerman sees to the development of a new retail outlet, there's nothing vague about it. The people he is leading will know exactly what sort of operation it will be even before he starts talking about it.

Leaders of super-performing companies, then, are able to exert an extraordinary focus on the activities around them because in their own minds they can actually picture what it is they are after. And picture it in detail.

What we find, in addition, is that not only are these demands explicit, but they are high. People like Raymond Ackerman, Peter Searle and Meyer Kahn will confess that they drive their people nuts. Robin Hamilton was even more explicit. "I'm probably a pain in the arse. Ja, I push."

193

For Philip Coutts-Trotter, Managing Director of SA Bias, this is a fundamental in dealing with people. He got quite carried away in talking about it:

"People perform exceptionally well here, and the reason is that we are pushing them to the absolute limit of their abilities and raising their expectations of their own ability. We are challenging them beyond what they believe they can do. I never take no for an answer, I push people exceptionally hard when I believe it necessary, I'm very demanding. I demand performance from people. I demand that they achieve what they are capable of achieving. I'm not prepared to let people under-achieve. It's just not on. I will not tolerate it. I know that sounds dictatorial, but it's a dictatorial approach that says to people 'You will achieve what you are capable of achieving'. Don't give me substandard performance if you're capable of giving first class performance. It's one of my beliefs in life — I tell my kids exactly the same thing — if you are going to do something, do it absolutely to the best of your ability. If you can't do it I accept that. I'm never going to kick somebody because they can't do a thing. But if they can do it, I want it done and I want it done to the best of their ability (by now banging on his desk)."

LEADERS HAVE A VISION

You think office furniture is dull? Listen to the starting point in Winky Ringo's visions:

"The organisations that are going to stay in business will need to compete. To compete, they will need information. That information will come through an electronic device. That electronic device will stand on a workstation — not a desk. The chances are that that workstation will come from one of our companies."

He continues to talk about the office of the future and what it will look like. And the organisation of the future and how the work of the individual will be structured within that organisation. It's not based on loose thinking. Mathieson & Ashley people have studied these things.

194

Leaders of the super-performers were able to talk about their vision with absolute clarity, in a way that simply made so much sense. And they were able to excite us with their vision (our clients tell us that we tend not to get excited easily). If you think office furniture is dull, spend some time with Winky Ringo. If you think the ordinary old potato chip (even with crinkles) is dull, go and talk to Mike Benn. Bruce Edmunds, Managing Director of Utico, will excite you about the cigarette industry. Because they've spent some time thinking about what sort of organisation they want to build and they've factored a lot of excitement into that.

LEADERS MAKE MEANING: THE POWER OF LANGUAGE

We made the point above that the leaders of super-performing companies are able to explain their vision in simple terms. **Having a vision is one thing, but turning it into something that has meaning, something people can put their arms around and cling to, is quite another. This is about making meaning, and language is the currency.**

The root of the concept is quite deep. That is, that reality is subjective. When is a freedom fighter a terrorist? When is our President "Die Groot Krokodil" or "Our Saviour"? And so one can go on. The point is, as the philosophers would tell us, that reality is the way you construct it. In a social organism, where there are power processes in play, people willingly give up their right to construct reality to a leader. So the leader is afforded an opportunity to construct reality for organisational members. Now, the more the noise, that is, the more information, contrary opinions, options, uncertainty and confusion, the more willing people will be to rally behind the leader who cuts through all this noise and is able to integrate facts and concepts into a reality that captures the imagination of organisational members. That is what we understand by the management of meaning.

The current situation pertaining to white parliamentary politics provides a good opportunity to illustrate the principle. Looking back at the history of the rise of the National Party one sees slogans, language and by-lines that have caught the imagination of the electorate. It started with Apartheid. This one word, more

195

than anything else, captured the imagination of the people. It rocketed the National Party into power. Apartheid then became Separate Development, then Plural Democracy. And there've been others, such as Total Onslaught, Co-federation of Southern African States. Pieter-Dirk Uys could give us a lot more. The National Party now finds itself unable to come up with these sorts of slogans — their message has become cluttered. Contrast this with Andries and the Conservative Party. His message is simple: Partition. This has captured the imagination of a large slice of the electorate.

While all this was going on, the Progressive Federal Party was never able to come up with anything to capture the imagination of the electorate. It tried with the idea of a National Convention, but a National Convention is not an outcome or end product. It's simply the start of a process. Most of its messages were cluttered with compromise and polemic. It possibly appealed to rational men, and even then only when they were thinking. It was therefore unable to ever capture the imagination of the electorate.

The same holds for organisational life. Time and time again we found the best leaders had verbalised their vision in a way that captured the imagination of their people. Raymond Ackerman says that "the customer is Queen". This tells us so much more than "the person buying our goods is supreme". The word "Queen" conjures up images of reverence, dignity, respect and worship. People latch onto that. Peter Searle talks about the Family Concept (see Chapter 8). In short, this is the vision that he holds for VW: that they should develop harmonious relationships with all parties that subscribe to their basic philosophy of pride (in a positive sense), quality and service. In using the word "family", there is no need to describe in detail the relationship. We know it. We've been brought up and are bringing up in it. It's also damn emotive. That is the management of meaning. And language is the critical currency.

Wherever we went in Toyota, we found people talking the same language. That is customer satisfaction, and care about customers, people and products. It starts at the top and works its way down. Toyota people use this language when they talk to each other. Brand Pretorius uses it in the frequent video messages he sends around the company. In analysing the transcripts of our interviews, we found that everyone we spoke to punctuated their discussion with these very words. They knew what they meant, where they come from, why they should strive towards their achievement and how they could make their best contribution to getting there.

This then becomes the vocabulary of the organisation. It forms the basis of the organisation's value system, the things organisational members identify with — culture. It becomes the basis on which "things are done around here". We pick up the theme in Chapter 10. The point of this juncture is that **the leaders of super-performing companies must be the people that define the culture and who act as custodians of that culture.** Peter Searle is our best example of this sort of leader. When asked how he considered a Managing Director of a large South African business could make his best contribution, he replied:

".. by understanding the corporate culture that he wants and living by that corporate culture. By getting everyone on board with that culture and living it himself."

LEADERS COMMUNICATE

We have already dealt with how the leader communicates his vision, and in doing so makes meaning. We deal here with the more mundane and everyday communication.

We have stressed the importance of communication as a vital element in liberating human potential. It is the conductor which carries the electricity around our super-performing companies. We have also spoken about how doing it properly involves a great deal of communication.

The point we make here is that the Chief Executive sets the level and tone of communication in the organisation. As with all processes, he drives communication. He is the wellspring. Certainly amongst the super-performers, we found Chief Executives spending an inordinate amount of time communicating.

We found leader communication to fall into two categories. One is of the informational type, i.e. communication to keep people informed and to keep the leader in touch. The other is of the motivational type.

Keeping People Informed and Keeping in Touch

Every evening of his working life Raymond Ackerman records on tape his thoughts on the events of the day. This is then typed up by his secretary and placed on file. It constitutes a detailed diary of his business life. As such, it serves a number of purposes, but most importantly, it provides him with material for his monthly open letter. It details all the events of the company in a very personal way, discussing openings, events at openings, promotions and various other factors affecting the company. He dishes out praise where it is due, comments on things needing improvement and, of course, reminds people of the company philosophy. Pick 'n Pay people simply love it.

As we all know, people get the mutters very easily. One of the favourite mutters is "We weren't told about that" or "They never tell us these things". People need to feel part of something, to know where their life's work fits into the broader scheme of things. This is what our super-performing companies pay attention to. People in companies like VW, Pick 'n Pay, Beer Division, Mathieson & Ashley and Seardel know these things. These companies are awash with open letters, in-house bulletins, staff letters, regular company gatherings and the like.

It goes without saying that the communication should be two way. Hence, the leader needs to listen to keep in touch. Says Ackerman:

> *"It's those little things. If top management can just try and keep in touch — and it's damn hard — it's the hardest thing to keep in touch. To go round and talk and listen and act on the small things. It makes people realise that you're not just a big amorphous company."*

Communicating for Motivation

Raymond Ackerman tells us: "I get communicated right through on weddings and graduations of children of all staff. And I invite them around and send them flowers — I probably send five or six bowls of flowers every day of my life. And I write about 60 letters a day, which may interest you." Wow! That's taking communication with staff seriously.

Again, you'll find leaders of super-performing companies

taking the time to tell people that their efforts were noted and appreciated. To tell them that they care. That the leader understands the pride a parent feels when a child graduates. It shows that the company cares for the employee. And this is reciprocated.

LEADERS DRAW PEOPLE AROUND THEM

With few exceptions, we found super-performing companies to have not only excellent leaders, but excellent management teams. These leaders are able to keep top people in all their key positions.

Clearly, good people will be attracted to the type of leader who knows where he's going and generates excitement. The point that really interested us was the best business leaders we met, whilst having big egos (almost without exception!) really believe that they can't do it on their own. They explicitly acknowledge that they need these good people to support them and turn their attention to getting and keeping these people.

ATTRIBUTES OF THE SUCCESSFUL LEADER

We are sure you will agree that the person who gets all of these things right is, well, quite a guy! We spent some time further analysing our research material and trying to find out as much as we could about these successful business leaders. That is, having seen some of the things that they do, what sort of people are they? Clearly, there are no universal statements that can be made — Peter Searle and Frankie Robarts are poles apart. However, our examination of the leaders of these super-performing companies suggests a personality and psychological profile that looks a bit like this: he is a strong character, ambitious, has a bold attitude to risk, is disciplined, has a strong people orientation, is committed almost to the point of obsession, consistent, an expert in his field and, most significantly, is both intellectual and emotional.

An important point that came through the research was that there is truth to the adage that for each organisation, there is the right leader at the right time. Fred Haupt, Group General Manager: Corporate Services of Edgars, dealt with this at some length and it certainly explains much of the success behind

Edgars. The company got off the ground with Sydney Press, the entrepreneur. Entrepreneurs tend to drive hard towards a vision and draw good people around them. However, they do not sit comfortably in formal structures. Yet most successful organisations require consolidation at some point. Enter Bellamy the consummate professional manager. Life cycle theory also suggests that the formalisation associated with consolidation tends to cause centralisation and a stifling of organisational skills. Enter Vic Hammond, the self-styled Mad Merchant, bent on improving merchant skills and on decentralising.

Having made this point, we went out a little more on each of the attributes of the successful South African business leader.

Leaders are Strong-Charactered

One would expect any business leader to be strong-willed, independent, forceful. We would like to suggest, however, that there are three other elements to the attribute of "strong-charactered" that we found to be prevalent in the leaders of the super-performers.

Trust and Reliability

Trust is essential to all organisations. And the main determinant of trust is reliability. That is, people who deal with the leader will always know where he is coming from and what he stands for. It is unlikely, therefore, that a response from this leader will surprise subordinates. People will always know where they stand with him.

There is a wonderful story about John Paul II on a visit to the USA. At a press conference, a reporter asked how the Pope could account for allocating funds to build a swimming pool at the papal summer palace. He responded quickly: "I like to swim. Next question." The point is that he did not, as many other people might have, rationalise about the health and fitness reasons or claim that the funds came from a special source. Research studies have shown time and time again that people would much rather follow individuals they can count on, even when they disagree with their viewpoint, than people they agree with but who shift positions frequently.

In speaking to the subordinates of the leaders of the super-performing companies, we found that this element of reliability was of major importance to them. Not all of them liked their leaders — but liking is much less important in a relationship of trust than is reliability.

Leadership Begins at Home

To us, it goes without saying that the successful business leader needs to be big-minded if he is genuinely going to give other people credit for the things he believes he did (remember Vic Hammond or Farrel Ratner?) or if he is to draw around him people who may be better than him without feeling threatened. This requires a deep inner self-confidence which comes from knowing oneself — one's strengths and weaknesses — and also from understanding the frailty of human competence. People do make mistakes! Including the best business leaders.

Almost without exception, leaders of super-performing companies know very well what they are good at and what they are bad at. People like Chris Seabrooke and Raymond Ackerman will tell you quite unashamedly of their mistakes — even failures.

Grinding the Grind

The third prevalent feature of the strong-charactered leader is that he is disciplined. Now, to get this concept of discipline in perspective you need to appreciate that most of the people we saw had f . . .-you money by anyone's standards. They really don't need to work. Also, that whilst many people aspire to the glamorous components of the leader's job, any leader will tell you that at least 50 per cent of his job is unexciting. It therefore requires discipline for Mike Benn to dictate the minutes for the tenth meeting of the day when he would rather engage the advertising people in marketing strategy. Or not to forego his Monday footstomp from café to café for something important that crops up. It requires discipline for Raymond Ackerman not to write five instead of 10 letters after a store visit. We could carry on and on with example after example. Yet the point is simple — **leaders of super-performing companies understand the grind that will inevitably envelop a goodly proportion of their working day, and discipline themselves to doing it.**

201

The application of this discipline extends well beyond the day-to-day grind. In Chapter 2 we dealt with the concept of focus. Quite frankly, focus requires discipline and this requires disciplined leadership. The sort of discipline that will lead Philip Coutts-Trotter to turn down an acquisition when the numbers look superb, but where the business fit looks problematic. The sort of discipline that will lead Winky Ringo to sit on a pile of cash until the right acquisition presents itself.

Leaders are Ambitious

It took us a while to get to see Dr Albert Wessels, founder of Toyota South Africa. This octogenarian still puts in a hard day's work. In his own polite way, he set aside our agenda. His belief is that if you want to understand what it has taken to build a successful company, you need to look to the leader. And then the most important thing in that leader is ambition. He related to us the story of his early years.

He was born in 1908. His parents had been wealthy farmers before the war, but their farm had been ruined during the war. They were, to use his words, economically ruined. He explained that he, like many Afrikaners in similar circumstances, was inflamed with three pervasive feelings: an overwhelming hatred for imperialism in general, and the British in particular; a burning desire to redress the economic ruination of their people; and a philosophy of not sitting on the *ashoop*, but going out and actively attending to the task of redressing the economic situation of their people. This was ambition! And in describing his own achievements — which he managed to do with the utmost humility — he ascribes these achievements to his burning ambition, which he traces back to the days when he began remembering.

Of course, the simple will to achieve is but a starting point. However, it is one of those *sine qua non* starting points and this makes it worthy of mention.

Leaders are Experts

Fred Haupt relates the story of the opening of the new Edgars store in Sandton — a big event in the development of the third generation store concept. The opening had been fully subjected

202

to the Edgars treatment of being carefully researched and thought through. They were poised for a spectacular success. Vic Hammond walked through the store and announced that it wasn't quite right; in spite of what the research said, there were some inconsistencies in the assortments. Out went the crimplene. A number of key displays were drastically changed. All would agree that the changes were for the better.

It's no surprise that each and every leader of our super-performing companies has spent the predominant portion of his working life in one industry. This is, in fact, the only characteristic that these business leaders have in common. A recent edition of *Fortune* magazine carried a cover story entitled "The Seven Keys to Business Leadership". Key number five is, "Be An Expert. From boardroom to mail room, everyone had better understand that you know what you're talking about." As *Fortune* sets it out **"The troops will follow a lot more willingly if they are confident that the man or woman in front knows at least as much as they do."**

We found that what Peter Searle doesn't know about cars probably isn't worth knowing. Likewise Philip Coutts-Trotter on the garment industry, Mike Benn on snacks, Frankie Robarts on stationery. And so on and so on.

Item 1 on Steve's agenda with Robin Hamilton centred on strategy. Hamilton responded:

> *"I've run into a bit of a brick wall on Item 1. It's not my kind of language, really, and when I read it, it isn't very clear to me."*

Hamilton enjoys playing simple. The fact of the matter is, he knows his business backwards and inside out. His employees know that, and that seems to focus the mind on doing it right. Said one:

> *"He's a clever bugger, actually — you don't have to tell him this for God's sake. When he asks you a question, he's just checking his answer, that's what he's doing. He's already worked it out."*

He spent time taking Steve through aerial photographs of bottling

203

plants, showing why this configuration worked and this one didn't. He knew all the nooks and crannies, and was clearly in his element.

Leaders Like People

It is surely a truism that the successful leader is the one who gets things done through people. He spends his working day interfacing with people. He drives them, inspects them, excites them, liberates their potential, makes meaning for them, draws them around him, cares about them. No surprise, then, that leaders of super-performing companies like people! Aaron Searll had this to say:

"I think the leader must take a deep interest in people. If he doesn't do that, I don't think he will be able to build morale or build up enthusiasm."

Leaders are Committed

The successful corporate leader is committed, and this commitment runs bone deep. Total commitment is one of the enabling factors between vision and success. Ability is also an enabling factor, but our research suggests that while ability is easy to find, commitment is in short supply.

Commitment involves facing some hard truths, such as the fact that like business and politics being inextricably bound, work and homelife also become inextricably bound. People like Raymond Ackerman can't wipe off their Pick 'n Pay commitment on the doormat with the dust from their shoes as they enter their homes in the evening. If he is to live it, that means all the time — wherever he is and whatever he does. It also means changing as a person, as Peter Searle found when he started changing the culture of Volkswagen. It will also mean that your life's work will consume your time and energy more than you would like it to.

Leaders Stride Boldly into the Dark

Innovation has become something of a buzzword, and not without reason. The research makes it clear that innovation is one of the critical factors distinguishing the super-performers from the also-rans. Unfortunately, one finds, innovation scares the hell out of most business leaders. "We're doing fine," they reason, which is exactly what happens in South Africa. In industry after industry, companies can make "acceptable" returns by doing well what they've done in the past.

Not so for the super-performers. We showed in Chapter 5 that **if the leader doesn't have a bold attitude to risk, there will be no ringing in of the new. Innovation will get stifled at the top.**

Some may remember a television interview with Raymond Ackerman some 10 years ago. When asked "What is it that you fear most?" he replied "The fear of losing what I have in Pick 'n Pay and having to start again — I could never risk that."

Sounds cautious, doesn't it? We studied with interest Pick 'n Pay's entry into Hypermarketing in 1975. Ackerman took a huge chance. Had the first hypermarket been a flop, it would have hurt them seriously. But he had made up his mind that the group needed it, and boldly set out to achieve success. Leaders such as Ackerman teach us that great things come from bold moves. Leaders, then, have to stride boldly into the dark.

Leaders are Intellectual and Emotional

Raymond Ackerman tells the story of an employee in Witbank who made an appeal to study further. The whole thing was complicated by the fact that his wife wasn't well and would be unable to work for a while. Ackerman arranged a meeting with the Personnel Director and local General Manager. He also sent flowers to the wife, and rang up to find out how the meeting had gone and how the wife was. The chap was moved to comment, "You know, Mr Ackerman, I just want you to know that whatever happens, I'll never leave Pick 'n Pay."

What we've said on leadership until now might apply with minor modification to business leaders the world over. What we have started to understand from our reading of American and British business literature, and from our admittedly limited contact with international executives, is that the western executive stereotype is that of a tough bastard, with the emphasis on bastard. Undoubtedly smart, but not the sort of person you would want as your friend — cold, calculating, unfeeling, programmed and, of course, totally ruthless.

How many of them have been parachuted into the company to

restructure, cut costs, squeeze out cash and then pull out? In those cosy social environments, it is quite possible to relegate the people issues to a top notch human resource department. If the chap is clever, he will factor their input into the decisions he makes.

South Africa, as we all know, is very different. Apart from anything else, the business leader needs to identify with totally different markets and categories of people, who may be driven by political philosophies ranging from ANC to AWB; with people whose means at the one extreme may dictate that they buy a Porsche and at the other extreme that they leave home at 05h00 to get three buses and one taxi to get to work at 07h30. This, the research suggests, requires a business leader who is able to use the heart and the gut as well as the head. Tough they all are, but bastards they ain't. The bastard would do for "sorting things out", but not to build a super-performer in the South African context.

---

10 Steps to Inspired Leadership

1. Develop a powerful vision of the organisation that embodies an invincible business concept and which captures the imagination of the people in the organisation and makes meaning for them.
2. Get into the driving seat, grip the steering wheel and put your foot down. It is the leader who sets the energy level and pace of the organisation.
3. Get to know the coalface, get down to it, and inspect it.
4. If your organisation doesn't excite you, bail out. Otherwise, show your excitement to all around you. It's infectious. So is apathy.
5. Demand the performance that your people are capable of. The chances are that they are more capable than you give them credit for.
6. Blaze the trail into new areas of opportunity.
7. Make meaning for the people in your organisation.
8. Communicate, communicate and communicate.
9. Draw people around you. The power of even the most impressive person is dwarfed by the power of a team that "hums".
10. Forget about the macho type who tells you that people's feelings and attitudes don't count. They are the bottom part of the iceberg. Understand them and engage the heart and the gut as well as the head. Soft is hard.

CHAPTER TEN

MAY THE FORCE BE WITH YOU

The Invisible Hand

Poised on the threshold of the 1980s, Volkswagen South Africa's management was looking forward to a very successful decade. On the strength of the ubiquitous Beetle, and their new model, the Golf, VW's market share had increased steadily to 20 per cent. Their market position was strong, profits were good. The new product was a big success. Dealers were profitable. By 1982, however, the picture had changed. In a declining market VW's market share had crashed from 21 per cent to 10,6 per cent. Profitability was appalling. The dealers — and their customers — had lost faith. Management knew they had to redefine the rules of the game at VW. A massive investment was made in facilities and a whole new approach to quality and customer satisfaction was implemented. The result? By 1988 delivery quality had increased 36 per cent. Customer complaints per vehicle in their first year of ownership had decreased by more than 40 per cent. By jolting market share back up above 20 per cent, VW SA had become the only motor manufacturer worldwide ever to double market share over so short a period. But how did VW get on top of their quality so effectively?

The next time you shop at a Pick 'n Pay supermarket ask any staffer what the company philosophy is. Odds are that "Consumer sovereignty" will be the reply. Ask how consumer sovereignty will be achieved. "By the four legs of the table", will be the answer. In Raymond Ackerman's own words, that simple philosophy — "The customer is Queen" — and the way that it is achieved "are very deeply embedded in every Pick 'n Pay person." How do Pick 'n Pay people come to share the philosophy so consistently, so deeply?

Durban-based Suncrush bottles Coca-Cola, Sparletta and Schweppes in probably the world's largest proliferation of pack sizes and flavours. The company operates 10 bottling plants which deliver directly to some 15 000 outlets around the country. In the year to June 1988 the company made pre-tax profits of R36 million on turnover of R230 million. The all-in annual return to shareholders over the five years 1983 to 1988 was a sparkling 58 per cent. Suncrush is a large and highly competent organisation. But don't ask Executive Chairman Robin Hamilton to show you the reports that the plant GM's send up the line. He can't give them to you — not because he doesn't want to, but because they don't exist. Incredibly, this tightly run company, the darling of the financial press, has no programme of formal reporting from operations to Head Office. Strange to tell, and stranger yet. Ask about the staff turnover at Head Office, and Hamilton will tell you this story:

"I had an interesting conversation with a guy once. He asked 'Why do people leave Suncrush?' And I said 'They don't leave.' And he said 'But what happens when you want them to leave, when you find them unsatisfactory?' I said 'They leave', and he said 'But you told me they don't leave.' I said 'Right.'

If you press him for statistics, Hamilton will tell you that only two managers have left the Head Office staff in 15 years. There have been no departures from the executive floor in all that time. What is this phenomenon that keeps a large successful company so stable yet so flexible?

Venturecomm is the name that Cashbuild uses for the five-person group in each branch that meets weekly to discuss matters of common concern and to take decisions on the running of the branch. Four of the five Venturecomm members are elected by branch personnel and take responsibility for the portfolios of Safety, Labour, Merchandise and Quality of Work Life. The fifth member of the team is the Branch Manager — who carries the Operations portfolio. Position in the branch is not a prerequisite for election; ordinary labourers (or "caddies") are eligible to be elected, and often are.

We attended a Venturecomm meeting in the Springs branch one morning in late 1988. The meeting starts when everyone is ready. It takes a while because two of the team are busy with a big order, but eventually all are clustered in the manager's small elevated office looking out over the main floor of the branch. We are formally welcomed as guests of the meeting, as is George Galela, the branch Stock Controller. Over the course of the following two hours, and in the most thorough, democratic and responsible way, the group works through the weekly agenda. Branch Manager Mannie Merckel reports the previous week's sales figures against budget, from which follows detailed discussion on pricing and discounting. Cosmo Busakwe (Quality of Worklife) raises items that were discussed at the previous evening's full-branch CARE Group meeting. Lucas Mabena (Labour) provides feedback on productivity. Edward Mtsweni (Safety), although only a labourer, offers wisdom beyond his 21 years. Daniel Mhlapo (Merchandising) suggests ways to prevent the theft of the small accessories that are boxed with taps. At one point Cosmo pops out for a few minutes to help load cement. As the meeting progresses it transpires that George Galela has been invited to the meeting to discuss a warning letter he recently received for insubordination. George had contravened the Cashbuild philosophy by threatening his superior in a moment of frustration. After presenting his case to the team and hearing their firm but good-natured decision that the warning letter should stand for six months, George appeared satisfied. Agenda dealt with, the meeting closed. Handwritten minutes were signed by all — including ourselves. We came away impressed by the very real self-regulation we had witnessed. These people know what is expected of them — as a group and as individuals. But *how* do they know?

Volkswagen, Pick 'n Pay, Suncrush and Cashbuild — and many others amongst the super-performers — share a hard-to-define characteristic; each company seems possessed of a powerful but intangible guiding force, a co-ordinating system that is not a system, a control mechanism that is not a mechanism. In each of these companies people simply seem to know what to do, how to behave, and how to react to circumstances both unusual and everyday. There is about these organisations a consistency of purpose that stems not only from the formal and evident system of management that turns a bunch of people into an organisation, but which also springs spontaneously from a concordance, a likemindedness amongst their people. What we are witnessing here is the behavioural phenomenon that has come to be called corporate culture.

Of course the concept of corporate or organisational culture has been around for years, so we knew a good deal about it before we started our research. But we weren't prepared for what we would learn. Having spent some time with some of South Africa's best companies, we are now convinced beyond all doubt that **corporate culture is the most powerful, most complete form of organisational control that a company could wish to have. We have seen how this unseen attribute can far exceed in effectiveness the formal management system it complements.** Newly exposed, as we are, to the potency of culture, we have been encouraged by the growing appreciation on the part of South African businessmen of the importance of corporate culture, and while there is still a generally limited understanding of the nuts and bolts of culture, the topic now receives regular airing.

In the remainder of this chapter we will try to describe the features of corporate culture in plain English. We will see how strong corporate cultures provide our super-performers with forceful but informal integrating mechanisms, controlling the organisation by guiding behaviour. We will see that a strong corporate culture can effectively bridge the diversity of ethnic and political subgroups that exist in almost every South African organisation. We'll see too that corporate culture helps motivate the organisation towards a common set of goals by communicating a shared vision to all employees. By reference to our top performing companies, we will describe some of the more frequently encountered attributes of successful corporate cultures. We will note that no two organisations have identical corporate cultures and we'll deduce that there is no one *right culture*, that each company needs something different to respond to the demands of its markets and to accommodate the needs of its own people. We will see that culture changes with time as the

210

firm grows and matures, and that, conversely, organisations change as culture strengthens. We will look at how to measure corporate culture and we will see how knowledge of its own culture affords a firm profound insight into the way that it operates. Perhaps most importantly we will see how the super-performers go about *managing* their cultures. We will look at the difficulties in merging two cultures. Zooming in, we will see that a range of subcultures exists within most organisations and that part of the challenge of culture management is the identification of these subcultures and the recognition of their value — and their threat. We will examine corporate climate, that manifestation of organisational happiness so closely related to organisational culture. Our chapter will close with the assertion that every organisation can harness the force-field of corporate culture, and that culture management activity should be on every South African executive's weekly agenda. But first . . .

Some Plain English

Ja, well no fine, but what exactly is corporate culture? We're glad you asked that question, because although "corporate culture" is one of today's trendiest business buzz-phrases, it is also one of the least understood. The burgeoning body of corporate culture literature offers many definitions, but we like to think of an organisation's culture as its *personality*.

A firm's culture dictates what sort of organisation it will be like to work in, to deal with, to compete against. It provides the answer to the question "What sort of place is this?" It gives pointers to "the way things are done around here". A corporation's culture is that set of unwritten behavioural norms that shapes individuals' responses to worklife occurrences. The stronger their culture the more quickly and easily will individuals make those responses and the more consistent and effective will those responses be — both over time and across the organisation.

And where does corporate culture come from? The most important of a culture's several sources is the Chief Executive, or the founder of the firm. The top man's personal values and beliefs, his management style, his *modus operandi,* his ambitions and his dreams — these are the weft and the warp of corporate culture. Weave through these the values of managers and of employees, the business style that prevails in the firm's particular industry; patch in some of those war stories — the legendary exploits of corporate heroes past and present that lend such colourful detail — and you have it; the complex, colourful and textured fabric of corporate culture.

Culture Power

We've talked in general terms about some of the results that a strong corporate culture can bring. Let's look more closely at the most powerful and important of those effects at work in the winning companies.

Organisational Integration

In Chapter 2 we saw how almost all the super-performers subscribe to the philosophy of decentralisation. They delegate as much activity as possible as far down the line as they can. With that delegated activity go authority and responsibility — devolved far away from Head Office. But decentralisation brings with it the need for co-ordination — formal and informal processes that keep the organisation from becoming disorganised. Organisational structures, lines of reporting, information systems, communication systems — these are the tools most obviously at hand for knitting the pieces of the decentralised organisation together. Readily offered in textbooks and by business schools, they are the integrating mechanisms that are easiest to think about, easiest to design, easiest to build. But while no organisation can do without structures, without communication and information systems, if these are all that the organisation relies on for co-ordination it is missing out on the most powerful integrating process of all: corporate culture. **Without exception, we saw culture power working in each of our top performers; like an invisible natural force field, corporate culture keeps the organisation aligned.**

Graham Mackay, SAB's Beer Division MD, is the manager's manager. Our own file note on Graham reads:

> *Ultimate managing machine/system, piercing intellect, efficient of word and action, unemotional, cool (but not cold), dispassionate, wise, long fuse, decisive, integrative.*

Macho stuff indeed. This man does not eat quiche! But if we have led you to think that Mackay isn't the kind of guy that would want any help from a fuzzy concept like corporate culture we have misled you. Graham understands culture power. He calls it a binding cohesive force; strong, spoken about and identified with. "Our culture makes it possible for us to run the company in a friendly, informal way — not in a grandiose style."

Meyer Kahn calls SAB a friendly place. "We're just a bunch of *losgatte*," he says. Notwithstanding Meyer's requirement for a *daily* sales report, Mackay says that SAB isn't a company that is run by the numbers.

A successful fashion retailer needs two kinds of people: it needs creative right-brained types to buy the ranges that are going to sell in the season ahead and it needs rational left-brained people to get those ranges into the stores at the right time and at the right cost. For business to hum, the fashion retailer must create conditions in his organisation for these two types to co-exist, to co-operate closely. Vic Hammond understands how culture power helps achieve this co-existence and co-operation. Edgars has strong values of discipline, doing the whole job and professionalism. With these shared concerns the high energy, high ego, high temperament fashion buyer can sit right next to her more rational, more cautious, more considered merchandising counterpart to plan the next season's ranges. Culture channels those strong creative impulses and provides a cushion for this critically important relationship, helping foster a condition that Hammond calls "stability in motion".

Bridging Human Diversity

Corporate culture offers too an integration of another kind. **A strong corporate culture will bridge across a bewildering array of ethnic and political subgroups whose influence might otherwise confuse the organisation's authority and responsibility structures.** On this score, the argument for strong corporate cultures becomes all the more compelling in the South African context. Particularly in Japan, but also in Europe, corporations function within very much more homogeneous ethnic milieux than we do here. While the ethnic origins of North Americans are perhaps as

213

diverse as our own, both the USA and Canada have relatively strong institutional value systems that are rooted in generations of commitment to democracy, equal rights and the free market economy. As has often been said before, South Africa is probably the most diverse society in the world, with every shade of political opinion, every conceivable skin pigment, dozens of different languages, and wildly diverse ethnic origins and customs. How, in all of this, do we create some cohesion, some consistency in our organisations?

In Chapter 8 we referred to Volkswagen's superb screen advertising. Aside from the product-specific commercials for Golfs, Jettas and Audis, are VW's wonderful corporate adverts. One in particular features a crowd of VW employees standing together to sing the company song; black and white, managers and workers, all stand side by side and sing. The camera pans across their faces, resting so briefly on Peter Searle's that you would miss him in the crowd if you didn't know what he looked like. There is real emotion in Searle's face, as there is in each of the faces around him. The screen fades to black. "Isn't that what you'd expect from Volkswagen?" is the closing question. In the course of a few short seconds, as you have watched, you have been impressed with the shared commitment that these VW people — The Volkswagen Family — have to building quality cars. Could that be real you ask, or is it just another clever commercial? Let us assure you that it is real. We were privileged to attend one of the regular regional presentations that VW gives to its dealers. In the course of the programme the entire gathering listened intently. You could have heard a pin drop. By the end of it there were tears in the eyes of many of those tough motor men.

Peter Searle has been carefully building this amazingly strong culture at Volkswagen since 1982. As he says, the only way to deal with the problems that occur when you have ANC and AWB members working side-by-side is to establish a corporate culture that is stronger than anything else. When values such as *pride* and *belonging* start taking hold in the workplace, he says, they will become the predominant force. At VW those myriad shades of ethnic origin and political persuasion have run together to make a new corporate colour that gently and pervasively tinges the whole organisation.

214

Shared Vision

As consultants, our work takes us into new organisations many times a year. Whether an assignment is large or small, we spend as much time as we possibly can getting to know the place, getting to know the products, getting to know the way things work. Most of all — and this is the real privilege our occupation affords — we spend time getting to know the people. We talk to both management staff and workers, sometimes in groups but usually one-to-one, because that's the best way to find out how a person really feels about his or her company, what the satisfactions are and what the frustrations are. Talking to people across the length and breadth of the organisation helps us understand the different perspectives different groups and individuals have of the company, and of each other. We find that these views usually differ — not unexpectedly. What is interesting is the *extent* to which they differ. Sometimes the divergence in perceptions of the same organisational reality is hardly credible, and as we talk to people we are staggered by how differently they see things. Are they all watching the same movie? we ask ourselves.

At Pick 'n Pay everyone is watching the same movie. They know what the organisation stands for, what it is trying to do. They know that the company's mission is consumerism — interpreting and satisfying customers' needs by selling quality products at competitive prices. They know that the customer is Queen and that the table symbolising the Pick 'n Pay philosophy has four legs: administration, merchandise, sales promotion and people. They know that their organisation is committed to organic growth, that it is actively involved in the communities it serves and that, as it grows, new positions will be filled only by promotion from within. Just one movie showing here folks — and everyone watching. It is a consistency of vision that flows from several sources; from leadership, from strategy, and most of all, from culture.

So we see that corporate culture, although mainly about values, is also about vision. To be strong, a culture will need to convey a sense of common purpose throughout the organisation, and at the same time, the stronger the culture the more effectively will it serve as the medium to convey that purpose. At SAB and

215

Suncrush, in Cashbuild, Toyota and Cadbury's, and in many of the other super-performers strong cultures promote shared vision.

Minimal Politics

Most of the super-performers evidenced a low level of political activity — corporate political activity that is. On reflection, that may not be surprising. Organisational politics thrives on uncertainty and personal insecurity, it thrives on divergent expectations and conflicting objectives. Choke off these nutrients with a strong corporate culture and the political parasite will recede, wither and perhaps even disappear altogether. The mainstay of their culture is supportiveness. Hugh Mathew, Foschini's outgoing Deputy Chairman;

> *"I'm sure that our success has something to do with this culture of supportiveness that we've engendered. People are confident. They don't have to worry about their jobs, or that someone is cutting their throats or stabbing them in the back. They have to worry about whether or not they are doing what they must do successfully, and whether someone else needs assistance."*

Continuity

Robin Hamilton, controlling shareholder and Executive Chairman of Suncrush, is quite evidently the wellspring of much of his company's culture. What if he were to fall ill, or God forbid, be run over by the proverbial bus — or Mynah? We put this question to Dennis Smit, one of Suncrush's two Divisional General Managers. "Would you sell your Suncrush shares if the unthinkable happened?" we asked.

> *"No, no. Robin has brought a certain sort of ethic into the place, but I think it's strong enough in the guys to carry on with it. There's this anti-bureaucracy thing that is very strong in all the GM's and myself. No, I wouldn't sell Suncrush shares if he was run over by a bus. I think the company is strong enough to run as it is."*

Cashbuild provides another example of the continuity that a strong culture brings. Although Albert Koopman was probably more responsible than any other individual for creating the Cashbuild culture, it has not only survived but probably continued to strengthen since his departure in 1987. It helped of course that most of the senior people at Cashbuild have been there almost from the start, and that the new MD, Gerald Haumant, was Albert's right-hand man from the outset, but the point is that a strong culture, once established, is likely to survive the passing on of some key individuals. Although the culture will undoubtedly change under the new order, it will provide important continuity through periods of management change.

We have seen in each of the winning companies the extraordinary power of a strong corporate culture. Organisational integration, bridging human diversity, shared vision, minimal politics and continuity all flow from it. Perhaps these benefits seem soft, but in reality they add up to superior bottom-line financial performance.

Cultural Types — a Rainbow of Flavours

Like fingerprints, no two corporate cultures are the same. Each organisation has its own unique culture that is the aggregate of that organisation's many cultural attributes. Corporate cultures don't come in plain vanilla; each is more like a special sundae made of little scoops of many flavours. When one starts to analyse each of these once-off culture recipes, however, one begins to isolate some common ingredients. In fact most corporate cultures are combinations of relatively few distinct traits or attributes. Let's pick out some of the most important from the cultural profiles of the super-performers.

A Performance Ethos

Performance is important to our top companies. Yes, that does sound trivial, but we do know of companies that would like to think of themselves as successful but which do not really subscribe to a performance ethos. **In a performance-based culture there is a focus on results at every level; corporate, group, divisional, departmental and especially personal.** Martin Glatt of Mathieson & Ashley talks about their "performance orientation". They have a "large infrastructure of profit incentives" aimed at rewarding

217

margins, not volume. Their targets, incentives, budgets and plans all combine to give the company a culture of performance.

Recall from Chapter 2 that when Peter Bester took over as Group Chief Executive of Cadbury-Schweppes he and his team identified the need to shift the organisation's culture. They had to make it more market-oriented, more innovative and more performance-based. Of the last, Bester says:

> *"We had to deal with complacency in the business. Quite interesting. It was the first time in my life I'd ever come across it. In some divisions for example salaries were averaged — all 14 guys in the same grade earned precisely the same amount. Almost as though there couldn't be any individualism and no emphasis on individual performance. The Divisional Director's philosophy was that that way there would be no destructive competition between them."*

Cadbury-Schweppes have since turned that around completely. Now they too have complex structures to stimulate and reward the kind of performance that the company regards as important; there is a share participation scheme, currently only extended to about 35 of the "top guys that do have a major impact on the business", and there is a strongly performance-orientated bonus scheme for senior and middle management. The performance-based component of remuneration at senior management level is around 40 per cent; at middle management level around 25 per cent. These are figures that focus the mind! Bester recognises that they need to push the reward-for-performance philosophy even further down the organisation, right to the factory floor in fact. It will take time, because it's not easy, but the complexity of the schemes at middle and senior level did not deter them, so they are not fazed by the complexity that the factory level programme might require. Shifting to a performance-based culture has already made a potent contribution to the group's strategic revitalisation — and being a bit of a stickler for performance himself, Bester isn't likely to stop halfway.

An Orientation To Customers

Super-performers do it with customers. As a bumper-sticker that phrase may not have a lot of potential, but there's no doubt about it: South Africa's best companies are besotted with their customers. We talked about this at some length in Chapter 3, on marketing. We saw how Raymond Ackerman — the walking, talking personification of customer care — has integrally bound consumerism into Pick 'n Pay's way of life. So too at Edgars, Cashbuild and Cadbury's; each organisation lives by a market-oriented attitude. At VW and at arch-rival Toyota, they believe that their customer interface — the dealer — must be as customer-oriented as they are themselves, so they spend real money getting the dealers up to speed. Both Toyota and VW check up on their dealers too, they constantly canvass their customers to make sure the dealers are looking after them. SAB have always considered themselves a marketing company. Yes, they worry about what their end user, the happy lager swiller, wants, but their first-line customer is the retailer, and be that retailer Jan Pickard, Lucky Michaels or one of Soweto's hundreds of shebeen operators, he gets SAB's full attention. **It's not just that these great organisations are good at marketing — they certainly are, but it's more than that; each of these companies has built into its collective psyche the conviction that the customer is the most important person in the world.**

Respect for the Individual

Cashbuild's participative approach to managing their organisation provides a fine example of another of corporate culture's fundamental dimensions. Respect for individual dignity is deeply embedded in Cashbuild's culture. Quantities of time, money and energy go into the development of each and every Cashbuild employee. Nevertheless it is not the rights of the individual that feature most prominently in the Cashbuild philosophy, but the rights, duties and obligations of the Team. Yes the philosophy booklet decrees in bold type that **People must be dealt with fairly** and that **We are an open and free culture with every person in the Organisation having access to any Line Manager in the event of grievances**, but the emphasis remains on the individual as part of the Team. The individual does get real respect, but at the same time he is left under no illusions as to where his duty lies.

219

Supportiveness

Closely akin to respect for the individual, supportiveness goes a little further. While individual respect is about giving cognisance to each employee's personal needs, aspirations and feelings, supportiveness is to do with backing that individual up in the workplace, providing support structures, safety nets, endorsing imperfect decisions that were made in good faith, spotting the signals that shout "I need help but I'm too proud to ask for it." Earlier in this chapter we heard Hugh Mathew talk about the supportiveness of Foschini's culture. Cashbuild, Pick 'n Pay, Suncrush, SAB and many more of the super-performers have a good measure of supportiveness in their respective culture recipes. But supportive doesn't mean soft. As Seardel's Aaron Searll says:

"If the guy's not doing the job you must change the situation quickly. Don't wait — it doesn't get better. One must cut the loss quickly or make a change as quickly as possible."

An Obsession with Quality

As we have seen in Chapter 3 on marketing and Chapter 7 on doing things properly, many of South Africa's top companies are almost obsessed with quality. VW and SAB both went through the quality trough — SAB in the late fifties and early sixties and VW 20 years later. Both companies saw improving product quality as central to their strategies for recovery. Both regard quality as the key component of their corporate culture. As Peter Searle says of Volkswagen's push for quality:

"Our sequence was, first of all, a tremendous concentration on quality which started back in 1982. That started to show itself in the product round about '83, '84, and was not really perceived by the public until perhaps '86, '87. We had to get the product right first and then we could start talking to our dealer organisations about customer service. The first thing we had to do was to get everyone to appreciate it was their responsibility — not just that of the Quality Assurance Department."

So Searle and his team embarked on a culture-building programme explicitly targeted at improving quality.

Innovation

Chapter 5 showed how prominently innovation features on the agendas of super-performing companies. **With increasing environmental turbulence and increasingly rapid change, innovation is becoming ever more important as a component of corporate culture.** Suncrush, as we have seen, is a particularly innovative company. Executive Chairman Robin Hamilton talks about the origination of some very innovative distribution initiatives the company is taking to increase penetration into the black market:

> *"The innovation in that regard has come from out in the field. If you're looking at what's different now to what was current a few years ago I would say that I'm trying to push the progress of the company — the innovation — to take place out there in the field. I'm trying to create a climate that encourages innovation and the appointment of the kind of people who are not going to be interested in reading the manual."*

Participation

Participation is at the core of Cashbuild's culture. It follows from the belief that **the opinion of a few is always better than the opinion of one, no matter how skilled or experienced the one may be.** Says Gerald Haumant:

> *"Common sense is something that is not so common, and it never emanates from one person. It's our problem in business, especially in the typical occidental environment, that as you go up the ladder you feel that your judgement is becoming sounder. It's not true. It's selectively sounder, but you've lost the overall perspective of things."*

Hence the company's emphasis on participative decision making. It follows too from the traditional black management system of Ubuntu, in terms of which the group predominates, and the individual emerges only from the group. As Albert Koopman says, "The concept of the *managed*, not the manager, shall apply!"

… And a Host of Other Speciality Tastes

The previous few paragraphs have dealt with some of the more common features discernible in the cultures of our super-performers. There are, of course, many more dimensions to corporate culture. Specific research conducted outside of this project together with our colleagues has identified at least 27 distinct and fairly commonly encountered dimensions, such as seriousness, response to change, risk propensity, independence of action, external diplomacy, internal competitiveness, level of discipline, loyalty, peer supportiveness, creativity, goal consistency, time consciousness, secrecy, experience, speed of decision making and many more.

Rum, Raisin and Chocolate Chip, Please

You have decided to go ahead with a culture change programme. You're standing at the culture counter, looking through the glass at the myriad options. The sales person is waiting, scoop poised. What combinations of cultural attributes will be best for your organisation?

Well, to begin with, **the culture that you need will be determined, at least in part, by the characteristics of the industry your company operates in. What does the customer value in your industry?** Quality? Build quality into your culture. Service? Build in customer service. Innovation? Safety? Creativity? Build them in. Perhaps you are in a commodity industry like sugar, cement or coal — where low-cost production is of paramount importance. Then build your culture on cost-consciousness. Or in a highly capital intensive industry where new production capacity takes a long time and a lot of money to install — the petrochemical industry for example. Then focus your culture on forecasting and planning-down the risk of those massive investment decisions.

More specifically, task is an important determinant of culture. Success in the construction business depends on superior planning and control of a host of related decisions and activities. The task thus dictates that the culture of a successful construction company is likely to be fairly formal — formal reporting, formal feedback and communication meetings and so on. A research laboratory or an advertising agency will be quite different. There the nature of the task will be more creative, less structured, to encourage intellectual or creative expression. Cultures in those organisations will need to be supportive of those conditions.

Culture must also be consistent with strategy. The two are inextricably interdependent. Culture can and should be built to give force to strategic initiatives — VW, Plessey, Pick 'n Pay, SAB, Cadbury-Schweppes and Suncrush all provide object lessons here. And, at the same time, strategic decisions cannot be made without cognisance of the existing corporate culture and the changes that might reasonably be effected to that culture over a period of time. It would be unreasonable, for instance, for a large insurance company to plan a rapid reorientation to the black market if its middle management structure is largely staffed by conservative whites.

Which leads to a final pointer towards the design of your desired corporate culture: your existing culture. Yes, you can change, but to a large extent how much you can change and even more importantly, how quickly you can change, depend critically on what you are now. **Understanding your existing corporate culture then is the first item on any agenda for culture management or culture change.** But more about that later.

The Wheel Turns

Not only does each company and industry situation require something special, but there's an added complication with corporate cultures: they aren't static. Cultures change as organisations grow and mature. We touched on this in our chapter on strategy when we suggested that different strategic management processes are going to be appropriate for different degrees of both centralisation and formalisation. The link here is that different combinations of centralisation and formalisation will create different corporate cultures — combinations that most firms will move through as they grow and mature. For example, the start-up company, typically characterised by high centralisation and low formalisation is likely to have a corporate culture in which "power" is the central value. As the level of formality increases the culture is likely to become "role" oriented — people doing things because the rule book says so. Moving to greater decentralisation, the emphasis is likely to shift away from "role" towards "achievement" — a culture which values what people actually achieve. (Hooray!) In the final combination, where decentralisation and informality come together, the culture is one that regards "support" as paramount — people support one another, perhaps even to the detriment of the organisation.[1] As we saw earlier, there are many more dimensions to corporate culture than formality and centralisation, so the model sketched here is rudimentary indeed, but we hope it serves to illustrate the point; as organisations grow and mature their cultures are likely to change.

There is a corollary to the previous paragraph, and for once, perhaps, the corollary affords more insight than the original proposition. We have said that culture changes as organisations grow and mature. Now we propose that organisations change as culture strengthens. Early on in the chapter we saw how corporate culture is a powerful informal mechanism for integrating and co-ordinating the activities of the organisations. It follows then that as its culture strengthens, an organisation can begin to replace formal control and co-ordination systems with the informal control that a strong culture brings. The organisation can afford actually to take out some of its formal systems. At the same time, strengthening the corporate culture should allow for greater decentralisation through the greater power of informal control. And the benefits? Well, informal systems typically operate much faster than formal ones and decentralised organisations are typically more responsive than centralised ones, so, as corporate culture strengthens, the organisation is likely to become more nimble, more responsive, more *flexible*.

Our best example of a highly decentralised, very informal organisation is — not coincidentally — one of our culture champions, Suncrush. We believe that some of that company's major strategic moves, and the speed with which they have been made, attest to exceptional flexibility. As examples one thinks of their lightning acquisition of Vaal Bottlers, their ground-breaking thrust into informal sector distribution of cold drinks and their

---

1 From Roger Harrison's Model.

ability to handle crazy demand peaks at staffing levels significantly lower than industry standards.

Measure it

Revisiting a point made earlier in this chapter, before you can begin to design your preferred corporate culture you will need to have a clear picture of your existing culture. Only by understanding the deficiencies in your cultural profile, can you map out the changes that you need to make, and the processes that you need to undergo to make those changes. We believe that the measurement of culture is important even for companies that already have strong cultures that are consistent with their strategies. For culture, like everything else in the organisation, must be *managed*, and, as you will remember Toyota's Brand Pretorius saying,

"If you can't measure it, you can't manage it."

The science of corporate culture measurement is a new one. In fact it is probably still more like art than science, but in the past 10 years a number of techniques and frameworks have been advanced for measuring and classifying corporate cultures. Deal and Kennedy, whose book *Corporate Culture*, published in 1982, was the first on the topic to gain wide readership, offer useful pointers for gauging a company's culture by observation.[2] For an outsider they suggest studying the company's physical setting, reading what the company says about its culture, testing how the company greets strangers, interviewing company people and observing how they spend their time. Other important indications are the career path progressions within the organisation, the typical duration of tenure in various jobs — particularly at middle management level, the content of discussions and writings and the anecdotes and stories that pass through the cultural network. Deal and Kennedy suggest a four-box grid for classifying corporate culture.

The grid categorises combinations of the risk of strategic decisions and the speed of feedback from those decisions. To quote Deal and Kennedy:

---

2 Terence Deal and Allen Kennedy, *Corporate Culture*, Addison Wesley, 1982.

The tough-guy, macho culture. A world of individualists who regularly take high risks and get quick feedback on whether their actions were right or wrong.

The work hard/play hard culture. Fun and action are the rule here, and employees take few risks, all with quick feedback. To succeed the culture encourages them to maintain a high level of relatively low-risk activity.

The bet-your-company culture. Cultures with big-stakes decisions, where years pass before employees know whether decisions have paid off. A high-risk, slow feedback environment.

The process culture. A world of little or no feedback where employees find it hard to measure what they do; instead they concentrate on how it's done. We have another name for this culture when the processes get out of control — bureaucracy!

The classification is interesting and, to a limited extent, quite useful. Indeed Deal and Kennedy concede that no company fits squarely into any one of the four boxes, and that different parts of the same organisation are likely to be classified differently. What other models are there? Earlier in this chapter, in the discussion on how a strengthening culture will change the nature of an organisation, we referred to the culture framework advanced by Roger Harrison, again a four-box grid but this time combining different degrees of formalisation and centralisation. We have certainly found this approach helpful in thinking about appropriate planning processes, and the effects of strong cultures, but once again, it offers little guidance to the design and management of a culture-change process.

Early in 1988, somewhat frustrated by the limited usefulness of the available culture measurement techniques, one of our own colleagues resolved to develop a more comprehensive culture measurement tool. At the time of writing the technique has been applied in a number of consulting assignments, each time with telling success. Based upon the survey of behaviour and attitudes right across the company, and employing a combination of skilled observation and sophisticated statistical analysis, the technique clearly profiles the culture of the organisation and its subcultures, affording powerful insight into the dynamics of the organisation. With culture measurement in hand, culture management becomes a whole lot easier to put into practice.

Manage it

Yes, you can manage your corporate culture. That good news comes to us loud and clear from the super-performers. Using a variety of skills, techniques and tools our top companies are shaping and strengthening their cultures. With care and dedication they are deliberately reinforcing and harnessing the power of corporate culture. Let's see how they go about it.

From the Top of the Heap

First things first. **The Chief Executive's role is fundamental to culture management. Like strategy, culture is the responsibility of the top man. He must acknowledge that his own personal values must very closely mirror the values that are so central to an organisation's culture.**

Indeed, if the CE is the founder of the enterprise, or if he has been at the top for a long time, the organisation's value system is likely to have developed directly from his own.

When Bruce Edmunds arrived at United Tobacco Company, for example, he found himself out of character with the organisation's casual, loose and comfortable culture. Through the Drive Policy, Edmunds deliberately swung the value system around to closely reflect his own more aggressive, more tightly managed style — a style then demanded by the newly competitive climate of the tobacco industry.

The organisation's style, too, follows from the Chief Executive's own personal style. Aaron Searll of Seardel puts it like this:

> "I've set certain standards of behaviour and style. I think it does revolve around standards. Standards vary. They vary according to the personality of the person in charge. They're based on personal standards, integrity — one's behaviour. If I ran around in jeans and smoked pot all day, I mean, what sort of guys would we have working here?"

The Chief Executive is indisputably the organisation's chief culture-builder. Raymond Ackerman is in world class here. Right alongside him is Peter Searle, who says:

"A Chief Executive is responsible to his shareholders for making a return on investment. Obviously that is true but at the end of the day, you only get there, quite frankly, if you can have a culture which supports what you are doing and has a long-term viability."

Searle goes on to say that the CE must lay the groundwork, and make sure the spirit of the organisation is right for the changes that lie ahead. He believes that the new culture must saturate the organisation — and that means the CE must drive it, must be passionate about it. Vic Hammond is passionate about the Edgars culture. The language that he uses constantly reinforces the important attributes of their culture. He talks about "fashion first", he refers to the customer as "she", he demands "pride in the merchandise". Hammond, Ackerman, Searle and Hamilton all demonstrate that the CE's style, behaviour and language are strong communicators of the essence of the culture.

The Tireless Horsemen

The CE is the central figure in culture management. He shapes the value system, kindles the passion and invents the language that culture management needs. But his efforts are critically dependent on his whole top management team. If they don't buy in to what the CE is trying to do, his message will not get through to the organisation at large. **Managers in our super-performing companies are the torch-bearers of culture; they demonstrate their corporate cultures — carrying the flame to the far corners of the company.** They make sure they are seen to be the most zealous and faithful converts. Cashbuild's Gerald Haumant talks about this visibility:

"Our open door policy is important. But we go a little bit further from a visibility of executives point of view. Any senior executive must be as visible as possible and that means spending about 50 per cent of your time in the country."

By "in the country" he means visiting Cashbuild's branches.

When they get there, he says, they don't just talk to the Branch Manager, they make sure they talk to people right across the board. And when they talk they will be asking the questions, using the language, lauding the behaviour that stress the Cashbuild corporate culture. VW's management, says Peter Searle, deliberately create fora for interactions. That means meetings, meetings, and more meetings.

Top Down, Bottom Up

Culture starts at the top and is managed from the top. But companies like VW, Cashbuild and Cadbury's tell us that **if the culture is to belong to the whole organisation, then all must feel involved in its creation.** Culture change is voluntary, Peter Searle reminds us, so you've got to make sure that people can identify with the new culture. Every day each employee brings to the workplace his or her own set of personal values. For the culture to grow, to be strong, those personal values must be allowed to influence the organisational value system. VW waited till their culture change programme had been running for two years before they committed a mission statement to paper. The Cashbuild philosophy, too, was fashioned with the intense involvement of employees. As Koopman says of the Cashbuild CARE philosophy:

> *"It is difficult now to reconstruct how the philosophy evolved. By no means was it a tidy sequence of events! We went into the whole process of change without any prerequisite or preconception. It was an article of faith that it should be an open ended process. There was constant discussion, managers would come up with some ideas, we'd talk to workers about them, find out what they thought. They'd come back to us with more ideas, suggestions, demands. So it went."*[3]

The Culture Tool Kit

The Mission Statement is the most evident artefact that the super-performers use to communicate their culture. Mission Statements have, of course, become *de rigueur* for every self-respecting

---

3 A. Koopman, *The Corporate Crusaders*, Lexicon Publishers, 1987.

modern organisation, but the top companies really do live out their Mission Statements. Aside from broad statements of the firm's goals, the effective Mission Statement clearly expresses the company's value system.

Cadbury's Mission centres on performance, quality, customer orientation and commitment to employees and their communities. The Mission Statement itself was presented to employees only as the culmination of a programme to convey to staff the fundamentals of the Cadbury's values and to build an understanding of their underlying commercial principles. The programme took the form of a seven-module video series, supported by multilingual pamphlets and posters, that was presented to groups of 30 to 40 workers at a time by their functional managers to encourage interaction. "It was a massive programme to get everybody through it," says Cadbury's MD Piet Beyers, "but I think it is only the start of entrenching our values and our goals." VW developed their Mission Statement in 1986 — two years after the start of their culture change programme. At that point they began a series of half-day Core Value Clinics that continue today. Nobody gets a copy of the Mission until they have gone through a CVC.

Cashbuild's Mission, or Philosophy as they call it, is contained in a pocket-sized 12-page booklet called *Welcome to our Company*, and subtitled *A Statement of belief and policy to help new employees orientate themselves to our company as to why things are done as they are at CASHBUILD*. The booklet is available in nine languages and is set out under the headings:

The Company
Our Customer
Our Team
— The Team
— The Individual
— The Management
— The Culture
Our Systems
Our Finances
Summary

Expressions of important Cashbuild values are highlighted in bold type. Some examples, including bold type as used:

Cashbuild frowns on insolent behaviour towards customers ...

Management displays low tolerance to game playing or politicizing ...

By virtue of the nature of our business as well as the company's stance towards individuals, **we place a high value on the aspect of assumed responsibility** ...

Good stock management separates the men from the boys. **The Team and Organisation's survival depends on good stock management** ...

The Cashbuild Philosophy is the basis of a contract between management and staff, between the company and employees generally. And they use it that way. Workers and managers pull the booklet out and quote from it to keep each other in line or to guide tricky or contentious decisions. The copy we were given was not new, it was grubby and well thumbed and had obviously been living in someone's pocket for months. That says a lot.

Several of the super-performers use symbols, messages and citations as effective culture management tools. Recall that Raymond Ackerman will write literally dozens of short notes to staffers he has met with during a day on his rounds. In a very similar way, Cashbuild's Gerald Haumant always writes a letter or two of commendation (and occasionally of censure) after visiting branches. These are an important part of what Haumant calls the information machine that communicates their corporate culture. He uses one of several special A5 size notepads, each of which has a cartoon featuring the Cashbuild lion with a message or slogan. "Keep up the good work," says one that has the lion looking awestruck at a large pile of money, "you are a true CASHBUILDER!" But another shows the lion angrily seeing someone off the left-hand side of the page, "You are turning away our Customer!" it rebukes.

A third type of culture management tool is affirmation — using slogans as mottos to declare some desired cultural attribute as unshakable fact. Plessey's memo pad has their slogan boldly emblazoned in blue in the bottom left corner, "PLESSEY the BEST". However if you look a little longer you will see that the same slogan is repeated in faint blue to cover the whole page in close type. MD John Temple was only slightly embarrassed by our suggestion that he was trying to get the message through on a subliminal level! It's going to get to you one way or the other, he agrees.

Anoint the Heroes, Again

It seems that one of the best ways to build or reinforce a culture is to publicly recognise exemplary behaviour. There is hardly a company anywhere that does not have some kind of award programme, even if only for long service, and of course the super-performers do too. But their award programmes are more carefully thought out, more accurately targeted at recognising the kind of behaviour that is consistent with their corporate objectives and corporate cultures.

In Chapter 2 we heard how Wellington Hlengwa won Pick 'n Pay's non-cash Pride in Performance award for handing in a diamond he found on the supermarket floor. Honesty and fair dealing with customers is an important part of Pick 'n Pay's culture. In Plessey, every division has several awards for heroic performance. There's no money involved — only a pen, say, or a cut-glass decanter. The important thing, says John Temple, is to make a public statement of the recognition. Company-wide Plessey has an Excellence Award for the person who single-handedly makes the greatest contribution to the company over the course of the year — something Temple introduced when he started with Plessey in 1985. The award is made on the strength of criteria-based nominations received from right across the company. The man who won it last year was Bob van Niekerk, the Research Manager in charge of Plessey's telecommunications research. Bob received over 100 nominations for his work on a new PABX, and for his enhancements to existing products. Temple calls him the finest telecommunications engineer in South Africa. But you don't have to be a high-level superstar to win an award. Says Temple:

"One of the awards that gave me the greatest pleasure to

present was to the female storelady in our Components Division in Johannesburg, who is a junior Black employee. And she kept that store absolutely impeccably. The management in that division figured that she was the person who had made the greatest single contribution to that division."

Choose the Right People

Several of the super-performers firmly hold that to build the culture you want, you must choose the people you hire very carefully. New people must be able to buy into the corporate culture fast. Initially Cashbuild struggled to get their participative culture up and running. They found that the Branch Manager was a key factor in the prospect for success in a branch. Some Branch Managers were moved out. The new ones that came in to replace them and to staff the new branches were chosen more carefully. Gerald Haumant again:

"So we really found a profile of the managers we would like to use. Instead of looking for a task-driven task-master, we suddenly looked at what a manager should be — a people integrator."

Volkswagen have come around to a similar view. Peter Searle:

"It has now reached the point where people have started questioning whether people who can't identify with the Mission should be brought into the organisation."

Suncrush have understood this for years. Their Head Office team do things together after hours — play tennis, go to the races, play bridge. They seem to like one another, says Hamilton. Their values as individuals are obviously closely congruent, and that has contributed enormously to the strength of the Suncrush culture. Hamilton believes that a culture will absorb more people of the same culture into it, and reject those that don't fit. There's had to be very little of that kind of rejection at Suncrush.

Take Time, Iterate and Have Courage

Perhaps one of the most important messages that our culture champions have for would-be culture builders is to prepare yourself for a long haul. Culture change takes a long time.

233

We have seen how VW's culture-change programme was laid out over 10 years from the mid-eighties to the mid-nineties. This is much longer than they thought they would need when they set out in 1982, says Peter Searle, and they found it frustrating. But real results have begun to come through now, and they have, at least partially, become accustomed to the slow pace of this kind of change. Cashbuild's experience has been similar. Their cultural reorientation began in 1984 and, by their own admission, still has a way to go.

Why does culture-change take so long? Well, the psychologists tell us that changing organisational cultures is achieved through changing people's attitudes, and attitudes that have formed over whole lifetimes are not changed overnight. The psychologists also tell us that the way to change attitudes is through behaviour. In terms of culture-change that means that people must see a clear and consistent behaviour change on the part of management. People themselves must repeatedly be involved in activity that influences their attitudes. Several years ago when VW were trying to convince their dealer network of the achievement of quality in manufacturing, they brought them to the plant again and again to show them that they were behaving differently. Changing people's attitudes and changing corporate culture is an iterative process. It needs time; it needs consistent, repetitive and demonstrative behaviour on the part of management; and it needs courage never to swerve from the path you have set yourself.

Managing Subcultures

Earlier in this chapter, when we were discussing frameworks for classifying corporate cultures, we touched on an interesting and important point: different parts of the same organisation may well have different cultures — or subcultures. Using the Deal and Kennedy classification, it may be that sales people would tend to be "work hard, play hard" types who get fast feedback on many low risk decisions, while the research and development people who live in a world of high risk might be the "bet-your-company" sort. This mix of subcultures is in fact quite typical. SAB's Beer Division provides a useful example; by far the most important performance measure at SAB is sales. Meyer Kahn, who is, remember, the *Group* CE, gets a Beer Division Sales report every single day. Sales, he says, is the issue that is discussed first — every time. At the same time Graham Mackay, the Beer Division MD, who is no doubt as focused on sales as Kahn is, can talk about taking a long-term perspective when deciding on investment in production capacity, pricing, branding, people development and so on. They are there for the long haul, says Mackay. Short-term sales and long-term investment, SAB is by no means unusual in this respect. The implication, though, is that the sales subculture in SAB is probably rather different from the engineering subculture, and should be so. How then do they hang together? Well they hang together under the shady canopy of SAB's overall corporate culture, which we see as having the following characteristics:

• Professional
• Friendly and informal
• Strong-minded
• Upfront
• Highly tolerant of debate
• Power seeking and political
• Developmental of people.

There seems no reason why the sales and engineering subcultures should not retain essential differences while having in common the qualities that shape the *corporate culture*. This perhaps should be the objective of subculture management. And if you get the balance right between the common and the different elements of your organisation's subcultures you will probably be well on the way to solving the eternal problem of intra-organisation competition.

Merging Cultures

The mergers and acquisitions trail is littered with wrecked hulks. Many of these failures, both in South Africa and abroad, came to grief on corporate culture. The trouble is merchant bankers, by and large, have vocabularies that include things like financial leverage, convertible prefs and tax shields, but which omit this phrase *corporate culture*. Fact is, most merger and acquisition decisions are taken on financial factors alone. The Metboard-Investec merger of 1987 is a case in point here. The deal looked great on paper, and may yet be so, but it's common cause that the two operations are having difficulty living under the same roof. Metboard's conservative, considered, old-school-tie approach isn't bedding down comfortably with the faster-paced, higher risk, deal-making culture at Investec.

The Cadbury-Schweppes acquisition of Bromor Foods provides a counter example. Bromor was previously in the Murray & Roberts stable. Bromor's MD, Mike Brownlee, recalls how little the two organisations had in common, culturally speaking: "When you're working in an engineering environment everything's very kind of work-a-day, somewhat short-term, that sort of approach." The M&R people weren't attuned to the idea of investing for four years in, say, a branding programme for Moirs jellies. They were more accustomed to getting a return in Year 2. It was the same with Bromor's motivations for capital investment. The horizon was too long for M&R, and Bromor had difficulty obtaining approval for capex projects.

Then Bromor was sold to Cadbury-Schweppes. Suddenly, says Brownlee, he was being encouraged to spend *more* on advertising, to strengthen brands, to develop "strategic" sections of the business that held prospect only in the long term. Even with the strong cultural compatibility between the two cultures, there has been a certain amount of give and take since the acquisition. Bromor had to adjust to Cadbury-Schweppes' "more considered, more thorough approach", recalls Brownlee. "They gave us a bit of a razzle on Patrick's side of the house." (Patrick Fleming is Cadbury-Schweppes' Group Financial Director.) There were new auditors, who went through Bromor like "Hurricane Charlie". "It wasn't easy, especially on our financial team, but there were absolutely no personal difficulties. It was good for us. We all learned a lot."

Perhaps the pre-merger lesson from this example is: know what you have in each organisation to start with, know what conflicts might arise, think about how to resolve them, and know what sort of merged organisation you hope to come out with at the end. In

this way even a cursory examination of the merging cultures might avert a disaster.

Corporate Climate — Sunny and Warm?

In many of our super-performers we quickly became aware of an unusually healthy corporate climate. These are simply happy companies. The business literature doesn't offer a clear distinction between corporate climate and corporate culture, but there does appear to be a general understanding that culture is about values and beliefs and climate is about satisfaction and contentment. **We like to think of corporate climate as the extent to which the personal values and expectations of employees correspond to the organisational values and goals embodied in the corporate culture. If employees' values closely match the corporate value system, then a healthy corporate climate will prevail. If there is mismatch the climate will be poor.**

We talked earlier about how well the Suncrush head office people get along with one another. Their values as individuals are closely congruent. They have a strong corporate culture. Appropriately, Suncrush's corporate climate *is* warm and sunny.

Culture Management — on Today's Agenda

Finally and importantly, **the culture champions of our super-performing companies show us that culture management can be planned and can be programmed. These companies have learnt how to grab hold of the warm fuzzy cloud of corporate culture and give it hard edges, defining it, shaping it to their advantage.**

Essential to a successful culture change programme, says Peter Searle of Volkswagen, is the appointment of an individual who will take responsibility for the programme's administration. Searle appointed Leon de Klerk, VW's Manager: Training and Education as Culture Change Co-ordinator. At Cashbuild the custodian of the corporate culture is Roy Bagattini, the Personnel Director. Culture management is a formal part of Leon's and Roy's jobs.

VW and Cashbuild have learnt that as soon as the management of culture is accorded formal recognition as a management activity, it goes onto the agenda, it gets done, and it brings incredible results. So don't wait in hope. Get started. Get the force of corporate culture working for you now!

---

11 Steps to Winning Corporate Culture

1. Turn on culture power to deliver
   - organisational integration
   - bridges across human diversity
   - shared corporate visions
   - minimal company politics
   - continuity in times of change.

2. Choose a culture appropriate to your industry, your strategy, your existing culture and the values of your people.
3. Pick your cultural attributes from a range that might include performance-orientation, customer-orientation, respect for the individual, supportiveness, an obsession for quality, innovation, participation and a host of other characteristics.
4. Recognise that your culture will change as your organisation grows and matures, and, conversely, that as your culture strengthens your organisation can become less formal, more flexible.
5. To manage your culture, you should first try to measure it, to define it.
6. Use these pointers to manage your culture:
   - start at the top
   - win the commitment of senior and middle management
   - build in employees' personal values
   - use the available tools — mission statements, philosophy booklets, symbols, messages, citations and slogans
   - encourage and recognise behaviour that is consistent with the desired culture
   - only employ new people who will buy into the culture
   - use consistent and repetitive behaviour (your own and employees') to change attitudes
   - allow plenty of time to make the changes you want — and don't give up!

7. Recognise the value — and the risks — inherent in subcultures. Manage these too.
8. Look at cultures before you merge companies, or even departments.

238

9. See your corporate climate as an indicator of the fit between employees' values and your corporate culture.
10. Nominate a custodian of your corporate culture.
11. Put culture management on today's agenda.

CHAPTER ELEVEN

THE WINNING WAY IN THE 1990s

This book has been written at a time when paradoxically the only constant we can cling to is that of change — if nothing else, we can expect change. The rate of change, we know too, will be faster than in the past and the direction more difficult to pinpoint.

Our study has focused on the past and present. We have distilled out of the research into 24 super-performers nine success factors. All very interesting, you may say, but will these factors apply to corporate South Africa in the 1990s?

To answer this question we will take you through some of the ideas and concepts of the future South Africa which are currently up for debate in the public forum. From this we will distil out the changes that we believe can be expected in corporate South Africa. We will then revisit the nine success factors and assess whether they are likely to apply in the 1990s.

SOUTH AFRICA IN THE 1990s

Obviously, business takes place in a socio-economic and political context. We do not purport to be experts in these things. Certainly, predicting the future in South Africa is hazardous — we shudder to think how we would feel reading something on South Africa in the 1980s which we had written in 1979. We will therefore restrict ourselves to the major trends that we believe hold special relevance for corporate South Africa in the 1990s.

THE POLITICAL FRAMEWORK — THE KEY TO EVERYTHING ELSE

Whilst it is expected that politicians will react to social and economic pressures, this reaction may take time and it may be in the wrong direction. For this reason, the focus of South African futurists is on what our political framework may look like. We now turn to some important trends that attract frequent comment.

The International Scene

If the last five years have taught us anything at all, it is that we are part of a world political and economic order. The most fascinating development that has taken place in this order has been the convergence of interests between the USSR and the USA — certainly where these interests pertain to regional conflicts. It has become clear that the USSR wishes to divest itself of expensive ideological exercises in off-beat places. They've pulled out of Afghanistan and are pulling out of the Namibian dynamic. This is the hard evidence. Both superpowers are focusing their energies on political, not violent, solutions to these regional conflicts. They have come to the realisation that negotiation, not revolution, is the way to solve regional conflicts.

The implication for South Africa is clear: the energies of the superpowers — and the powers that follow — will be to resolve the South African problem through negotiation. The cards they will be playing will force our local actors to the negotiating table, not to continue killing each other.

The Domestic Scene

When our governing politicians talk about a "Reform Programme", it is tempting to envisage a clearly set out list of activities, each with a completion date and responsibility allocated to it. Of course we know this to be far from the truth. Instead the process has been a bit like this: a senior cabinet minister makes a public utterance about a reform issue. This quickly attracts public interest and it is much discussed. Then the backpeddling and uncertainty set in, and the minister is at pains to point out that what he really meant was . . .

The chances are, however, that this reform will, in time, take place. The abolition of influx control, repeal of the immorality legislation and mixed residential areas are but a few examples of changes that have already taken place.

241

In our opinion exactly the same will apply to the concept of "Negotiation of power-sharing within a unitary state". Both De Klerk, albeit in a very guarded fashion, and Heunis, in swansong fashion, have irrevocably placed this on the reform agenda. That is, that the concepts of power-sharing and a unitary state, not a multi-nation state, will be achieved through a process of negotiation.

So, whilst it is not possible at this point to pinpoint the nature and form of these things, these negotiations are likely to be the predominant political theme of the 1990s. We should expect the politically astute De Klerk to consolidate the National Party, and through the party determine the pace of the negotiations. We can expect that, by legitimising a negotiating process, the left-wing extra-parliamentary actors will see their military paradigm severely undermined. There will be strong moral pressure to take a seat — even if initially gingerly, at the negotiating table. We would also expect to see that by legitimising negotiation (which is surely the path of all reasonable people?), the National Party will effectively marginalise the right wing. They will become another principled opposition, relegated to the fringes of power politics.

Such are the possibilities. One would be foolish to suggest that this is the only scenario. It is a likely one. One would also be foolish to suggest a date on which the negotiation process will have run its course. Our own feeling is that meaningful changes in the political framework, in the sense of a fundamental change to the power structure in South African politics, is unlikely to occur in the planning period in all but companies with the longest planning periods. Rather, it is expected that the National Party will pursue the course of negotiation politics, and this will involve an easing up of discriminatory laws and further accommodations, but which will fall short of the aspirations of the majority of South Africans.

Juxtaposed against this, we are witnessing certain developments which suggest that the pressure for fundamental change is becoming an unstoppable force. The recent developments in Namibia are an example. Also, the understanding (albeit a reluctant one) of the need for politicians to adapt to the laws of economics. Racial legislation has become costly, as are the policies which inhibit South Africa's ability to attract foreign capital and to export. The need to adapt to the laws of economics is particularly strident if one looks for a minute at the changes to the composition of our society and the associated structure of income in that society. Our population, more particularly our Third World population, is exploding. Our population is expected to reach the 100 million mark by 2035. The formal bureaucratic structures and the formal economy are simply no longer able to cope. Hallmarks of racial separation like the Group Areas Act are quickly becoming a sick joke, as are laws and regulations which impede the growth of the informal sector.

Yet given these pressures, we suggest that a fundamental change to the political framework would constitute a discontinuity — something difficult to plan for, but for which contingency plans should exist. Below we deal more specifically with what this means for the economy and corporate South Africa.

THE ECONOMY

We need little reminding of the problems faced by the South African economy. To recap:

- The growth of a developing economy such as South Africa's is critically dependent on foreign capital. The debt crisis precipitated by the withdrawal of foreign lines of credit has turned the country into a net exporter of capital. This is considered to impose a ceiling on the growth in GDP of about 3 per cent. The population is growing at something close to that.
- Unlike our major trading partners, we have been unable to contain the economic monster that is inflation. One of the insidious effects this has is to impair our export competitiveness — and this at a time when political factors are also affecting export competitiveness.
- The composition of our exports remains heavily skewed towards mining output — particularly gold. The world outlook for these products does not look promising.
- The State's share of GDP continues to grow and has reached unacceptable proportions. The processes of privatisation and deregulation have begun, albeit slowly. Nevertheless, the State's outlay on recurrent expenditure needed to feed its

243

bureaucracy and security machine remains something of a political necessity for the ruling party. At this juncture, this political necessity is no match for plaintive calls from the private sector to reduce recurrent expenditure.

In summary, it would take some tough action on the part of the government to turn the economy around. It would require, for example, slicing the State bureaucracy, allowing interest rates to rise to market levels and deregulating and privatising on a serious scale. It would require winding up exports and attracting capital, which are both largely dependent on political accommodation at home. The political price for the ruling party is too great, particularly during a protracted negotiation process, when it becomes all the more necessary to attend to the economic whims of all the constituencies of the various actors in the process. This is not the time for decisive and unpopular remedies. We therefore take the view that features of our economy such as slow growth (1 to 3 per cent), capital shortages, high inflation, foreign exchange shortages and high taxes will remain features of the South Africa of the 1990s.

The Social Environment: a Moving Landscape

Within this low growth scenario, we will witness the continuation of the movement of the landscape of the social environment. The hard data of this landscape, in the form of incomes, will show a growing redistribution of income. Crudely expressed, this will be from white to black. Black incomes will continue to rise in the light of unionisation, growth in the informal sector, improvements in the educational standards and the sheer force of urbanisation in its own right. According to some estimates, black spending power is likely to outstrip that of whites by the year 2000.

Companies marketing fast-moving consumer goods, such as beer, soft-drinks, confectionery, cigarettes, washing powder, deodorant and shoe polish are focusing on the mass, and that happens to be predominantly black. This trend will continue.

Furthermore, we are finding that the very term "black market" is an outdated one. Successfully positioning branded goods requires a quantum leap from this outdated thinking. This presumes the old rule of black = poor, white = affluent. The income bands are merging at a rapid pace. Particularly in the middle, successful marketeers have moved into horizontal marketing — targeting a product at a type of appeal which may be black or white — it really doesn't matter. Remember Vic Hammond's comment about Sales House? Much of their merchandise with classical appeal is sold mainly to Afrikaner women and blacks.

It is also fundamentally affecting distribution patterns. Take SAB's Beer Division — about 70 per cent of their product is now sold through shebeens in the townships. Suncrush is in the process of setting up a distribution system that will allow consumers to buy cold Coke from a spaza shop. About R3 billion worth of product is now sold annually through this backyard retailing mechanism. That's pretty close to Pick 'n Pay's annual turnover!

What South Africa is witnessing, then, is a fundamental shift in the consumption patterns. This will be a feature of South Africa in the 1990s.

WHAT DOES THIS MEAN FOR CORPORATE SOUTH AFRICA?

Given this broadly sketched scenario, we now move on to look at some of the important implications that this raises for corporate South Africa and some suggested responses.

The overriding theme in this discussion is that the somewhat static nature of the features of this scenario belies the one and only constant that we can cling to, and that is change itself. We will suggest that winning companies in the 1990s will need to drastically change the way they conduct their business.

The Need for a Resilient Business Psyche

The negotiating process in the context of a weak and contracting economy is going to knock business confidence from pillar to post. At times we will take two steps forward and three backward. Then three forward and one backward. Our business psyche is fragile to start with.

Winning companies will need to cut through the noise of the

rapid changes to business confidence. If a capex proposal is justified in terms of the economics, it will need to go ahead even if a key actor suddenly ditches the negotiating process. The chances are that, in time, he will be coaxed back again. That overseas investment will also need to go ahead, if the economics look right, even if the financial rand takes yet another smack because yet another multinational pulls out. And so on. Decisiveness, resilience and consistency of purpose will be needed to win in the 1990s.

The Role of Business in Society: Redefining the Concept of Self Interest

Consistency in message is a vital ingredient in any marketing strategy. It therefore jars when a company positions its product at a market which is predominantly black, appealing to lifestyle values of sharing, outdoor living, fun and laughter, yet doesn't follow through in the workplace. Following through may mean bumping heads with important customers, like government and local authorities, as well as with strong racist attitudes in the workplace itself.

Organisations are beginning to see that care for customers cannot be separated from care for employees. Both happen to be predominantly black, and, as such, have been subjected to social engineering on a scale unprecedented in the post-war world. Super-performing companies have nailed their flags to the mast, and organisations that want to compete for customers and employees in the 1990s will have to follow suit. It will reach the point where nailing the flag to the mast doesn't mean deliberately taking an anti-government stance. It will mean simply acting in response to self interest.

It will also mean broadening the role of business in society to dealing with societal issues that have a very direct bearing on corporate success. Education is a good example. A workforce that is to meet the challenges that lie ahead will have to be a much better educated workforce than the current education system is providing for. And that will need to begin with primary school education. Tertiary education schemes for employee dependants, already part of the scene in many super-performers, will be expanded downward into the organisation and downward to secondary and primary school education. Company schools for dependants are a distinct possibility in the South Africa of the 1990s.

Self interest is also going to mean engineering opportunities to interface with the informal sector. We have already made the point about the growth in the informal sector. Certainly, there has been a plethora of euphoric prose in recent years about the promise of the informal sector. Our own firm recently conducted a market research exercise on the accounting, auditing and consulting needs of the informal sector. We came away from the exercise with a stronger understanding of the need for informal sector growth, but also with a heightened sense of despair — primarily because of the lack of interface that this section had with the formal economy. A dual logic economy is desperately needed. But it will only work if the informal sector develops from hawkers to consumers, to suppliers to big business. We have personally attempted to get informal sector suppliers to contract with big companies. Talk about a highly regulated State bureaucracy! The poor guys don't know where to begin — tender documents, sourcing specifications, product specifications, delivery schedules, stocking requirements, and so on and so on. In the 1990s, organisations are going to find that their cost structures make functions such as cleaning, garden maintenance, tea services and many of the labour-intensive services far more cost effective when provided by the informal sector. Self interest is already starting to dictate interfacing with the informal sector.

Creating a More Caring World

It's a tough place, South Africa. The future scenario doesn't look as if it's going to soften much either. Yet people's expectations of fair treatment are becoming more strident.

Laurens van der Post recently delivered a talk to the Society of Civil Engineers. His theme was that the western world, whilst it had advanced economically in moving to more free-market and less socialism, had become hard and masculine. He urged the world to allow the feminine side to express itself, i.e. more sensitive, less macho; more intuition, less rational; more caring, less directing; more listening, less talking. In our opinion his message has special relevance for South Africa. Our customers and employees do live in a tough environment. Expectations of fair treatment will drive them into organisations — as customers and employees — if they can take refuge in a more caring environment.

We made the point in Chapter 9 that inspired leaders know how to touch the heart. It is going to be a prerequisite for successfully competing in the 1990s.

Developing People, Developing Managers

We have dwelt at length on the focus which super-performing companies bring to bear on developing their people and developing their managers.

We need little reminding of the critical skills shortage in South Africa. In the past, organisations have relied almost exclusively on the growing number of white school leavers to fill the skilled ranks. We are now finding that the number of white school leavers is declining. The number of blacks is expanding exponentially. We need not say much about the black educational system, but suffice it to say that organisations are already having to work much harder at skill development than they did in the past. Companies wishing to be super-performers in the 1990s will have to become fanatical about developing their people.

In particular, the need to develop *real* black managers will become a burning issue for all of corporate South Africa in the 1990s. Try this for a statistic: We didn't interview a single black manager in the course of our research. Try this too: In 1987 two of our colleagues delivered a series of lectures to the senior financial staff at a large Zimbabwean group. Seventeen out of the 25 were black. These were real black managers, qualified and in charge of large staffs. We only have 17 black qualified chartered accountants in the whole of South Africa.

If for no other reason than self interest, organisations that aspire to super-performer status in the 1990s will have to have a cadre of black managers. We do not underestimate the size of the task in getting there. It's big, and it's fraught with problems. But we find that organisations like Pick 'n Pay tackle these problems with the vigour and enthusiasm that they apply to the retailing market.

Becoming More African, Understanding Black South Africa

Lucky Michaels, shebeener, restaurateur and founder of the National Taverner's Association, was quoted in *The Executive*, November 1988 as saying:

> *"You can't claim to understand black business if you don't know the way to Soweto."*

They always say that great poets would marvel at the depth of interpretation placed on their great works. Well, we aren't sure if Lucky Michaels intended it, but we read an awful lot into this. The fact is that white people control corporate South Africa. The vast majority of these white people have a severely limited understanding of black South Africa (and really, this *is* South Africa), developed mainly from contact with their domestic staff. We were sharply reminded of this when conducting a consulting assignment on the black home loan market. We kicked off the assignment by interviewing 25 (white) people who were reputed to have some understanding of the issues. Of these, 18 related at length the housing situations of their domestic staff. Fine, but then they would proceed to define the market based on this understanding.

The point is, few whites have had the privilege of sharing with blacks classes, play groups, rugby teams, choirs, military training, dinners, parties or any other form of social interaction on which an understanding of each perspective is based. Yet, as we mentioned earlier, corporate South Africa's market and employee body are dominated by blacks! Reflecting black South African values in our organisations will become a feature of corporate life in the 1990s. Organisations will become more communicative, less fraught with hidden agendas; more open and less reserved; more friendly and less uptight; more communal and less individualistic; more group oriented and less hierarchical; more value driven and less systems driven.

Work-life Enrichment

Corporate members, in line with international trends, will increasingly look to their organisations for personal development opportunities. Super-performing companies in the 1990s will need to focus on enriching the working life of their members — the best and the brightest people will gravitate towards these organisations and they will become winners.

In order to provide these growth opportunities, participative systems will become the order of the day. Command post management will be restricted to the army and State bureaucracy. Organisations that don't offer people participation in decision making and action taking will be bled white and relegated to the ranks of the also-rans.

Sharing the Spoils

The expectation of sharing in the spoils is becoming more widespread. ESOPS, performance awards, generous bonus schemes deep down in the bowels of the organisation, so prevalent in the super-performers of today, will become prerequisites for the super-performers of tomorrow.

Flexibility: Keeping on Your Toes for an Uncertain Tomorrow

We have spoken about the only constant being change, about the increase in the rate of change and about the possibility of discontinuities. How do you plan for this? Flexibility is one way — making sure that your organisation can turn on a tickey should the environment change. Flexibility has two dimensions: resilience and speed of response.

Resilience is about having a less than optimal amount of debt in the balance sheet, having a diversified turnover, having a well-balanced customer base, having a range of distribution channels, a range of supply channels, having access to one of the major power groupings, having succession plans for key positions, and stocking up more than an EOQ model would suggest.

There is certainly a cost associated with resilience. As such, resilience should become part of the leader's management agenda.

The other part of flexibility is the ability to perceive change and respond speedily. The super-performers of today have shown us that they have the mechanisms in place to feel the environment, and then to respond with lightning speed — before the also-rans have even noted that change is taking place.

Perceiving change means having feelers out there in the environment. This requires not only ongoing market research, but that organisational members understand what is going on in society — being out there living and feeling it. It also requires managers doing a lot of "horseback" research — getting out, feeling and understanding what is going on in the country.

Whilst perceiving the change is obviously important, actually responding is the trick. How will companies see to lightning response in the 1990s? The super-performing companies of today are showing the way:

- **Pushing responsibility to the lowest level of decision-making.** That means buyers — not corporate executives — making buying decisions, salesmen doing the selling, negotiating terms and conditions without having to wait for an okay from Head Office; assembly line workers deciding on productivity improvement schemes; and so on. Remember, though, that this will require an enormous investment in developing the people to equip them to discharge this responsibility.
- **Eliminating the red tape.** A bureaucracy can only change gradually, and cannot possibly hope to compete with the speed of change that South Africa will experience in the 1990s.
- **Building flexibility into capital projects.** In a rapidly changing environment, it is essential to build alternative uses into plants, buildings and other capital projects. This will invariably cost, but not as much as if the whole thing were rendered redundant by some unforeseen change in circumstances.
- **Building flexibility into systems.** Systems are essential to the orderly conduct of business. The problem is that they implicitly embody business models, data structures and decision rules appropriate to a particular time in history. They render the organisation less responsive to new rules of the game in a rapidly reshaping business environment. Furthermore, they are difficult to adapt to changing circumstances. Flexibility is usually available but it costs and it retards the initial implementation.
- **Keeping liquid.** Opportunities are likely to arise at short

notice, just as easily as unexpected surprises can knock your cash flow.

- **Building quick response into corporate culture.** We have dwelt at length elsewhere on the power of corporate culture. The super-performers of today have built into their culture one value: that change is the only constant. What follows from this is the need to be in touch with this change and respond quickly. Corporate members should not be threatened by it, but challenged, and take pride in being the first to respond to this change. This will become an absolute requirement for super-performance in the 1990s.

In short, management decisions in the 1990s will have to factor in the need for flexibility. Managers will need to deal specifically with the implications that decisions have for the organisation's resilience and speed of response. Where these build rigidity into the organisation, plans will need to be developed to counter the inherent risk.

Suncrush is, to our mind, an example of the type of flexible organisation of the 1990s. It is resilient — it has a strong balance sheet, a range of distribution channels, a range of supply channels and depth of management. Its speed of response is formidable: responsibility is pushed down to the lowest level, it is informally driven, systems are simple and flexible and focused on the important things, it is liquid, and it has a set of values which willingly embrace change. We expect to see Suncrush flex and flex, turn itself inside-out and outside-in over the next decade and remain a leader in its industry. Super-performers of the 1990s could learn much from this winner.

International Isolation: Bridging the Growing Gap

Inherent in the scenario for the 1990s is increasing isolation from the international community. Corporate South Africa needs these links for a number of reasons: from production to management we are dependent on overseas technology, overseas markets and supply routes, overseas skilled personnel and, importantly, overseas money. We need not labour the point. Some politicians may think we can go it alone, but leaders of super-

252

performing companies stress the critical importance of maintaining these links.

We would like to focus here on the widening gap that we perceive in management technology and management thinking. This follows from the rising cost of sending people overseas, the reluctance of people overseas to talk to us and, most importantly, from the exit of some of the world's best companies. ISM, for example, will find it increasingly difficult to implement the management techniques of IBM. The impact of this is more profound than most people think.

We believe that the super-performers of the 1990s will need to go to extraordinary lengths to bridge the growing gap. They will need to send people overseas more, not less; to send more managers on courses at Harvard and Stanford, to pay more for overseas skilled personnel, and so on. It will become part of the management agenda of the 1990s.

Sanction-busting has become a national pastime over the last few years, so we need not talk of the importance of this. We would like to re-emphasise the importance of exports. Some of the reasons why they are so important are:

- We have small local markets, which aren't able to justify capacity for capital-intensive industries.
- Export-led economic strategies in countries like Taiwan and South Korea have really worked.
- We are under-the-gun to meet debt repayments.
- As a developing country, we need international technology, which costs in terms of foreign currency.
- From the corporate perspective, the South African economy looks set to grow only marginally. Organisations will find themselves with enormous capital investments in industries which are set to contract. Survival will depend on the ability to export.

For these reasons, and many more which we could mention, super-performers in the 1990s will have to exert an extraordinary focus on exports.

At Last: a More Competitive Economy

There is a way to go, but the South African economy has become more competitive. The Competitions Act, lower growth, the State's slow retreat from interference, a stronger Department of Trade and Industries and a growing understanding on the part of politicians of the debilitating effects of interference and protectionism, have combined to make the South African economy more competitive.

In fact, there are now a number of industries which are competitive by world standards. Banking is a good example. Whereas 10 years ago the industry was locked in a cosy cartel with the Department of Finance decreeing deposit and lending rates, and controlling entry by not issuing new banking licences, the industry is today fiercely competitive. Banks are now at each other's throats, competing for borrowers and lenders. They are racing to get the competitive edge through customer-care campaigns, product development, corporate image and information systems. They are restructuring themselves to get closer to their markets and to lower the cost of doing business. There is going to be a shake-out, and the race is on to be a survivor in the 1990s. In spite of all the bleating, this is as it should be. Organisations in industries which are starting to feel real competitive pressures should take note — they have much to learn from the banking industry.

The improved competitive climate is fundamental to the development of the South African economy. Super-performers of the 1990s will need to recognise this and focus their energies on adapting their organisations to it, rather than complaining about it. Gone are the days when making money in South Africa was a bit like falling off a log. Being a super-performer in the 1990s will require managers to be far more analytical about their businesses and to answer some fundamental questions: How do we create value for our customer? Is there a smarter or lower cost way of doing it? How are we going to offer improved price/performance for our customers? Certain hard-to-achieve factors will become absolute requirements for being in the game. Already customer care is such a factor in the auto business — VW and Toyota have gone that route. Together they hold more than 50 per cent of the passenger market. Smaller competitors won't even be in the game if they aren't able to offer the same level of customer care. The banking industry is heading the same way, following on the lead taken by Volkskas. It's driving corporate executives nuts, but consumers love it. And that's what business is all about.

The Relationship Between Government and Business: a More Constructive Tomorrow

The relationship between business and government has an interesting history. Business has been predominantly English, and government predominantly Afrikaans. A study of the history of English speakers in South Africa shows that there has been little determination to hold the reins of political power. The focus has been on developing the private sector of the economy. The Afrikaner agenda has been to firmly hold the reins of power. It has been intensely nationalistic. The earlier decision-makers in the National Party cabinet were drawn from the academics, the agricultural sector and from the ranks of the professional politicians. It is fair to say that until only recently, the matters of business never achieved a position of power and prominence at a cabinet level. This has now changed.

Meanwhile, there have been some interesting developments in business. It is certainly fair to say that a growing number of Afrikaner-controlled organisations are coming out trumps in the hurly-burly of the corporate sector. Also, that more and more positions in the senior ranks of organisations are being filled by Afrikaners. What we have witnessed, then, has been a *toenadering* of the two positions, in the sense of a heightened understanding of each other's perspectives. We have started to see a constructive relationship between business and government in matters pertaining to economic policy.

This constructive relationship at the level of economic policy is likely to be a feature of the landscape in the 1990s. Super-performers of the 1990s will increasingly look to this relationship, to nurture it, and constructively develop it.

The Rising Cost of Capital Equipment: the Time-Bomb

A deteriorating exchange rate which incorporates a discount for political uncertainty, pressure on the balance of payments and our increasing isolation are combining to put the replacement of capital equipment out of reach. This is a time-bomb, because if South Africa's stock of capital equipment skips a generation, it is bound to price our products out of world markets. This has been the time-bomb of post-colonial Africa, and we now face the same prospect.

Super-performers in the 1990s which rely on big investments in capital equipment — one thinks particularly of the manufacturing sector — are faced with a range of responses. These include:

- Reworking the costs of the various factors of production. In particular, labour intensity will have to bear deep consideration as an alternative to capital intensity.
- Actively seeking out advantages to the local situation to offset this disadvantage, and winding-up the exports. This may mean relocation to reduce transport or labour costs, or to improve raw material sourcing.

The problem is a real one, and super-performers of the 1990s will need to respond. That is not to say that organisations won't be able to make money without responding. Rather, organisations aiming to compete in world markets in the 1990s and beyond will have to address this problem.

REVISITING THE NINE SUCCESS FACTORS

We turn now to the nine success factors distilled out of the research and assess their relevance to the scenario for the 1990s and to the implications of this scenario for corporate South Africa.

Mastering Your Corporate Destiny

The lesson we learnt was that super-performing companies manage their organisations strategically. That is, they take the future into their own hands, position themselves to compete in the marketplace and focus on offering their customers something different. The processes for getting there may vary, but all involve a strategy.

We have noted above that super-performers in the 1990s will operate in a far more competitive economy; that change is the only constant. This will require becoming more proactive, more analytical and constantly flexing the organisations around the whims of the marketplace. This requires strategy, for without strategy the organisations of the 1990s will be tossed about the oceans of change without rudder or direction. The costs of being rudderless will mount — whilst this would have meant mediocre performance in the past, it will mean extinction in the 1990s.

Giving the Lady What She Wants

The lesson here is that super-performing companies go to extraordinary lengths to give the customer what she wants. They devote enormous resources to understanding her and then build the organisation around her. Customer care is something of a religion in these companies.

As we've noted above, our markets are changing — rapidly. Surely, then, it becomes even more important to understand one's market and to understand the dynamics of change within that market? Surely, too, it becomes more important to consistently reposition one's organisation around the needs of the customer? When industry leaders start treating their customer as the focal point of all organisational activity, how can one even be in the game without giving the lady what she wants?

Liberating Human Potential

Super-performing organisations see their organisations as nothing more than a collection of people. In an environment in which there is a chronic skills shortage and multiple opportunities for all but the unskilled, they are adept at getting them to perform beyond their own expectations of their abilities. They are adept at the art of liberating human potential.

The skills shortage will get worse, the multiple opportunities for the skilled will multiply and the expectations of a "fair deal" will continue to change. The art of liberating human potential will attract an extraordinary focus from managers in the 1990s. Managers will have to find new ways of eking out performance improvements from organisational members. But implementing the principle itself will sap the talent and energy of corporate leaders in the 1990s.

Ringing in the New

Super-performing companies constantly explore the possibilities of offering their customers something different to their competitors. They build this into their structures and their *modus operandi*.

We have noted that the 1990s will be characterised by more competition; that it will be more difficult to show growth; that customer care will become the order of the day. Organisations aiming for super-performer status in the 1990s will have to exert an even greater focus on innovating, of outsmarting the competition by giving the customer something new, of doing things within the organisation which drives down the cost of doing business. Organisations that fail to do this will be like the twelfth man in a losing football team — they will watch all the action and experience excruciating frustration as the other side scores all the goals.

Doing What Comes Logically

Super-performing companies turn themselves into schools for developing skills in their fundamental areas of operation. They set themselves the target of being the best in their industry and work out what skills they need to develop to get there. They then build these skills.

They also focus their attention on a small number of indicators which enable them to feel the pulse of the business and take rapid action.

We have noted above the need to continually develop people and develop managers; that the game is going to become more competitive. Organisations wishing to play the game will have to develop distinctive skills in that game. Otherwise they will lose hands down every time.

Organisations are likely to become more complex environments as they grow and as people come to expect more from them. Feeling the pulse will, accordingly, become more difficult. Yet the need will become greater in the light of a rapidly changing environment. To be a super-performer in the 1990s, organisations are going to have to cut through that complexity and focus on the fundamentals.

Doing it Properly

Super-performers do it properly, are careful and don't push their

258

luck. They keep things simple, they think ahead, consider consequences of actions, adopt a "right first time" philosophy, act professionally, focus on the detail, focus on delivering and aim at being accomplished at all things they do.

It sounds easy, but it extracts enormous energy and focus to get there. As the going gets tougher and the competition smarter, as it will in the 1990s, organisations which display a propensity to botch it will lose more frequently. The cost of the botch-ups will increase and performance will suffer. Losing will also become the order of the day and the organisation will be driven down continually in a cycle of despair.

Moving Beyond 15-Man Rugby

Super-performers understand that there are off-the-field players that vitally affect the fortunes of their organisations. Controlling these players by owning them doesn't always work. Far better, they have taught us, is to develop mutually beneficial relationships with them. These companies have become superb at developing relationships with the wide network that surrounds the typical business enterprise.

Trends such as third party contracting, breaking down of vertically integrated businesses, the special effort that is required by business to win the hearts and minds of the community — these will all continue with new vigour in the 1990s. Organisations aiming for the super-performing tag will have to become adept at moving beyond 15-man rugby. Organisations that aim to control the network by owning it, and that base their business systems on a ruthless kind of adversarial relationship will go the way of the dinosaur.

Inspired Leadership

The super-performers have taught us a lot about leadership in South Africa. They drive their organisations to the limit; they fire-up their troops; they have an intimate knowledge of operations; they make meaning for people; they spell out a vision of the organisation for the future and, importantly, they are both intellectual and emotional.

It is obvious to us that with all the challenges that lie ahead,

259

leadership will be one of those factors separating the sinkers from the swimmers. The concept of the manager as an operator will have its important role in organisational life. However, far more important, we believe, will be the role of the leader — the person who makes the future happen for the organisation. The person for whom organisational members will spill their blood and guts.

Strong Culture

Sure, we'd known that corporate culture was important before we began the research. But we were nevertheless dazzled by the awesome power of this forceful, yet informal integrating mechanism that guides behaviour in super-performing companies.

Organisations aspiring to super-performance are going to have to engage and manage a control system that provides for both consistency of purpose and flexibility amid the oceans of uncertainty and change. Corporate culture is the most complete form of organisational control that we know of.

This research has been a deeply enriching experience for us both. The lessons that the super-performers have taught us are, we believe, robust and enduring. This is because they are well grounded in a rugged playing field, and are based on some very clear thinking on the part of the most successful operators in a lively corporate environment. We believe, too, that they are durable because at the end of the day, they are about basic common sense. And who could fault that?

INDEX

261

Modise, Tlhopheho, 89
Mtsweni, Edward, 209

Natbolt, 56

Ogilvy, David, 116, 117
Oppenheimer, Harry, 14

Pick 'n Pay, 12, 184, 185
  corporate culture, 207, 208, 215,
  219, 232
  decentralisation, 37, 39
  human resource development, 66
  incentives, 83, 84
  leadership, 187
  marketing strategy, 27, 29, 31, 46,
  59-60, 77, 170
  rewards, 40, 232
  strategic planning, 15, 23, 27-28
Player, Gary, 14
Plessey, 77
  communication, 155
  corporate culture, 36, 78, 231, 232
  doing things properly, 150
  innovation, 99, 105, 106, 115
  marketing strategy, 59, 60, 62
  quality, 153
  rewards, 232, 233
  strategic planning, 17-19, 23
  strategy implementation, 35
Plessey UK, 18
Press, Sydney, 200
Pretoria Portland Cement, 14, 23, 44,
158
Pretorius, Brand, 39, 86, 117, 174-
175, 197
Putco, 181

Quality, 30, 32, 39, 151-154, 167-168
207, 220-221

Ratner, Farrel, 187, 201
Relly, Gavin, 4
Rembrandt, 9, 12, 126, 134, 174
Rewards, 39, 40, 118, 232, 233
Ringo, Winky, 12, 202
  communication, 88

corporate culture, 127
human resource development, 67
leadership, 189-191, 194-195
quality, 154
Robarts, Frankie, 12, 78, 79, 133
  leadership, 199, 203
  marketing strategy, 55, 61
  strategy implementation, 34
  Waltons success story, 122, 123
Rolfe, Terry, 55
Rosevear, Ken, 190
Rupert, Anton, 3, 9

SA Bias Binding Manufacturers Ltd,
12
  acquisitions, 161, 162, 163
  corporate culture, 75, 117
  decentralisation, 38
  doing things properly, 154
  financial strategy, 144, 179, 180
  human resource development, 64,
  65, 72
  incentives, 79
  information systems, 138
  innovation, 98, 99
  marketing strategy, 30, 31, 77, 177
  strategic planning, 17, 25, 28
  strategy implementation, 34, 35, 40
SAB, Beer Division,
  corporate culture, 17, 124, 126, 131-
  132, 213, 219-220, 234-235
  cost control, 134, 135
  doing things properly, 149, 150
  incentives, 83
  marketing strategy, 31, 44, 49, 56,
  100, 170, 174-175
  quality, 152, 220
  strategic planning, 21-23, 28
Sales House, 37, 46, 69
Samcor, 173
Savage, Richard, 22
Savory, Peter, 112, 131, 142, 149-150,
152
Schmidt, Rudi, 154
Scott, Carol, 30, 57, 58
Seabrooke, Chris, 12, 201
  acquisitions, 161, 162, 163, 164